Latin America in the Era
of the Cuban Revolution
and Beyond

Latin America in the Era of the Cuban Revolution and Beyond

Third Edition

Thomas C. Wright

 PRAEGER™

An Imprint of ABC-CLIO, LLC

Santa Barbara, California • Denver, Colorado

Library of Congress Cataloging-in-Publication Data

Names: Wright, Thomas C., author.
Title: Latin America in the era of the Cuban Revolution and beyond /
  Thomas C. Wright.
Description: Third edition. | Santa Barbara, California : Praeger, 2018. | Includes
  bibliographical references and index.
Identifiers: LCCN 2017042464 (print) | LCCN 2017057817 (ebook) |
  ISBN 9781440857683 (ebook) | ISBN 9781440857676 (hardcover : alk. paper) |
  ISBN 9781440858468 (papercover)
Subjects: LCSH: Latin America—Politics and government—1948- | Cuba—
  History—Revolution, 1959—Influence. | Radicalism—Latin America—
  History—20th century. | Violence—Latin America—History—20th century. |
  United States—Military policy.
Classification: LCC F1414.2 (ebook) | LCC F1414.2 .W75 2017 (print) |
  DDC 980.03—dc23
LC record available at https://lccn.loc.gov/2017042464

ISBN: 978-1-4408-5767-6 (print)
      978-1-4408-5846-8 (pbk)
      978-1-4408-5768-3 (ebook)

22 21 20 19 18   1 2 3 4 5

This book is also available as an eBook.

Praeger
An Imprint of ABC-CLIO, LLC

ABC-CLIO, LLC
130 Cremona Drive, P.O. Box 1911
Santa Barbara, California 93116-1911
www.abc-clio.com

This book is printed on acid-free paper ∞

Manufactured in the United States of America

para mi querida Dina

Contents

Part Five   The Reaction

Part Six   The Continuing Impact of the Cuban Revolution

Acknowledgments

This book owes much to many friends and colleagues. James Kohl, Robert J. Alexander, John Super, Thomas Walker, E. Bradford Burns, Catherine Zubel, and Daniel Barber read the manuscript of the first edition and offered invaluable critiques, while Marion Sumners, Jamie Coughtry, and Randy Hale provided essential assistance. The insights of Garry Leech, Kirk Bowman, and Monica Barczak strengthened the second edition. Jerry L. Simich read the text of this edition, and Angela Moor, Heather Nepa, and Shontai Beltran provided expert technical support. My long-suffering friend and colleague, Joseph A. (Andy) Fry, read and critiqued all three editions and offered both editorial and substantive suggestions.

The love of my life, Dina Titus, has been involved since the gestation of the first edition in the summer of 1987 in San Miguel de Allende, Guanajuato, Mexico. Her encouragement and support have been indispensable.

Finally, I wish to thank the many students who took my class "Revolution and Reaction in Latin America" over the years and sharpened my focus on the era of the Cuban Revolution.

Acronyms[*]

AAA	Argentine Anticommunist Alliance
AD	Democratic Action (Venezuela)
ALBA	Bolivarian Alliance for the Peoples of Our America (Venezuela)
APRA	American Popular Revolutionary Alliance (Peru)
CAEM	Center for Advanced Military Studies (Peru)
CDR	Committee for the Defense of the Revolution (Cuba)
CDS	Sandinista Defense Committee (Nicaragua)
CELS	Center for Legal and Social Studies (Argentina)
CIA	Central Intelligence Agency (United States)
COMECON	Council for Mutual Economic Assistance (Soviet Bloc)
DINA	Directorate of National Intelligence (Chile)
DR	Revolutionary Directorate (Cuba)
ELN	Army of National Liberation (Colombia)
ERP	People's Revolutionary Army (Argentina)
EZLN	Zapatista National Liberation Army (Mexico)
FALN	Armed Forces of National Liberation (Venezuela)
FAO	Broad Opposition Front (Nicaragua)
FAR	Rebel Armed Forces (Guatemala)
FARC	Revolutionary Armed Forces of Colombia

---

[*] This list includes only the acronyms that appear in the text more than once.

FMLN	Farabundo Martí National Liberation Front (El Salvador)
FSLN	Sandinista National Liberation Front (Nicaragua)
IMF	International Monetary Fund
IPC	International Petroleum Company (Peru)
ITT	International Telephone and Telegraph
M-26-7	26th of July Movement (Cuba)
MAAG	Military Assistance Advisory Group (United States)
MAPU	Popular Unity Action Movement (Chile)
MIR	Movement of the Revolutionary Left (Chile)
MIR	Movement of the Revolutionary Left (Peru)
MLN	Movement of National Liberation (Uruguay)
OAS	Organization of American States
OLAS	Latin American Solidarity Organization (Cuba)
OPEC	Organization of Petroleum Exporting Countries
ORDEN	Democratic Nationalist Organization (El Salvador)
PDC	Christian Democratic Party (Chile)
PRI	Party of the Institutionalized Revolution (Mexico)
PSP	Popular Socialist [Communist] Party (Cuba)
SINAMOS	National System to Support Social Mobilization (Peru)
UDEL	Democratic Liberation Union (Nicaragua)
UFCO	United Fruit Company
UN	United Nations
UNAG	National Union of Farmers and Cattlemen (Nicaragua)
UNO	National Opposition Union (Nicaragua)
UP	People's Unity (Chile)
URNG	Guatemalan National Revolutionary Union
USAID	U.S. Agency for International Development

Introduction: The Cuban Revolution and Latin America

"January 1, 1959, when Fidel Castro triumphed, began a new era in Latin America." So wrote *New York Times* senior editor Herbert Matthews, a close observer of Fidel Castro's guerrilla war against dictator Fulgencio Batista.[1] Echoing Matthews' words, dozens of academic and journalistic studies written in the 1960s proclaimed the Cuban Revolution a major watershed in Latin America's history.

The six decades since Castro's victory have marginalized Cuba from the Latin American mainstream. As a result, it may appear from today's perspective that the Cuban Revolution had been an exotic, aberrant growth on the Latin American body politic. In fact, quite the opposite is true. The Cuban Revolution owed its vast influence in Latin America to the fact that—most evidently in its early years—it embodied the aspirations and captured the imagination of Latin America's masses as no other political movement had ever done.

Beginning with the Mexican Revolution of 1910, Latin America witnessed the rise of reformist and revolutionary forces dedicated to bettering the material condition of the workers, the dark peoples, the poor, the illiterate, the exploited—those who lived their lives on the margin of society and outside the realm of politics. Mexico's revolutionary 1917 constitution not only set goals for Mexico, but its commitment to political democracy, social justice, and national liberation from foreign economic dominance—in sum, to freedom and human dignity—also set the agenda for 20th-century Latin American politics. Following the Mexican Revolution, mass movements such as Peru's American Popular Revolutionary Alliance (Alianza Popular Revolucionaria Americana, APRA) and Venezuela's

LATIN AMERICA AND THE CARIBBEAN POST-1945

Mexico

Bahamas

Cuba

Dominican Republic

Belize
Guatemala
El Salvador

Jamaica
Honduras
Nicaragua

Haiti

Panama

Costa Rica

Trinidad & Tobago

Venezuela

Guyana

French Guiana

Colombia

Suriname

Ecuador

Peru

Brazil

Bolivia

Paraguay

Chile

Argentina

Uruguay

Democratic Action (Acción Democrática, AD) struggled to create new societies with a place for the downtrodden. Leaders such as Nicaragua's
Augusto César Sandino and Colombia's Jorge Eliécer Gaitán fought with
arms or with their political skills for the same goals. Bolivia experienced
Latin America's second social revolution in 1952 when the Indian peasants seized much of the country's agricultural land; the government nationalized the country's basic industry, tin mining; and the enactment of
universal suffrage gave the Indian majority a voice in national politics for
the first time.

Despite two revolutions and the unstinting efforts of reformist parties
and leaders, Latin America on the whole moved only slowly and tentatively
toward the goals of political and social democracy and national liberation.
The power and resilience of Latin America's elites, ingrained attitudes of
obedience and resignation among the masses, and U.S. opposition to
change combined repeatedly to thwart the forces of progress. With Castro's
rise to power in Cuba, however, the waters of revolution poured over the
dam, submerging Latin America in political and social ferment that threatened the very foundations of the established order.

Compared with the Mexican and Bolivian revolutions and the few
reformist governments that had held power in Latin America up to 1959,
the Cuban Revolution had far greater ramifications for Latin America. There
were several reasons for the potency of Castro's revolution outside of Cuba.
It provided an explicit blueprint for successful insurrection by reducing
the overthrow of governments to a simple matter of faithfully following
Che Guevara's handbook on guerrilla warfare. Cuba went far beyond the
previous revolutions, carrying out Latin America's most thorough social
transformation and becoming the hemisphere's first, and only, country to
break completely from U.S. domination. The Cuban Revolution also had a
dynamic, charismatic leader who symbolized the revolution and elicited
popular sympathy and support throughout the hemisphere. Rejecting territorial limits to his revolution, Castro actively promoted insurrection
against established governments and bourgeois power throughout Latin
America.

The immense popularity of the Cuban Revolution, especially in the years
of the great transformation from 1959 through the early 1960s, is easy to
understand. During these years Castro constantly made headlines with
his social reforms and his measures to throw off what many Latin Americans regarded as the yoke of Yankee imperialism. The abortive 1961 Bay
of Pigs invasion—the improbable victory of a Cuban David over a Yankee
Goliath—cemented Castro's hold over the Latin American masses. After

that high point, fulfillment of the revolution's promises became increasingly selective: political democracy was indefinitely postponed, then discarded, as Castro embraced Communism; individual liberties were subordinated to social justice for the collective; and after the first decade, growing dependence on the Soviet Union compromised the quest for Cuban sovereignty. Yet Cuban influence remained strong for many years, long after failures began to tarnish the revolution's image, because for many Latin Americans the hope and the example that the Cuban Revolution provided in its youth transcended the shortcomings of its later years.

The Cuban Revolution was responsible not only for the revolutionary ferment that spread across Latin America. Because it posed an existential threat to Latin America's elites and to U.S. economic and geopolitical interests, that wave of revolution created a powerful wave of reaction that engulfed the region. Supported by the United States, the militaries took power in all but four Latin American countries in the 1960s and 1970s and instituted severe repression against advocates of reform or revolution that, in several instances, reached the level of state terrorism. Unconstrained by constitutions that protected human rights, the militaries harassed, exiled, jailed, tortured, murdered, and disappeared hundreds of thousands of people in their quest to exterminate those they considered Communists or simply "subversives."

This book offers an interpretation of the era of the Cuban Revolution, the period when the forces of change that first burst forth in the Mexican Revolution of 1910 mounted an all-out challenge to the status quo in Latin America—a time when the threat or hope of reform and revolution was never stronger. This was also the period of the most extreme reaction in Latin America's history—a period that witnessed the institutionalization of dictatorships and repression that extinguished democracy and human rights. This era that began with Fidel Castro's triumph in 1959 lasted through three decades until global forces and developments within Latin America signaled its end in 1990.

In arguing that the Cuban Revolution dictated the broad sweep of Latin American politics for some 30 years, I am not advancing a single-cause explanation of the political life of a huge and diverse area. Clearly, the mobilizations and the revolutionary movements that swept the hemisphere beginning in 1959 had indigenous roots. They sprang from the poverty and social inequities that characterized Latin America and from the efforts of preexisting political forces advocating reform and revolution. Castro certainly did not create revolutionary ferment from thin air; but by its example, reinforced by Castro's ambitious efforts to promote insurrection throughout Latin America, the Cuban Revolution served as a catalyst to the spread and the intensification of social and political conflict to unprecedented levels.

Likewise, the Cuban Revolution was not the only cause of the extreme reaction of the 1970s and 1980s. With rare exceptions, Latin America's military establishments were historically conservative, and thus the generals and admirals normally supported the elites' resistance to revolution and reform. But the threat posed by the Cuban Revolution was an unprecedented challenge to the status quo that threatened both the elites' privileged way of life and their very survival. Moreover, military leaders were acutely aware that upon coming to power with his guerrillas, Fidel Castro dissolved Cuba's national armed forces and replaced them with his own rebel army. As a result, the Latin American militaries, with U.S. encouragement and support, rarely hesitated to use the full extent of their power to quash the forces of revolution unleashed by developments in Cuba.

Thus the Cuban Revolution was paramount in setting the general terms of political debate in Latin America. The heightening of demands for change, the pan–Latin American scope of the ferment, and the transcendence of the issues—the very survival of existing economic, social, and political systems was at stake—made the years after 1959 the period of greatest political upheaval in Latin American history. These same forces drove the wave of extreme reaction that swept over Latin America in the 1970s and 1980s. This overarching influence of the Cuban Revolution—sometimes explicit, often implicit, but never absent—is what distinguishes the period from 1959 to 1990.

Rather than taking a country-by-country approach, this study synthesizes the broad trends and phases of the Cuban Revolution's impact on Latin America. Chapters 1 and 2 cover the Cuban Revolution itself. They are not intended to provide an exhaustive history of the revolution; rather, they are designed to emphasize those features of Castro's revolution that made Cuba so influential in Latin America during three decades of revolution and reaction. Chapters 3 and 4 examine the Cuban Revolution's destabilizing impact on Latin America and the United States' responses to the threat of the spread of Communist revolution beyond the island. Chapters 5 and 6 focus on guerrilla warfare, first on rural guerrilla warfare as practiced in Cuba and popularized by Che Guevara, then on the urban variant that emerged following Che's 1967 death. Chapters 7 through 9 analyze revolutions in Peru, Chile, and Nicaragua. Although differing greatly in provenance and policies, these revolutions experienced similar outcomes: all ended prematurely before completing their missions. Chapters 10 and 11 examine the reaction, focusing on state terrorism in South America and Central America, respectively. The final chapter deals with developments that brought the era of the Cuban Revolution to an end in 1990 and surveys major political trends since that time, including those that reflect the residual influence of Fidel Castro and his revolution.

Note

1. Herbert L. Matthews, *The Cuban Story* (New York: George Braziller, 1961), 273–74.

PART 1

Revolution in Cuba

CHAPTER ONE

Fidel Castro's Road to Power, 1952–1959

On March 13, 1952, three days after Fulgencio Batista seized power in a military coup, a young Fidel Castro denounced that coup as "a brutal snatching of power!" and called on his Cuban compatriots to "sacrifice and fight back!"[1] On July 26, 1953, Castro took up arms against the dictator. Five and a half years later, after many twists and turns, Castro drove Batista off the island and launched the Cuban Revolution—a revolution that radically changed not only Cuba but also Latin America and U.S.–Latin American relations for three decades. These three decades constitute the era of the Cuban Revolution.

Background to Revolution: The Condition of Cuba

Most observers of Latin America were surprised that the most radical revolution in the Western Hemisphere should have taken place in Cuba. By most of the standard indicators, Cuba was near the upper end of the scale in development and modernization. In per capita gross national product, Cuba in the 1950s was fourth in Latin America; its literacy rate was within the top quarter. Cuba ranked third in medical doctors and hospital beds per capita, and it had Latin America's lowest infant mortality rate. Union membership was among the strongest in Latin America—approximately half the labor force—and Cuba ranked second in the proportion of the working population covered by social security. In two indices of consumerism, television sets and radios per capita, Cuba ranked first and second, respectively. Although not particularly dynamic, Cuba's economy in the early

1950s was relatively stable. Finally, Cuba's government had the strong and explicit backing of the U.S. government and business sector. By the conventional wisdom that backwardness and poverty breed revolution, then, many Latin American countries seemed more susceptible than Cuba to radical change.

The post-1958 boom in Cuban studies yielded volumes on the question: Why Cuba? Researchers probed Cuban history and reexamined the island's economy, society, and political system to bare the roots of Castro's revolution. The picture that took shape was not a rosy one, but neither did it appear to have presaged a successful popular insurrection and a radical revolution. The elements that made Castro's revolution possible, not inevitable—the conditions that he was able to exploit in building the anti-Batista movement and, once in power, in conducting a sweeping revolution—can be set forth in four broad categories: strong and pervasive anti-U.S. sentiment, the deleterious effects of excessive dependence on sugar culture, fragmentation of Cuban society, and the disrepute in which Cuba's political system and institutions were held.

The endemic anti-Americanism that Fidel Castro was able to draw upon to build support for his struggle against dictator Fulgencio Batista, and subsequently for his revolution, had its roots in the United States' historic and continuing dominance of Cuba. Beginning early in the 19th century, while Cuba was still a Spanish colony, U.S. expansionists looked to the island as a potential new state. This prospect was especially attractive to Southerners, who recognized the potential compatibility of another slave society. While internal U.S. politics worked to check the expansionists, American businessmen invested heavily in Spanish Cuba in the closing decades of the 19th century. With a growing geopolitical interest in the Caribbean and substantial investments to protect, the United States watched closely when the second Cuban independence war broke out in

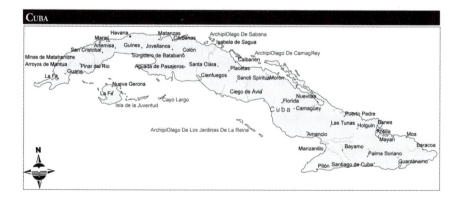

1895. When the sinking of the *Maine* in Havana harbor generated support for intervention, U.S. troops entered the fray in 1898 and easily defeated the Spanish, assuring the victory of the independence forces.

Cubans quickly learned the truth of what many had feared: independence from Spain did not mean an independent Cuban nation. Although pledged to granting Cuba independence, the United States, entering a phase of expansionism in the Caribbean, could not resist conditioning the withdrawal of its troops on Cuba's adoption of a constitutional provision making the island a protectorate. The Platt Amendment denied Cuba the essence of nationhood—sovereignty—by granting the U.S. government "the right to intervene for the preservation of Cuban independence [and] the maintenance of a government adequate for the protection of life, property, and individual liberty."[2] The United States also acquired a perpetual lease over Guantánamo, which it initially used as a coaling station for its navy. These and other restrictions written into the 1901 Cuban constitution and confirmed in the 1903 U.S.-Cuban Treaty of Relations were bitter pills for those patriots who had fought two wars for genuine independence. A result of American tutelage during the three-plus decades of the "Platt Amendment Republic," wrote Cuban intellectual Jorge Mañach, was "general civic indolence, a tepid indifference to national dangers."[3]

The United States exercised its right of military intervention by reoccupying the island between 1906 and 1909 and landing troops in 1912 and 1917. Equally debilitating to the development of an independent Cuba were the many instances of overt political intervention supported by the implicit or explicit threat of military action. General Enoch Crowder usurped most of the powers of President Alfredo Zayas (1921–1925), choosing his cabinet and ordering fiscal reforms that left U.S. banks in a dominant position. Perhaps the most significant political intervention was that of 1933, when ambassador-at-large Sumner Welles refused diplomatic recognition to the reform-oriented government of Ramón Grau San Martín, which followed the overthrow of long-term dictator Gerardo Machado. Facing U.S. opposition, the fledgling government was unable to consolidate its power and was quickly replaced by the more conservative and subservient military regime of Fulgencio Batista. Many Cubans look back to 1933 as a critical turning point—a lost opportunity to address Cuba's mounting economic, social, and political problems while moderate solutions were still possible.

U.S. control over Cuba changed complexion, but not substance, after 1934 when President Franklin D. Roosevelt, in keeping with his Good Neighbor Policy toward Latin America, agreed to a new treaty that abrogated the Platt Amendment. The United States honored its renunciation of military intervention, but, as before, U.S. economic and geopolitical interests dictated constant oversight and close political control over the island. By 1927 direct U.S. investment in Cuba had ballooned to over a billion dollars, the largest amount invested in any Latin American country, and U.S. capital dominated the major sectors of the economy, including sugar, transportation, banking, and utilities. U.S. investment declined subsequently through the 1940s, not reaching the billion-dollar level again until the late 1950s; as the U.S. presence shrank, Cubans gained the dominant position in sugar and banking, while the later influx of American capital went into newer sectors such as mining, petroleum, manufacturing, and tourism.

Cuba's dependence on the U.S. market, on the other hand, remained strong. Although the proportion of Cuba's sugar going to the United States fell from some 80 percent in the 1920s to less than 55 percent in the 1950s, Cuba still placed approximately two-thirds of all its exports in the traditional American market. In the 1930s sugar imports were put on a quota basis, subject to annual congressional review and approval. This economic control with its accompanying leverage over Cuban politics kept Cuba in a dependent position long after the Platt Amendment disappeared. The pervasive U.S. economic presence combined with the highly visible political constraints on Cuba's freedom of action continued to engender resentment of U.S. power over the island.

In addition to making Cuba economically subservient to the United States, the heavy reliance on sugar cultivation and export posed both economic and social problems for Cuba. As a primary commodity, sugar was and is subject to the vagaries of climate and the world market. Sugar constituted approximately 85 percent of Cuba's export earnings in the 1950s and over a third of its gross national product; thus even minor price fluctuations had far-reaching effects on the sugar labor force and on the island's economic stability. Tariff agreements and quotas giving Cuban sugar preferential treatment in the American market, moreover, were based on reciprocity. The favored status of U.S. manufactured goods in the Cuban market limited the possibilities for Cuba's economic diversification and development.

Reliance on sugar had important social ramifications as well. As sugar planting expanded across the island, sugar came to dominate the prime agricultural lands, pushing out peasant farmers and creating a huge rural proletariat, which in the 1950s numbered some 600,000. These landless rural workers outnumbered the poor peasant farmers by more than three to one and constituted nearly a third of the country's labor force. The majority of the rural proletariat worked the cycle imposed by cane cultivation and harvesting, finding regular employment only four or five months per year. Government road maintenance and public works jobs, scheduled during the dead seasons, ameliorated conditions for some but did not substantially alter the poverty and chronic underemployment that prevailed in rural Cuba. The sugar proletariat had demonstrated its potential for radical action during the 1933 uprising against Machado when workers seized sugar mills and established Soviet councils in several parts of the island.

Along with the social cleavages typified by the contrast between wealthy sugar planters and their proletariat, two other pronounced divisions impaired the cohesiveness of Cuban society. To sustain the institution of slavery, which it preserved until 1886, Spanish Cuba imported large numbers of Africans through the late 1860s. The result was a racially divided population, which, despite steady Spanish immigration over the next century, was still officially 27 percent black or mulatto in the 1950s; these descendants of slaves suffered economic and social discrimination in various forms. Although the racial division was mitigated somewhat by easier social relations than those found in the United States, it occasionally broke into the open as it did in the 1912 "Race War of Oriente."

Another notable fissure in Cuban society was the widely perceived generation gap. Each "generation" of Cuban youth in the 20th century tended to deprecate the failed efforts of the preceding generation to rectify Cuba's problems. Thus the generation of 1930 blamed that of 1895 for failing to win true independence, and Fidel's generation, that of 1953, blamed the 1930 group for the failure to consolidate reform. The wholesale dismissal of the efforts and values of preceding groups of national leaders left young Cubans with few models and traditions, predisposing them to radical and bold approaches to solving Cuba's national problems.

Rounding out the "condition of Cuba" was the widespread disenchantment with Cuba's politicians and its public institutions. From its inception, the Cuban government had been too weak and too subject to foreign manipulation to command the respect of its citizens. Added to the antinational *vendepatria* (selling out of the homeland) reputation of leaders, parties, and government were the open, massive corruption and the partisan violence that pervaded even the progressive Auténtico Party administrations of Ramón Grau San Martín (1944–1948) and Carlos Prío Socarrás (1948–1952). Nonetheless, many still entertained the hope that better government could be achieved through elections until Fulgencio Batista's 1952 coup d'état.

Batista was a well-known and widely disliked figure in Cuban politics. As a sergeant, he led the 1933 revolt that put the reformist government of Grau San Martín in power; four months later, with strong U.S. backing, he engineered the overthrow of Grau. As leader of the military, Batista had exercised considerable influence over the governments of the 1930s and had served a presidential term from 1940 to 1944. Although his administration proved more progressive than most observers expected, Batista never escaped his identity as the United States' instrument for thwarting reform in 1933–1934.

A candidate for the presidency in the scheduled June 1952 election, Batista trailed in the polls; rather than suffer defeat, he overthrew the Prío Socarrás government on March 10. As Cuba was not experiencing economic or political crisis in 1952, Batista's seizure of power was commonly viewed as an act of naked self-interest. As a result, his government was resented and resisted from its inception, and the dictator was unable to consolidate his regime and govern with any degree of normalcy. In order to retain power, he instituted a regime of repression characterized by states of siege, censorship, closings of universities, arbitrary arrests, and assassinations—all of which broadened the opposition. Batista periodically lifted the censorship, reopened universities, and freed political prisoners as conciliatory gestures, but despite these overtures, the opposition to his regime steadily expanded during his nearly seven years in office. Batista's dictatorship, then, left Cuba's political institutions in disarray and completed the erosion of the political system's legitimacy.

U.S. domination of Cuba, subjugation to a vulnerable sugar economy, strong cleavages in the social fabric, and the absence of legitimacy that characterized Cuba's political system gave Fidel Castro and other Batista opponents ample material with which to build mass followings. The poor, the dark, the nationalists, the disenchanted—among them, the majority of the Cuban population—were attracted by talk of change and improvements in their lives. Invoking nationalistic slogans and promising economic diversification, social justice, and political democracy, Castro and his counterparts found legions of willing followers and sympathizers. The generalized absence of allegiance to the government and its institutions further opened Cuba to radical change.

Fidel Castro: From the Moncada Barracks to the Sierra Maestra

From the outset of his dictatorship, Batista faced an active and diverse opposition. The major progressive political parties, the leftist Ortodoxos and the more moderate Auténticos, followed a variety of approaches to ridding Cuba of Batista. The Ortodoxos quickly organized underground cells and mounted a campaign of propaganda, street demonstrations, strikes, and sabotage, while some of the Auténticos initially opted to participate in politics under Batista's rules but soon adopted a more militant stance. The Revolutionary Directorate (Directorio Revolucionario, DR), founded in 1955 by the University of Havana student federation, was a radical group that used both civil protest and armed struggle against the dictator. In addition, disaffected military officers attempted coups against Batista, exile groups mounted armed invasions, labor unions struck, and resistance groups burned cane fields from time to time.

One of the early opposition leaders was Fidel Castro, a lawyer in his mid-twenties who had been an Ortodoxo candidate for a congressional seat in the aborted 1952 election. Castro was the son of a wealthy landowner in Oriente province. He attended Jesuit schools, obtained a law degree from the University of Havana, and had extensive experience in university politics. Castro was one of the most active Ortodoxos, organizing cells and publishing an underground paper called *El Acusador.*

Castro first achieved prominence as a result of his attack on the Moncada Barracks on July 26, 1953, the date for which Castro would name his own movement after breaking with the Ortodoxos. This formative event continues to be central to the lore of the Cuban Revolution and provided the occasion for Castro's major annual speech. With some 165 followers, he set out to attack the 1,000 troops staffing Cuba's second-largest army base in the eastern city of Santiago. The maximalist notion, typical of Castro's approach to taking power and carrying out revolution, was that a successful attack would produce such shock waves as to ignite popular insurrection and bring down the regime.

Predictably, Castro's approach failed, leaving half his followers dead and most of the survivors, including himself, captured. Typical also of Fidel was the bungling of some basic preparations. He later admitted: "Due to a most unfortunate error, half of our forces, and the better armed half at that, went astray at the entrance to the city and were not on hand to help us at the decisive moment."[4] Half a century later, Castro gave a different explanation of the defeat: "What failed there was that we lacked sufficient combat experience."[5] Defending himself in a military court-martial, Fidel presented a historical analysis of Cuba's ills and eloquently argued the duty of patriotic Cubans to take up arms against Batista. His courtroom speech ended: "Condemn me, it does not matter. *History will absolve me!*"[6] Although he failed to persuade the military judges, who sentenced him to 15 years on the Isle of Pines, his arguments appeared in a clandestinely circulated pamphlet that disseminated Castro's name and message throughout the republic.

The story of Fidel Castro might have ended with his imprisonment had it not been for a general amnesty declared by Batista in May 1955 in an attempt to court the support of moderates. Castro immediately left Cuba for Mexico where, with his indefatigable energy and indomitable will, he raised funds and recruited fighters, including the young Argentine medical doctor Ernesto "Che" Guevara. Meanwhile in Cuba, Castro's followers organized and developed his new 26th of July Movement (Movimiento 26 de Julio, M-26-7), absorbing much of the Ortodoxo Party membership and developing cells nationwide. Before embarking on the second phase of his fight against Batista, Fidel developed relations with the major anti-Batista forces and signed the Mexico City Pact of September 1956 with the DR, agreeing to coordinate efforts, reject all compromise with Batista, and, after victory, establish a government based on a 19-point program. And Castro announced that he would return to liberate Cuba before the end of 1956.

The plan of attack, developed in coordination with M-26-7 operatives in Cuba, was another maximalist attempt to defeat Batista by shock—to accomplish a seemingly impossible feat, expose the regime's weakness, and provoke a generalized uprising against the dictator. The target, even less plausible than the Moncada Barracks, was the entire city of Santiago, Cuba's second largest, which would be captured by a combination of marine assault from Mexico and a simultaneous uprising within the city on November 30. This time Fidel planned for the eventuality of defeat. He engaged Colonel Alberto Bayo, a republican veteran of the Spanish Civil War, to instruct his men in military skills and tactics that might enable survivors to continue the fight in the Sierra Maestra outside of Santiago. This precaution would serve Castro well.

As in the Moncada case, the attack on Santiago was plagued by mistakes and miscalculations. The launch *Granma* departed from the Mexican port of Tuxpan on November 25 in a storm, an inauspicious start that Che Guevara recorded in his diary: "We began a frenzied search for the anti-seasickness pills, which we did not find. We sang the Cuban national anthem and the 'Hymn of the 26th of July' for perhaps five minutes and then the entire boat took on an aspect both ridiculous and tragic: men with anguished faces holding their stomachs, some with their heads in buckets, others lying in the strangest positions, immobile."[7] Arriving two days late, Castro's 82 men landed in the wrong place and after three days of wandering were discovered by army units. Had they arrived on the appointed day, their presence might have secured the victory of the urban insurgents who took control of Santiago for a few hours. Some 15 of Castro's contingent from the *Granma* were soon able to regroup and make their way into the Sierra Maestra; the rest were dispersed, captured, or killed.

Following his second defeat, the ever-ebullient Fidel, with his brother Raúl, Che Guevara, and the others, had to choose between abandoning the fight and falling back to a strategy that was clearly not the preferred one. Out of desperation rather than choice, then, was born the rural guerrilla war.

While Castro languished in prison and later prepared in Mexico, his followers in Cuba and the members of other opposition groups skirmished with the Batista regime, primarily in the cities and towns. During 1957 and the early months of 1958, the cities continued to be the main theater of war between Batista and the opposition. This offered Castro the great advantage of being virtually neglected while the government's security forces concentrated on beating back the urban-centered opposition. Batista's initial public response to Castro was to claim that he had been killed along with the other invaders from Mexico and to deny the existence of armed rebels in the mountains. His military response was to try to isolate Castro in the Sierra Maestra, where presumably he could do no harm, and to prevent reinforcements of men and supplies from reaching the guerrillas. Thus Batista's commanders strengthened military outposts on the perimeter of the Sierra Maestra, sent additional patrols into the mountains, and carried out sporadic aerial bombing, but did not mount large-scale offensive operations against the rebels.

Left in relative peace, Castro's *foco*, or guerrilla band, evolved in 17 months, from the humblest of beginnings with a handful of defeated men seeking refuge in the mountains, into a force capable of turning back the best offensive that Batista could mount against it. In the first weeks after the disastrous landing, the rag-tag band aspired to little more than day-to-day survival. Che described the early period in the Sierra Maestra: "In that period it was very difficult to enlarge our army; a few men came, but others left; the physical conditions of the struggle were very hard, but the spiritual conditions were even more so, and we lived with the feeling of being continually under siege."[8] The rebels benefited from the cooperation of the scattered peasantry of the Sierra Maestra, some of whom had been recruited in advance by M-26-7 operatives from Santiago. This peasant support, combined with the army's strategy of cordoning off the entire mountainous zone to contain the guerrillas, gave Castro's group the ability to scout the terrain and establish ever-expanding networks of trusted peasants. Free from concerted government pressure, the guerrillas were gradually able to establish a "liberated zone"—an area in which they could operate with relative security from army attack—in the Sierra Maestra.

The guerrilla band was still tiny and virtually untested when *New York Times* senior editor Herbert Matthews introduced it to the world in

February 1957. Desperately seeking the publicity that Batista's censorship denied him, Castro arranged for Matthews to cross army lines into the *sierra* and be taken to the rebel camp for an extensive interview and a look at the guerrilla operation. Fidel knew how to take advantage of such a providential opportunity. Although having only 18 men at the time, he told Matthews that his troops operated in "groups of ten to forty" and claimed that "we are winning." Deeply impressed, the veteran correspondent wrote that Castro had "mastery of the Sierra Maestra" and opined that "General Batista cannot possibly hope to suppress the Castro revolt."[9] Matthews' story appeared in the *Times* on February 24. Due to a temporary lifting of press censorship, even Cubans were able to read about Castro for the first time.

The Matthews interview disproved Batista's claim that Fidel and his followers had been wiped out. The publicity helped recruiting, and the force grew substantially. At the time of its second military victory—an attack on a 53-man garrison at El Uvero on May 28, 1957—the guerrilla band boasted approximately 100 men. El Uvero, according to Che, was "the victory which marked our coming of age."[10]

The strategy at this stage was not to conquer and hold additional territory, but to engage the enemy in carefully prepared ambushes at the perimeter of the liberated zone, inflict casualties, and retreat to safety before reinforcements or air power could arrive. It was critical for the guerrillas to choose the engagements, avoiding confrontations with superior forces that could defeat them. The goals of this phase were to cause increasing numbers of troops to be committed to the perimeter of the Sierra Maestra and to score enough small victories to establish military credibility and demoralize the army. Following several months of successful small-scale offensive operations, Castro was able to set up his own broadcast station, *Radio Rebelde*, with the power to reach much of the eastern end of Cuba. Castro took another major step in March 1958 by sending a column under the command of his brother Raúl to establish a second front in the Sierra Cristal mountains of northern Oriente province.

Castro and His Competition

After retreating to the Sierra Maestra, Castro was still only one of several leaders competing for the prize of defeating the dictator and shaping post-Batista Cuba according to their own views. While Fidel worked to cultivate peasant support and establish secure perimeters, the urban resistance intensified its efforts during 1957. On March 13, DR carried out a bold strike on the presidential palace in an attempt to assassinate Batista,

who narrowly escaped. The DR paid dearly for its f.
Antonio Echeverría, was killed in the attack and the
out most of the remaining leadership. A second maj(
taneous uprising sparked by the July 30 police assas
of popular M-26-7 leader Frank País, a potential riv.
movement's leadership. This uprising became a genera\
throughout the country, supported by all anti-Batista gr(...u the populace at large, but it fizzled after a few days. On September 5, a naval revolt
broke out in Cienfuegos but collapsed after a coordinated uprising in
Havana was called off.

The success of any one of these 1957 actions might have preempted
Castro's drive for power, but their failure smoothed his path. In response
to these 1957 uprisings, Batista increased the repression on the urban
underground, severely weakening Castro's competition within the armed
resistance. In fact, Batista's success in the cities drove several groups to
emulate Castro and take up the struggle in what appeared to be a less dangerous setting. Beginning in mid-1957, the DR, the Auténticos, the Ortodoxos, and an independent group set up guerrilla operations in the
Escambray Mountains of central Cuba.

In February 1958 the Popular Socialist Party (Partido Socialista Popular, PSP, the Cuban Communists) finally declared against Batista. The PSP
had remained on the sidelines of the anti-Batista struggle due to an arrangement by which, although technically illegal, the party and its central role
in the labor movement were tolerated in exchange for the PSP's tacit support of the dictator. The PSP earlier had denounced Castro as a "bourgeois
adventurer," but the erosion of Batista's support made the party's position
untenable.

Meanwhile, Batista's states of siege, mass arrests, and murders alienated
growing segments of the population, broadening the non-armed opposition to include moderate to conservative political and business leaders. The
Auténticos stepped up their nonviolent activities, and by early 1958 the
Catholic Church hierarchy called for mediation of the conflict. In March,
the country's major economic interest associations called for Batista's
resignation.

The beginnings of the unraveling of Batista's regime elicited serious concern in the United States. Deciding that Batista was no longer viable, the
Eisenhower administration began seeking a controlled presidential succession and in March 1958 embargoed arms for his army as a means of pressuring him to cooperate. As Cubans recognized, the United States was
historically the final arbiter of Cuban politics: regardless of the relative
strengths or popularity of the opposition leaders, the leader or coalition

cured U.S. backing was likely to prevail in the rivalry to succeed
..ista. With a range of safe, moderate contenders from whom to choose,
Washington would certainly not tap the unpredictable and mercurial Castro to be its man in Havana. But the rivalries among parties and factions
and Batista's refusal to cooperate prevented Washington and the Cuban
elites from arranging a succession on their terms and made Batista's removal
a military rather than a political matter.

Seeking to exploit the dictator's shrinking support, the major opposition groups called a national general strike, to be accompanied by armed
uprisings against the dictator, in April 1958. This was to be the final blow
to Batista. Fidel Castro and his urban M-26-7 cadre were fully committed
to the strike, which began on the morning of April 9. However, the strike
effort suffered from poor planning, insufficient arms, and faulty collaboration among the various groups. Whereas the strike seriously disrupted
Santiago, it barely affected the daily routine in Havana. As reported by an
M-26-7 leader, "The strike in Havana was 'paralyzed,' and its tragic consequences have been incalculable."[11] As usual, Batista's forces exacted a heavy
toll on the opposition, killing around 200 M-26-7 militants and numerous members of other factions.

The Fall of Batista

The failed general strike was a major turning point for Castro. The defeat
confirmed his growing doubts about the efficacy of the urban resistance,
including his fellow M-26-7 members in the cities. Batista's harsh reprisals, moreover, made it unlikely that the urban resistance could recover
any time soon. Having seen urban operations fail time after time, Castro
and his fellow *barbudos* (bearded ones) in the Sierra Maestra essentially
decided that the burden of defeating Batista was theirs.

The failed general strike was also a turning point for Batista. Strengthened by his victory, Batista finally decided to turn his fire power on the
guerrillas in the mountains, whose momentum had grown in the previous few months. With considerable fanfare and the appearance of complete confidence, the army in May 1958 launched what it announced would
be a quick campaign to exterminate Castro's guerrillas. Nonetheless, unable
to get its tanks, half-tracks, mortars, and even jeeps into the mountainous
terrain, the army could only mass on Castro's perimeter or send foot patrols
into the Sierra Maestra in search of the rebels. This strategy played directly
into Fidel's hands. His troops merely taunted the massed army and then,
controlling the terrain, freely ambushed the columns dispatched to find
and finish them. After three months of frustration and substantial losses

of men and equipment, Batista's commanders called off the campaign in August and returned to the strategy of sealing off the guerrillas.

Having repelled the national army, Castro surged in prestige and power. The failure of the offensive against Castro revealed that the 28,000-man Cuban army was far less capable than it appeared to be. Having fought no wars, officers and soldiers were inexperienced in combat. Like other armies schooled in conventional warfare, it was frustrated by the innovative guerrilla approach. And as the pillars of Batista's support, army commanders were chosen first for their loyalty, second for their military abilities. Corruption was also rampant within the army, and Castro found it easy to bribe officers to permit personnel and supplies to slip through army lines into the *sierra*.

By the latter months of 1958, Batista's grip on power was slipping. Under renewed U.S. pressure to resign in time for a caretaker government to conduct elections, Batista instead held his own elections for Congress and a president on November 3, backing his prime minister Andrés Rivero Agüero. With the exception of the dwindling number of Batista loyalists, most eligible voters boycotted, either voluntarily or under pressure from the rebels, making the elections a farce and denying any possibility of legitimacy to the hand-picked government slated to succeed the dictator in February 1959. Rather than arresting the regime's collapse, the sham elections hastened it.

Even before the elections, the military tide had turned against Batista. Buoyed by the defeat of Batista's summer offensive, Castro expanded his military operations to central Cuba in late August when he dispatched a column of 150 fighters from the Sierra Maestra, under Che Guevara, to the mountains of Las Villas province. Its objectives were to cut communications between Havana and Santiago, take control of the DR and other guerrillas already operating in the Escambray Mountains, and strike a decisive blow that would bring down the regime. A second column under Camilo Cienfuegos, headed originally to Pinar del Río in the island's far west, also arrived in Las Villas after a seven-week march through army-held territory. When the final offensive began in early November, Castro's total guerrilla forces had reached roughly 1,000 troops.

After capturing numerous villages and cutting the central highway and railroad, Che's guerrillas attacked Santa Clara, Cuba's fourth-largest city with a population of some 80,000, on December 29. The city fell after heavy fighting on January 1, 1959. News of the imminent fall of Santa Clara prompted Batista to abandon a New Year's Eve party at his palace and take a waiting plane to the Dominican Republic and the fraternal embrace of dictator Rafael Trujillo. After a triumphant tour through the Cuban heartland,

Fidel and his guerrillas from the Sierra Maestra, their ranks swollen by last-minute converts, rolled into Havana on January 8 to a thunderous welcome. Total guerrilla strength at the fall of Batista did not exceed 3,000.

Mythogenesis, or the Myth of the Heroic Guerrilla

Even before Castro's seizure of power, the myth of the heroic guerrilla had begun to gain currency. The myth of the heroic guerrilla is the founding myth of the new Cuba; just as any new nation embellishes the heroic deeds and character traits of its founders in the process of forging national identity and institutional legitimacy, a society created by revolution creates its own founding myth by exaggerating the faults of the *ancien régime* and embellishing the feats and qualities of its revolutionary leaders. The founding myth of the Cuban Revolution, like other founding myths, is a selective recounting of history. It tells the story of the victory from the viewpoint of the victors.

Having struggled and suffered for 25 months in the Sierra Maestra against overwhelming odds and at great personal sacrifice, and having developed an attitude of superiority vis-à-vis the urban resistance for its repeated failures to dislodge Batista, Fidel and his cadre of guerrilla fighters quite understandably claimed credit for the victory and the beginning of a new Cuba. It was the guerrillas, after all, who won the decisive victory over the army and paved the way to Batista's defeat. In believing and in broadcasting the heroic guerrilla message, they were not wrong, nor were they lying; theirs was truly a heroic struggle. However, they overlooked and, perhaps inadvertently, discredited the work and sacrifice of thousands of members of the urban resistance, including the great bulk of M-26-7. Some of these men and women had been on the front lines of resistance for four and a half years before Fidel and his little band retreated to the Sierra Maestra to launch a new front in the war. Fidel acknowledged this distortion in a 1968 article written during a period of reassessment following the death of Che Guevara in his attempt to replicate the Cuban model in Bolivia: "Almost all attention, almost all recognition, almost all the admiration, and almost all the history of the Revolution [have] centered on the guerrilla movement in the mountains . . . This fact tended to play down the role of those who fought in the cities, the role of those who fought in the clandestine movement, and the extraordinary heroism of young persons who died fighting under very difficult conditions."[12]

As Castro implicitly admitted, the myth of the heroic guerrilla omits the work of the urban resistance in tying down Batista's forces in the cities during all of 1957 and the first four months of 1958. Without the repeated demonstrations, strikes, assassination attempts, acts of sabotage, and uprisings carried out by DR, M-26-7, students, political parties, organized labor, and military dissidents, Batista almost certainly would not have neglected Castro, allowing his forces to grow without significant military pressure until the army's belated offensive in May 1958. The myth also downplays the role of the urban cadres of M-26-7 in supplying weapons and recruits to the Sierra Maestra and fails to credit the same group with proselytizing among the peasantry of the area prior to Castro's arrival—a matter of considerable importance in view of the universal peasant distrust of outsiders.

The myth of the heroic guerrilla, firmly anchored in the history of the guerrilla war, evolved as the result of several circumstances. Most fundamental were the undeniable heroism and the epic quality of the guerrilla phase of the struggle against Batista. When the charisma and commanding presence of Fidel and the colorful and engaging personality of Che Guevara are added, the figure of the guerrilla fighter assumes a larger-than-life quality. From the appearance of Herbert Matthews's story in February 1957, the international press found the guerrillas more appealing and newsworthy than the student protests, general strikes, and military revolts which were the standard stuff of Latin American politics. Fidel's highly developed sense for publicity further helped to focus news coverage on the guerrillas. After the victory, Fidel institutionalized the guerrilla struggle in the new regime by installing Sierra Maestra veterans in the most important positions, thus making guerrilla fatigues, boots, and beards the official attire as well as the symbol of the revolution. Finally, Che Guevara's *Guerrilla Warfare* and other writings gave the Cuban guerrilla war the status of a holy crusade, completing the formulation of the myth of the heroic guerrilla.

The guerrillas also attained their preeminence in the founding myth by default. In the power struggle over the succession to Batista, Fidel had swept aside numerous leaders of the urban resistance; in the authoritarian climate that Castro quickly imposed after taking power, there was no room for questioning the official version of the war. Thus the great majority of those involved in the anti-Batista movement had no one to tell their story until much later, after the heroic guerrilla was firmly established.

The founding myth of the heroic guerrilla was an important asset to Fidel Castro in legitimizing the revolution and in maintaining popular support during times of external threat and economic hardship. One of the myth's functions was to link the revolution to Cuban history, reassuring Cubans that however radical or unorthodox Fidel and his policies appeared, they were rooted in the national experience. Both his method—guerrilla warfare—and his goal—national independence—placed Castro squarely in the tradition of José Martí, Antonio Maceo, and Máximo Gómez, who had fought guerrilla wars for independence from Spain. The suffering, sacrifice, perseverance, and indomitable will of the guerrilla also served as models for the behavior of citizens struggling to throw off Yankee imperialism and build a new Cuba at times when massive amounts of volunteer labor were needed and material rewards were scarce. In his speeches, Fidel frequently exhorted the people to sacrifice in the spirit of the Sierra Maestra, and generations of children were indoctrinated in the values of self-abnegation and struggle characteristic of the heroic guerrilla. In these and other ways, the myth of the heroic guerrilla became an explicit and central part of the political culture of Castro's Cuba.

The myth of the heroic guerrilla also became a major Cuban export. For those Latin Americans already committed to revolution, the example of Cuba's successful guerrilla war provided hope and a model for successful insurrection. For the many others who had not been committed to radical politics before, the romantic version of the Cuban revolutionary war and its heroic guerrillas was a siren song that lured them to action. After Che Guevara published *Guerrilla Warfare* in 1960, Latin Americans had available a handbook on how to emulate Castro's victory. Unfortunately for the many who died trying to follow the Cuban example, the myth of the heroic guerrilla was a very selective, even misleading, recounting of Fidel Castro's road to power.

Notes

1. Fidel Castro, *Revolutionary Struggle, 1947–1958*, ed. Rolando E. Bonachea and Nelson P. Valdés (Cambridge, MA: MIT Press, 1972), 147, 149.

2. https://ourdocuments.gov/doc.php?flash=true&doc=55.

3. Jaime Suchlicki, *Cuba from Columbus to Castro and Beyond*, 5th ed. (Washington, D.C.: Brassey's, 2002), 78.

4. Castro, *Revolutionary Struggle*, 174–75.

5. Fidel Castro and Ignacio Ramonet, *Fidel Castro: My Life, a Spoken Autobiography*, trans. Andrew Hurley (New York: Scribner, 2008), 115.

6. Castro, *Revolutionary Struggle*, 221.

7. Ernesto (Che) Guevara, *Reminiscences of the Cuban Revolutionary War*, trans. Victoria Ortiz (New York: Grove Press, 1968), 40.

8. Guevara, *Reminiscences*, 81.

9. *New York Times*, February 24, 1957.

10. Guevara, *Reminiscences*, 117.

11. Julia E. Sweig, *Inside the Cuban Revolution: Fidel Castro and the Urban Underground* (Cambridge, MA: Harvard University Press, 2002), 136.

12. Edward González, *Cuba under Castro: The Limits of Charisma* (Boston: Houghton Mifflin, 1974), 92. Despite this admission, the official line had not changed over two decades later. In a small display in Havana's Museum of the Revolution, the urban fighters were acknowledged to have "played an important role as an *element of support* [italics added] for the struggle that unfolded in the mountains." Author's observation, 1991; author's translation.

CHAPTER TWO

Cuba: The Making of a Revolution

Within months of coming to power, Fidel Castro demonstrated his commitment to creating a new Cuba. Within two years, Castro had laid the foundations for a thorough revolution in Cuba's social, economic, and political structures and in 1968 completed the transition to socialism with the "revolutionary offensive" against the last vestiges of capitalism on the island. In Cuba's foreign affairs the shape of revolution was clear by 1962 when, after breaking with and being attacked by the United States, Fidel cemented his alliance with the Soviet Union. Compared with the other iconic 20th-century revolutions—the 1917 Bolshevik revolution in Russian and Mao Zedong's 1949 Chinese revolution—the Cuban Revolution developed with lighting speed. The pace and thoroughness of Cuba's transformation provided example and inspiration to the poor masses and political left of Latin America while causing grave concern among Latin America's elites and political conservatives and raising alarms in Washington, D.C.

Although Castro soon adopted socialism as the model for Cuba's new economy and society, it is important to note that it was in the first three years of his government—prior to his public embrace of Marxism-Leninism—that Fidel instituted the most dramatic revolutionary changes. He was guided in part by the well-known program that M-26-7 had been proclaiming for several years before the triumph: its 10 points included national sovereignty, economic independence, work for all, social justice, education, political democracy, civil authority, religious freedom, public morality, and constructive friendship with all countries. Evident in the

M-26-7 program was the intention of addressing Cuba's historic ills: U.S. dominance, lopsided reliance on sugar with its attendant social and economic problems, social fragmentation and injustice, and a discredited political system.

Castro was also guided during his early years in office by his own maximalist proclivities. Beginning with the 1953 assault on the Moncada Barracks, Fidel had exhibited a tendency to attack the greatest challenges in order to have the maximum impact. The period of seasoning in the Sierra Maestra demonstrated the persistence and dedication of Fidel and his followers. These experiences and characteristics, which one scholar has called the "Moncada Barracks mentality" and the "Sierra Maestra complex," quickly came to the fore in Castro's Cuba as Fidel set out to rectify, almost overnight, Cuba's historic condition.[1]

Finally, Castro had an unusual opportunity during his early years in power to tackle Cuba's problems head-on. Although the political system was already in disrepute before Batista's coup, the last semblance of legitimate authority disappeared under the dictator. Thus Batista's flight left a power vacuum that no individual, group, or institution associated with the old regime could pretend to fill. And the Auténticos and other moderates who claimed a role in the new government as a result of their opposition to Batista lacked influence alongside Fidel, whose enormous popularity and control over the rebel army made him the uncontested leader of post-Batista Cuba. In this situation, there were no restraints on Castro's appetite for change. In fact, with his support based on the poor, on the working and some of the middle classes, and on youth, and with the elites effectively out of the political equation, momentum for radical innovation grew quickly after the victory.

A Communist Revolution

For the first four and a half months following his victory, Castro's posture was fairly moderate. He and the other principal anti-Batista forces had agreed in advance on Manuel Urrutia, a respected jurist, as acting president. Urrutia selected a cabinet balanced between bourgeois figures and Castro supporters. The United States recognized the Urrutia government a week after Batista's flight, maintaining correct, if not cordial, relations. Castro visited the United States in April 1959, invited by the Newspaper Editors Association to address its convention. His 15-day visit became a successful goodwill tour.

Beneath the facade of moderation, there were early signs of Castro's quest for power and his commitment to breaking with the past. As commander of the Rebel Armed Forces, Castro held de facto veto power over the government. In mid-February 1959, Castro had President Urrutia appoint him prime minister, formalizing his control. The summary trial and execution of several hundred Batista officials and collaborators was a further sign of Castro's seriousness of purpose and confirmation of his pledge from the Sierra Maestra to punish those most responsible for the repression, torture, and assassination of Batista opponents. Given the normal scenario of exiling, not killing, the operatives of deposed Latin American regimes, the executions raised significant concerns. Apprehension among U.S. leaders and some Cubans grew when Castro called off the elections he had been promising throughout the struggle against Batista, saying "Revolution first, elections later."[2]

Even more vexing to U.S. officials and Cuban elites were increasing signs of Castro's accommodation with Cuba's Communists, the PSP, a move that presaged his formal embrace of Marxism and construction of an alliance with the Soviet Union. For Castro, forging the PSP alliance was a pragmatic decision designed to help him consolidate power. Despite the antagonisms resulting from the Communists' late entry into the anti-Batista struggle and their characterizing him as a "bourgeois adventurer," Castro quickly established a close working relationship with the PSP and its leader, Carlos Rafael Rodríguez. The PSP had a highly centralized organization and historic control of major blocs of the labor movement. Moreover, having remained on the sidelines of the anti-Batista struggle until near the end, the PSP had not experienced the degree of repression suffered by other rebel groups and emerged from the fray intact and functional. To cement the alliance, in July 1959 Castro removed President Urrutia, who resisted the growing Communist ties, and replaced him in the presidency with long-time PSP militant and lawyer Osvaldo Dorticós.

The PSP alliance was just the beginning of Castro's move toward Communism and the Soviet Union. On April 15, 1961, he publicly affirmed that Cuba's transformation in progress was a "socialist revolution carried out under the very noses of the Yankees."[3] He created a new governing organization three months later with the merger of M-26-7, the PSP, and the smaller DR into the Integrated Revolutionary Organizations (Organizaciones Revolucionarias Integradas, ORI). After months of public hints of his Marxist sentiments, Castro declared in a long speech on December 2, 1961: "I am a Marxist-Leninist and I will be a Marxist-Leninist until the last day of my life."[4] The founding of the Communist Party of Cuba (Partido Comunista de Cuba, PCC) in 1965 completed the Castro–Communist merger and formalized the revolution's Communist character.

Participants, observers, and scholars have addressed the intriguing question of Castro's turn to Marxism and his motivations for working with the Cuban Communists, establishing socialism, and aligning Cuba with the Soviet Union. This is a critical question, as it had profound implications for Cuban citizens and for U.S.–Cuban relations. Establishing Communism meant that Western norms of civil and political human rights were subordinated to economic and social human rights, as in all Communist regimes and as embedded in Cuba's 1976 constitution, which formally established a Communist state. Castro's decision to embrace Communism also alienated Cuba from the United States during the Cold War and for a quarter of a century thereafter, subjecting its people to an economic embargo that failed in its objective of bringing down the Castro government but retarded Cuba's economic development and subjected its citizens to serious material depravations.

An early hypothesis explaining the Communist path of the Cuban Revolution was that Castro had been a Communist all along but had hidden his true colors until firmly entrenched in power to avoid alienating many Cubans and inviting U.S. intervention. This conspiracy theory, understandably popular with Cubans who felt betrayed by Castro, gained little credence among scholars and objective analysts.

Most observers of the Cuban Revolution assume that Castro converted to Marxism after taking power; the debate focused on whether he embraced Marxism of his own volition or whether the United States forced him into Marxism and the Soviet alliance. The latter interpretation holds that strong U.S. opposition to Castro's radical agenda drove him to seek an alliance with the Soviet Union, the only power in the bipolar world of the 1960s potentially capable of protecting his revolution from U.S. military intervention. In order to achieve Soviet support in the dangerous game of confronting the United States in its own backyard, he had to demonstrate a firm commitment to Marxism and the Soviet Union.

While acknowledging the effects of U.S. pressure, others have argued that the turn to Communism was Castro's free choice. Enjoying immense personal prestige and power following his triumph, Castro was in a position to take the revolution in any direction he might have chosen. In explaining his transition toward Communism, he alleged a gradual conversion, basically completed by 1959, to a Marxist-Leninist worldview and a conviction that Cuba's and Latin America's problems could not be resolved within the framework of capitalism: "I have had a very interesting and very effective schooling. That is simply . . . the process which, from my first questionings until the present moment, made me into a Marxist revolutionary."[5]

In embracing Marxism and establishing a Communist state, Castro was part of a broader pattern. Whereas today we tend to view Communism as an antiquated, failed experiment, when Castro came to power in 1959, Communism was attractive to many in the developing world because it promised to solve problems of underdevelopment and social injustice. Communism, moreover, had momentum at the time. Following the defeat of Nazi Germany in World War II, the USSR imposed Communist rule on the Eastern European countries it occupied. Mao Zedong established a Communist regime in China, the world's most populous country, just 10 years before Castro came to power, and several African countries emerging from colonialism flirted with Communism. Communist expansion in the former French colonies of Indochina was well underway, and U.S. governments from the 1950s into the 1970s were so concerned about Communist momentum in Southeast Asia that they conducted the long and frustrating Vietnam War in a vain attempt to stop it. During the 1950s and 1960s, the competition between the two rival systems—capitalism and Communism—was intense, and it was unclear which would prevail. In 1956 Soviet premier Nikita Khrushchev famously told a group of diplomats from capitalist countries: "Whether you like it or not, history is on our side. We will bury you."[6] His boast appeared credible at the time.

Whatever the exact circumstances of Castro's decision to carry out a Communist revolution, his Marxism was incompatible with the political democracy promised in the M-26-7 program. He rejected Western-style democracy, calling it "the dictatorship of the capitalists."[7] He was undoubtedly correct in recognizing the incompatibility between Western democracy and social revolution; the constraints on action inherent in constitutional democracies and the power of money in the electoral and legislative processes would have thwarted Castro's ability to carry out the radical changes to which he was committed. Yet the establishment of a Communist state, even though it carried Fidel's distinctive imprint, disillusioned some of his early supporters in Latin America as it did many in Cuba. It also confirmed the views of those conservatives in Washington and Latin America who argued that reform must be resisted because of its unpredictable course and potentially dangerous outcomes.

It is important to note that the establishment of Communist Party rule in Cuba followed a course unique in the annals of Communism. Rather than the Communists capturing the revolution, Castro captured the Communists for his own ends. He was either titular or de facto head of all government and party organizations, and his trusted veterans of the Sierra

Maestra—rather than PSP cadres—completely dominated the remaining positions of power. This relationship between long-time Communists and those whose first loyalty was to Fidel remained stable over the years. Following the establishment of a formal Communist state in 1976, Castro held the positions of head of state and head of party without interruption until ceding power to his brother Raúl in 2008, while Sierra Maestra veterans continued to dominate the political and military leadership, eventually promoting a younger generation to top positions in the 1990s.

The Domestic Revolution

By the end of 1960, both the domestic revolution and the realignment of Cuba's international relations were well advanced. Influenced by the M-26-7 program in its broad outlines, by the Marxists within Castro's inner circle, and by Fidel's unfolding vision of a new Cuba, the dual revolution proceeded without any strict guidelines or preexisting blueprint. Rather, the far-reaching changes were often guided by impulse and improvisation, reflecting the maximalism of the Moncada Barracks approach and the reliance on will, sacrifice, and dedication that characterized the Sierra Maestra experience.

In March 1959, Castro implemented three populist measures that hinted at the shape of the revolution to come: he took over the management of the U.S.-owned telephone company and cut its rates, decreed the forced sale of vacant urban lots to end land speculation and reduce prices, and slashed urban rents by 50 percent. Two months later, he unveiled the centerpiece of his emerging plan for transforming Cuba at a televised ceremony in the Sierra Maestra. The agrarian reform law of May 17, 1959, launched the redistributive phase of the revolution by mandating the expropriation of large agricultural properties. The declaration of agrarian reform began the revolutionary transformation of Cuba's economy and, as a consequence, of Cuban society. The social revolution unfolded as a result of the state's incremental appropriation of businesses and property, which eventually made nearly every Cuban worker a state employee subject to wages and benefits set by a government committed to an egalitarian society.

The agrarian reform law realized a long-standing aspiration of many Cubans. The progressive 1940 constitution had banned *latifundia* (very large rural holdings) but left definition and implementation to future governments which, given the power of U.S. and Cuban sugar interests, did nothing until Castro's initiative. The law established the maximum legal holding at 30 *caballerías* (403 hectares or 995 acres), with exceptions for

unusually efficient units of up to 1,342 hectares. It also abolished renting
and sharecropping and severely restricted foreign ownership of agricultural
land. The land taken, much of it owned by large U.S. sugar and cattle companies, passed into different types of holdings. Nearly 100,000 renters and
sharecroppers of expropriated land received 27 hectares and had the right
to purchase 40 hectares more where the land was available; unutilized land
became state property; and large sugar and cattle holdings worked by wage
labor became cooperatives or state enterprises rather than being broken
into inefficient small parcels. Compensation was to be awarded to expropriated owners in 20-year government bonds bearing 4.5 percent interest,
with prices to be based on declared value as reflected in the tax rolls. As
owners typically undervalued their land in order to save on taxes, compensation would be well below market value—leading the U.S. government on
June 11 to demand "prompt, adequate, and effective compensation" for
its citizens.[8]

By 1961 implementation of the agrarian reform law and other government actions had created a mixed agricultural economy in which small
and medium private holdings of 67 hectares or less constituted approximately 39 percent of Cuba's total agricultural surface, large private holdings of over 67 hectares 19 percent, and cooperatives and state farms
42 percent. In only two years, Fidel's agrarian reform had progressed
remarkably, but with the adoption of socialism as the revolution's goal, further measures to reduce the capitalist sector in agriculture were implemented. By 1962 the cooperatives were converted to state farms, and a
second agrarian reform law of October 1963 limited private holdings to
67 hectares. Some 10,000 properties exceeding that size were expropriated and their land was incorporated into the state farm sector, which by
1965 encompassed approximately 60 percent of Cuba's agricultural surface and continued to grow through purchase and selective expropriation
to reach 68 percent in 1971 and 79 percent in 1977.

The continued existence of a large private farm sector—some 250,000
holdings averaging 13 hectares and occupying nearly 40 percent of total
agricultural surface in 1965—was an anomaly in the context of Cuba's
socialist economy. Castro addressed this problem through the mechanism
of the National Association of Small Farmers (Asociación Nacional de Agricultores Pequeños, ANAP), which organized a large majority of the smallholders into production cooperatives. This, combined with close regulation
of all aspects of small farms, including the obligatory sale of produce at
fixed prices to the state and the prohibition against selling land except to
the state, blurred the distinction between peasant farmers and workers on

state farms. This transformation of agriculture put the most valuable sector of the Cuban economy and approximately half of the country's economically active population under state control.

Complementing the agrarian reform program, nationalization of the Cuban economy proceeded on several other fronts. A major impetus to the growth of the state sector was the confiscation of all properties of enemies of the regime and of exiles. Within weeks of coming to power, Castro created the Ministry for the Recovery of Embezzled Property (Ministerio de Recuperación de Bienes Malversados), with sweeping powers to seize the assets of Batista and his collaborators, "counterrevolutionaries," and after 1960, of all exiles. During most of his first 15 years in power, Castro maintained a policy of fairly easy emigration that removed real and potential enemies as well as promoting the transfer of major economic assets to the state. Initially composed primarily of Batista collaborators and supporters, the flow of exiles swelled with Cubans' deepening realization of Castro's revolutionary intentions. Whereas all socioeconomic groups were represented among the emigrants, the upper and middle classes predominated in the exodus which reached some 600,000, or nearly a tenth of Cuba's 1958 population, by 1974. As a result, the state inherited a significant share of the Cuban-owned businesses, real estate, and rural land through the phenomenon of mass exile.

Another major blow to private property in Cuba came between August and October 1960 in the midst of a flurry of actions and counter-actions pitting Havana against Washington. In response to the cancellation of the Cuban sugar quota in the U.S. market, Castro decreed the expropriation of all U.S.-owned property in Cuba without compensation. Agricultural land had already been affected by the agrarian reform law, but the extent of U.S. investment was such—over a billion dollars—that the expropriations transferred major portions of the public utilities, banking, transportation, communications, sugar refining, insurance, industrial, mining, and tourism sectors of the economy to the Cuban state and made it the employer of hundreds of thousands of additional workers.

The onslaught against U.S. holdings was a signal for the accelerated expropriation of the remaining Cuban-and foreign-owned enterprises. By 1964 the only remaining significant private activities outside of agriculture were retail business and services. The final thrust of the drive to eliminate private business was the "revolutionary offensive" of 1968. In one blow the nearly 56,000 remaining private businesses throughout the country were expropriated: restaurants, laundries, mechanic shops, and beauty parlors became part of the state-owned economy overnight. After the elimination of small business, the only remaining vestiges of the capitalist economy were the small farmers, whose economic rights were severely limited.

After the revolutionary offensive, every working Cuban was subject to state-set wages or other income. In 1968 the scale ran from 96 pesos per month for a cane cutter to 900 pesos per month for a supreme court judge. All unskilled and most skilled workers earned between 96 and 250 pesos monthly, with most salaries above that level reserved for ranking government functionaries. The minimum retirement pension was 60 pesos per month.[9] On one hand, this wage scale reveals pragmatic concessions designed to keep needed talent from emigrating. On the other hand, the great compaction of wage differences since 1959 clearly reveals Castro's interpretation of social justice as egalitarianism.

Two other elements of government policy were as revolutionary as the leveling trend of wages. First, full-time, year-round work was guaranteed for all Cubans. To underscore the significance of work for all, even at the wage of a cane cutter, one only needs to compare the new order with the 1950s, when Cuba had approximately 10 percent year-round unemployment and 25 percent of the labor force worked less than half the year. For the poor masses of Cubans, 96 pesos per month year-round was a monumental gain. The second policy that raised living standards for the less well paid was the provision of free social services: Castro redirected much of the national budget toward establishing cradle-to-grave social welfare—health care, education, housing, transportation, retirement benefits, and vacations.

Establishment of the socialist variant of the welfare state should be seen in the context of the major economic problems of the 1960s, which set back Cuba's development, caused aggravating shortages of food and other essentials as well as consumer goods, and failed to reduce the island's dependence on sugar monoculture. Fidel's Moncada Barracks approach to economic development simply did not work. His impatience to end Cuba's excessive dependence on sugar motivated a major cutback in cane planting after 1959, but a concurrent program of crash industrialization and agricultural diversification failed to compensate for the decline of sugar revenues.

As minister of industry between 1961 and 1965, Che Guevara experimented with moral incentives and various kinds of planning and market strategies, honestly attempting to revolutionize the norms of work and production in pursuit of Communism and the "New Cuban Man"—a variant of the "New Soviet Man" or worker hero of the 1930s Soviet Union. However, his goals were thwarted by the hard realities of imbedded attitudes, infrastructural weaknesses, heavy defense expenditures, and the damaging

U.S. embargo. Reacting to the failed plans of the early 1960s, in 1963 Fidel reversed his approach to sugar, extending plantings and setting the maximalist goal of a 10-million-ton harvest in 1970—nearly twice the average harvest of the 1950s. Having made the 10 million tons the national priority of the late 1960s, Fidel directed all available investment capital and labor to sugar, weakening the recently established industrial and agricultural enterprises but missing the goal by 1.5 million tons. By the 1970s the period of greatest experimentation was over and modest economic growth resumed.

The economic failures of the 1960s prevented the full development of social services for all Cubans, especially those in remote rural areas. Nonetheless, with full-time, year-round employment available at fixed wages and a host of free social services developed as fully as austere conditions permitted, a large share of Cuba's population, probably a majority, was materially better off after a few years of revolution than it had been under the old order. Despite the imperfections of the system and the glaring shortages that required the establishment of rationing in 1962, life improved markedly in terms of health, nutrition, housing, educational opportunity, and economic security. The redistribution of resources threatened the wealthy and the better-off middle classes, of course; the majority of the upper class and substantial numbers of the middle class chose exile over loss of status and, for many, a greatly reduced standard of living. This picture of changes in living standards in revolutionary Cuba sums up the social revolution: it took from the rich and the comfortable and gave to the poor and needy. Even though the Cuban economy failed to develop as projected, the revolution was an austere success. It was this redistribution of societal goods, not the statistics on economic performance, that made the Cuban Revolution so appealing to millions of Latin Americans.

The Revolution in Foreign Affairs

The domestic revolution and the revolution in international relations were closely intertwined. The linkage between domestic and foreign policy was nothing new: throughout Cuba's republican history, U.S. dominance closely circumscribed Cuban governments' freedom of action in domestic policy. So long as Cuba's economic health depended on favorable U.S. sugar tariffs and quotas, no government could afford to antagonize Washington with policies detrimental to U.S. business interests in Cuba. This meant that any legislation granting labor benefits, raising taxes, regulating utility rates, or in any way affecting the profits or security of the ubiquitous American companies had to be moderate or, as in several cases, had to remain on the books without implementation. As demonstrated in 1933, reformist governments were not welcome.

Despite the connections between the revolutions in domestic and foreign affairs, one should not conclude that one drove the other. Castro took power convinced that Cuba needed both a social revolution and a release from historic subservience to the United States, and he quickly set out to achieve both. The timing of certain domestic events inevitably affected the timing of developments in international relations, and vice versa; but Castro's commitment to creating a new Cuba clearly involved both arenas.

The agrarian reform law was the first substantive issue to drive a wedge between Cuba and the United States, and its impact was heightened by the already tense climate of relations resulting from provocations by both sides. In addition to the mass executions of Batista officials and Fidel's open domination of the government, Castro's cooperation with the PSP unnerved Washington. His strident calls for revolution and aid to exile invasions of Panama, Nicaragua, Haiti, and the Dominican Republic rankled U.S. officials. And Castro's growing popularity in Latin America was a matter of serious concern in Washington.

Meanwhile Washington contributed to the provocations. From early 1959, Cuban exiles, at first primarily Batista supporters and officials, conducted air and sea raids from Florida unhindered by U.S. authorities. During his April visit, Fidel was continually harassed by questions about his possible Communist inclinations—questions that were surely legitimate but that reminded Fidel of the United States' pretensions to veto power in Cuban politics. U.S. officials, among them Vice President Richard Nixon, openly urged the Eisenhower administration to take a strong stand against Castro. In December, Secretary of State Christian Herter publicly hinted at possible cuts in Cuba's sugar quota, thus invoking the long-established levers of control over Cuba. What Washington did not realize, however, was that rather than bullying Castro into submission, the use of economic leverage and military threats only reinforced his conviction that radical change was needed in Cuba's economy and its foreign relations.

The first concrete step in Cuba's realignment in international relations came when Soviet Deputy Prime Minister Anastas Mikoyan visited Cuba in February 1960 to sign a large-scale trade and loan agreement with Castro. Tensions with Washington escalated in early March when the French ship *La Coubre*, delivering arms from Belgium, blew up in Havana harbor, killing 75 dock workers and wounding some 200; Fidel accused the United States of sabotage. On March 17 President Eisenhower approved a Central Intelligence Agency (CIA) plan to train and equip an army of Cuban exiles for guerrilla action on the island or an invasion patterned loosely after the

U.S.-orchestrated 1954 invasion of Guatemala that overthrew the progressive government of Jacobo Árbenz. The CIA plan, intended as a clandestine operation, promptly became an open secret when recruitment of exiles began.

Skirmishing soon gave way to all-out economic warfare. When the first shipment of Soviet-supplied oil arrived in Cuba in April 1960, the U.S.-owned refineries, prompted by Washington, refused to process the crude. After a standoff, Castro expropriated the refineries between June 29 and July 2. On July 6, invoking powers granted by a law passed just a few days earlier, Eisenhower cancelled the Cuban sugar quota for the remainder of 1960, leaving Cuba with some 700,000 tons of unsold sugar. In response to that measure, Castro completed the expropriation of all U.S. holdings on the island. This bold action locked in the collision course that was already set.

The Eisenhower administration refrained from military action but increased diplomatic pressures against Castro. In August 1960 it attempted unsuccessfully to have the Organization of American States (OAS) condemn Cuba. On January 2, 1961, alleging that the U.S. embassy was full of CIA operatives, Castro asked the Eisenhower administration to reduce the size of its embassy staff to the number that Cuba had in Washington. In response, Eisenhower broke diplomatic relations the following day. The incoming Kennedy administration promptly extended the economic pressure on Castro by setting the 1961 sugar quota at zero. From the break in diplomatic relations, it was only a short step to war. Although he had campaigned on getting tough with Castro, Kennedy hesitated after being informed of the CIA's training of exiles in Guatemala. By April, two new factors pushed him toward action. The use of Guatemalan territory for training the exile army was becoming a volatile issue in that country; thus, despite its strong anti-Castro sentiment, the government of Miguel Ydígoras Fuentes began pressuring Washington to remove the irritant. Concurrently, U.S. intelligence learned that Cuban pilots being trained in Czechoslovakia to fly Soviet MiGs were scheduled to return shortly to Cuba, combat ready and with their new planes. The necessity of dealing with an expanded and modernized air force would mean more overt U.S. involvement than Kennedy wanted. After extensive debate among his advisors and escalating pressure from some, on April 5, Kennedy decided to strike; five days later, the invasion force was moved to its embarkation point in Nicaragua.

The Bay of Pigs operation had primary and secondary objectives. The first, reminiscent of Fidel's own Moncada Barracks approach, was to set off a general uprising against Castro that would lead to his rapid overthrow. This objective rested on the false assumptions that Castro lacked popular support and that a strong opposition stood ready to assist the invaders. The secondary objective, to be pursued if the first failed, was to capture and hold sufficient territory to allow the landing of a Cuban government in exile that would then call for U.S. aid in a "civil war" against Castro. The operation was designed to appear as an exclusively Cuban exile affair, with no U.S. involvement. The CIA plan failed in both objectives. Estimates of public disenchantment with the regime and of the strength of resistance groups were greatly exaggerated. Having expected U.S. military action for several months, moreover, Castro had prepared for the invasion. He had created a 200,000-person militia to back the army. In September 1960, he had called for the creation of Committees for the Defense of the Revolution (Comités de Defensa de la Revolución, CDRs) to exercise "revolutionary collective vigilance;" these mass organizations had grown rapidly and spread throughout the island by the time of the invasion.[10] Finally, upon learning of the imminence of the invasion, he arrested over 100,000 people of questionable loyalty to forestall collaboration with the invaders. Thus the hoped-for popular rising against Castro did not even begin.

The secondary objective also failed, due to miscalculations and the constraints on U.S. involvement imposed by the official line that the invasion was a Cuban exercise. The greatest miscalculation was that 1,400 men could succeed against Castro's army and militia. Nonetheless, as a prelude to the landing, planes with Cuban markings bombed air fields on April 15 to take out Castro's small air force. Cuban spokesmen immediately denounced the bombing in the United Nations as a U.S. action, which the Kennedy administration denied. But fearing more adverse publicity and a strong international reaction, Kennedy cancelled a second raid scheduled for the following morning, despite the failure of the first bombing to eliminate all of Castro's air power. When Brigade 2506 hit Girón beach at the Bay of Pigs on April 17, it encountered not only troops but also planes, which sank two supply ships of the exile flotilla and pinned down the landing party in swamps. Over 1,100 of the invaders surrendered by April 20, to be held captive for 20 months until ransomed by U.S. shipments of food and medicines. In addition to humiliating the United States, the Bay of Pigs fiasco strengthened Fidel's popular support and control in Cuba, heightened his popularity in Latin America, and accelerated Cuba's realignment with the Soviet Union.

The revolution in Cuba's international relations was complete by late 1962, when the United States and the Soviet Union reached the brink of nuclear war over the placement of Soviet nuclear missiles in Cuba earlier that year. From the perspective of global nuclear strategy, Cuba offered the Soviets their first opportunity to deploy short-range missiles capable of striking the United States and offsetting the American advantage of missile sites in Europe. For Castro, they represented protection against further U.S. aggression. Upon learning of the missiles' presence, Kennedy deployed a naval blockade to intercept a Soviet convoy bringing additional missiles to the island. The world watched tensely as the Soviet fleet steamed toward the blockade until, at the last minute, the ships turned back. Premier Nikita Khrushchev subsequently agreed to remove the missiles already installed; in return, the United States pledged not to invade Cuba and secretly agreed to remove its missiles from Turkey, the closest U.S. missile site to the USSR. Despite Castro's anger over the Soviets' unilateral action, from this point forward the Cuba–Soviet alliance was firm, if not always smooth, and the Cold War entered the Western Hemisphere in full force.

The years from 1962 through 1968 were a period of testing the alliance. Always an ardent nationalist, Fidel was not content for Cuba to fall from the eagle's talons into an equally dominant bear's hug. Thus Fidel and his regime gave various signals that, despite a growing reliance on Soviet economic and military aid, Cuba aspired to exercise an independent foreign policy. The major Cuban deviation from the Soviet line was Castro's active support of revolution in Latin America—a policy that countered the traditional Soviet approach of working gradually to build Communist parties and allies for revolution at some future time. In addition to exhorting revolutionaries to act, Fidel offered material aid, training, and financing to insurrectionary groups throughout Latin America. In 1966 he hosted the Tricontinental Conference, a meeting of revolutionary governments and organizations from Latin America, Africa, and Asia, whose purpose was to accelerate revolution throughout the Third World. The following year Castro established the Latin American Solidarity Organization (Organización Latinoamericana de Solidaridad, OLAS), a bureau of Latin American revolutionary parties and guerrilla groups provocatively designed as a parallel organization to the Washington-dominated OAS. The scope of his activities suggests that Castro may have been attempting to make Havana the seat of a third camp in international Communism, alongside Moscow and Beijing.

While Fidel overtly pushed the overthrow of governments, the Soviet Union attempted to maintain correct relations and to broaden its formal diplomatic contacts in Latin America so as to foster good working conditions for local Communist parties. The resultant friction between Havana and Moscow surfaced in several conflicts, most notably Castro's 1962 purge of a "microfaction" led by PSP veteran Aníbal Escalante and a second purge of the reinstated Escalante clique in 1968 on charges of fostering Soviet interests against those of Cuba. The testing period effectively ended in

1968, when to the dismay of many of his supporters Castro endorsed the Soviet intervention that ended Alexander Dubcek's "Prague spring" in Czechoslovakia. To many observers, this gesture of subservience to Moscow signaled Castro's reluctant abandonment of the quest for an independent foreign policy.

Cuba strengthened its ties to Moscow during the 1970s. It joined the Soviet-led trade organization Council for Mutual Economic Assistance (COMECON) in 1972, cementing the island's role as sugar purveyor to the Eastern bloc. Soviet aid became increasingly important to sustaining Cuba's economy. Although Fidel had his own reasons for involvement in Africa—Cuba's historic and ethnic ties to Africa, the opportunity to pursue revolution in a promising setting, and the aggrandizement of Cuba's international power—the dispatch of 50,000 Cuban troops to Angola, Ethiopia, and other African countries in the mid-1970s was widely interpreted as Cuba's playing the role of Soviet surrogate. Overall, as the 1970s wore on, Cuba exhibited more of the traits of a Soviet client state. Despite the ultimate failure of his aspirations for a truly independent Cuban foreign policy, in his first few years in power Castro had exceeded the dreams of the most ardent Latin American nationalists: he had removed Cuba from the U.S. orbit and challenged Yankee supremacy throughout the hemisphere. In fulfilling the anti-imperialist aspirations of the Latin American left, Castro set an example that enflamed nationalist sentiment throughout the hemisphere. For many years the fact that Cuba had failed to achieve full sovereignty was far less important to Latin American progressives than the fact that Castro had broken the ties of subservience to Washington and Wall Street—ties as strong in the Cuban case as they were in any Latin American country.

The Style of the Revolution

The popularity of the Cuban Revolution in Latin America was based primarily on the concrete accomplishments of the first few years: the victory of Castro's guerrillas over Batista's army, the institution of drastic changes in Cuba's economy and society for the benefit of the masses, and breaking U.S. economic and political dominance over the island. Dramatic as these developments were, they alone do not explain the enthusiasm that Castro's revolution generated in Latin America. The other ingredient that made the Cuban Revolution such an intoxicating brew was the style of the revolution. This style contributed not only to the revolution's initial impact in Latin America but also to sustaining its popularity long after the early accomplishments began to be overshadowed by the loss of independence to the Soviet Union, the lackluster economic record, and the prolongation of Castro's personal dictatorship.

Castro's credentials as a charismatic leader are well established. Even after decades in power, he remained a spellbinding orator and a dominant presence in any setting. During his early years in office he repeatedly demonstrated his remarkable ability to inspire crowds with emotional, extemporaneous four-or five-hour speeches rallying support for volunteer harvest labor or calling for vigilance against Yankee aggression. His exhortations to greater sacrifice and the deferral of material rewards were the sustenance that kept the revolution going during the period of economic hardships in the 1960s. Fidel's ascetic style; his proclivity for personal contacts with ordinary Cubans; his physical size and athletic prowess; the martial image that he projected with fatigues, boots, beard, and cigar—all of these traits complemented Fidel's intelligence, perseverance, flair for publicity, and extraordinary powers of persuasion to make him one of the 20th century's most fascinating and durable political leaders.

The David and Goliath quality of Castro's challenge to Washington was another element that cemented Fidel's power at home and gained sympathy and support for the revolution throughout Latin America. Through his defiance of the United States, which often amounted to taunting, open provocation, his refusal to back down under escalating U.S. pressure, his nationalization of U.S. assets, and finally through his defeat of the Washington-sponsored Bay of Pigs invasion, Castro acquired the international stature of a second Bolívar—a new liberator of Latin America. This successful challenge to the hegemonic power of the hemisphere resonated throughout Latin America, where almost every country had a primary symbol of U.S. imperialism—United Fruit Company in Central America, International Petroleum Company in Peru, Anaconda and Kennecott Copper in Chile, the canal in Panama, and so on—against which nationalist politicians railed but rarely acted. Fidel's actions against the United States, then, combined with his flamboyant and provocative style of pulling Uncle Sam's beard, gave vicarious satisfaction to the millions who possessed even a modestly nationalistic outlook.

Another characteristic that made the Cuban Revolution so influential in Latin America was the active support that Castro's government enjoyed within Cuba. The massive turnouts for Fidel's speeches and the obvious enthusiasm of the crowds for the revolution and its policies were but a partial barometer of popular support. More impressive was the widespread participation of millions of Cubans in the tasks of the revolution such as volunteer labor, the literacy campaign, and the CDRs, which continued to grow after the Bay of Pigs invasion until some 2 million, or half the island's adult population, were enrolled by 1964. After the invasion crisis, the CDRs became more routinized and diversified in their functions, assuming the roles of neighborhood civic association, organizer of volunteer labor, overseer of the rationing system, and dispenser of justice in petty matters while continuing their original mission of exercising vigilance and enforcing conformity.

In addition to the ongoing work of the CDRs, volunteer labor was solicited as needs arose. Castro declared 1961 the "year of education" and launched a drive to eradicate illiteracy in Cuba. Some 270,000 volunteers, mainly students, spent up to nine months in every corner of the island instructing the illiterate 24 percent of the adult population in the fundamentals of reading and writing. Their efforts reportedly reduced the illiteracy rate to under 4 percent, a respectable rate even for developed countries. With the rapid expansion of sugar cane after 1963, great amounts of volunteer labor were needed for harvest. Construction of the Havana Green Belt also depended on volunteer labor.

Observers have raised questions about volunteer labor in revolutionary Cuba. Did individuals volunteer out of love of the revolution, or were they motivated by self-promotion and a quest for rewards? Was extra labor really volunteered or subtly coerced? Regardless of the answers, the fact is that in the 1960s millions of Cubans participated in their government's work. This is the picture that reached Latin America where the poor and the disenfranchised—a majority in most countries—saw government as their oppressor at the service of vested interests. They could hardly avoid being favorably impressed by their perception of a government which, in contrast to their own, enjoyed the active support and benefited from the volunteered sweat of its citizens.

Castro's impatience for change, his Moncada Barracks approach to getting things done, contributed to the style that made the Cuban Revolution appealing to the Latin American masses. Although Fidel's impatience for economic development, especially evident in the failed crash industrialization program, was a dysfunctional approach to economic management, his maximalist approach worked in other areas. The speed and scope of the agrarian reform, the boldness of the literacy campaign, and the brashness of the nationalization of U.S. investments gave the revolution its momentum and broadcast the message that nothing was impossible if the political will and the support of the masses were in place.

Fidel was well aware of the value of style in selling his revolution abroad. Throughout the struggle against Batista, he had repeatedly demonstrated his mastery of public relations skills, and once in power his use of radio and television, symbols, and his own charismatic powers helped him to portray the revolution in the most positive light. Castro announced his major policy moves in symbolic settings and in dramatic speeches. Newspaper, magazine, and book publishing became servants of the state and of Castro's publicity needs, much of their production aimed for export. Radio Havana set up a special section to broadcast throughout Latin America, not only in Spanish and Portuguese but also in the Indian languages spoken by significant numbers, such as Quechua and Aymara. No opportunity was lost to bring student, labor, and other groups to Cuba to show off the socialist paradise in the tropics.

In sum, although based primarily on Castro's guerrilla campaign and on the changes in Cuba's economy, society, and foreign relations, the impact of the Cuban Revolution on Latin America was greatly enhanced by the style that characterized the Castro regime during the 1960s and beyond. There is no doubt that the same concrete accomplishments, carried out by a leader lacking Fidel's charisma and style, would have excited the masses of Latin America considerably less than Castro's revolution did. It was evident at every turn that Fidel and the revolution were inseparable.

Notes

1. Edward González, *Cuba under Castro: The Limits of Charisma* (Boston: Houghton Mifflin, 1974).

2. Jorge I. Domínguez, *Cuba: Order and Revolution* (Cambridge, MA: Harvard University Press, 1978), 144.

3. Martin Kenner and James Petras, eds., *Fidel Castro Speaks* (New York: Grove Press, 1969), 74.

4. Lars Schoultz, *That Infernal Little Cuban Republic: The United States and the Cuban Revolution* (Chapel Hill: University of North Carolina Press, 2009), 174.

5. Lee Lockwood, *Castro's Cuba, Cuba's Fidel*, 2nd ed. (Boulder, CO: Westview Press, 1990), 160.

6. William Taubman, *Khrushchev: The Man and His Era* (New York: W. W. Norton, 2003), 427.

7. Lockwood, *Castro's Cuba,* 147.

8. Hugh Thomas, *Cuba, or, The Pursuit of Freedom,* updated ed. (New York: Da Capo Press, 1998), 1223.

9. The difference between official and black market exchange rates precludes accurately translating Cuban pesos into U.S. dollars.

10. Richard R. Fagen, *The Transformation of Political Culture in Cuba* (Stanford, CA: Stanford University Press, 1969), 69.

PART 2

The Promise and Threat
of Hemispheric Revolution

CHAPTER THREE

Fidelismo and the Radicalization of Latin American Politics

Fidel Castro's improbable victory over Batista sent a tremor throughout Latin America at the beginning of 1959. During the next three years, each bold stroke in the social transformation of Cuba and each clash with the United States set off an aftershock. The example of Castro's actions combined with his and Che Guevara's strident calls for revolution in the hemisphere had an immediate and profound effect on Latin American politics. In the words of journalist Herbert Matthews, who interviewed Castro in the Sierra Maestra in 1957, "something new, exciting, dangerous, and infectious has come into the Western Hemisphere with the Cuban Revolution."[1] This something was *fidelismo*. Reduced to essentials, *fidelismo* was simply the attitude that revolution should be pursued immediately. As Castro put it, "The duty of every revolutionary is to make the revolution," and he meant *now*.[2]

The most visible symptom of *fidelismo* was a dramatic growth of demand for change. In virtually every country, the intensity of political activity increased after Castro's victory as new actors, new social issues, and more aggressive challenges to the existing order came to the fore. The connection between the Cuban Revolution and the political ferment in Latin America was explicit. Fidel Castro and the Cuban Revolution dominated discussion and debate in the press, on the streets, and in the universities; the slogan "*Cuba sí, Yanqui no*" covered the walls of Latin America; and the term "*fidelista*" entered the political lexicon as new movements appeared and existing ones embraced the new faith in revolutionary action.

Latin American governments blamed Castro for the political agitation affecting their countries. They were often correct in alleging Cuban interference in their internal affairs, for, in contrast to Russia following the Bolshevik Revolution, there was no debate in Castro's Cuba between consolidating the revolution at home and immediately promoting revolution abroad. Castro mounted invasions, trained guerrillas, sent propaganda and money to *fidelista* groups, and occasionally dispatched arms and even personnel to support guerrilla activities. Nor was he reticent in calling for revolution, as in his speech on July 26, 1960, when he threatened to "convert the Cordillera of the Andes to the Sierra Maestra of the Hemisphere."[3] But it was the example of Cuba, translated into *fidelismo*, that was the driving force of political destabilization throughout Latin America. As Che Guevara observed: "Each time that an impudent people cries out for liberation, Cuba is accused; and it is true in a sense that Cuba is guilty, because Cuba has shown the way . . . This Cuban example is bad, a very bad example."[4]

Initial Impact of the Cuban Revolution

The magnitude of the Cuban Revolution's impact on Latin America was due in part to timing. First, the battery-powered transistor radio, invented just five years before Castro's rise to power, was mass produced and thus affordable even to many of Latin America's poorest. The transistor radio transcended the barrier of illiteracy and put the millions living beyond the reach of electricity, illiterate or not, in touch with developments in Cuba. Although the new medium of television was beyond the means of most Latin Americans, it was common to see knots of people in cities and towns congregating in front of shops displaying television sets and watching, among other features, news from Cuba

Second, the Cuban Revolution occurred at a time when civilian, democratically elected governments held sway in Latin America. The mid-to late 1950s, labeled by an observer as "the twilight of the tyrants," witnessed the demise of the authoritarian Juan Perón government in Argentina (1946–1955) and the dictatorships of Manuel Odría in Peru (1948–1956), Gustavo Rojas Pinilla in Colombia (1953–1957), and Marcos Pérez Jiménez in Venezuela (1952–1958).[5] With the exception of Castro's own emerging personalist regime, only five dictators remained after the fall of Batista, all in small, poor countries. Four of these regimes were long-term personal or family dictatorships: those of the Somoza family in Nicaragua, François "Papa

Doc" Duvalier in Haiti, Rafael Trujillo in the Dominican Republic, and Alfredo Stroessner in Paraguay. The fifth was a military-dominated regime in El Salvador. Despite these exceptions to the democratic trend, the proportion of Latin America's population living under elected governments had never been higher than in 1959.

Due to the predominance of civilian, democratic governments, Latin America was particularly vulnerable to destabilization by the impact of the Cuban Revolution. Media censorship was minimal under the democratic governments, and freedom to demonstrate, strike, and organize new political groups and parties, including explicitly pro-Castro organizations, was optimal in most of the hemisphere. Thus the political climate in most of Latin America allowed *fidelismo* to take root and even flourish, at least temporarily. Had it occurred a decade earlier, when authoritarian and dictatorial governments ruled in much of Latin America and before the transistor radio, the Cuban Revolution's impact would have been significantly reduced.

Despite the ascendancy of democratic governance, civilian political institutions in most countries had shallow roots and were ill prepared to weather the tempest unleashed by the Cuban Revolution. With the exceptions of Chile, Uruguay, Mexico, and Costa Rica, Latin American countries were subject to periodic coups and periods of military government. The armed forces were accustomed to intervening when crises created disorder and destabilized elected governments. When *fidelismo* swept over Latin America, many of the civilian regimes were threatened by the political awakening of previously inert groups such as peasants and urban slum dwellers, the surge in demands for reform, and the attempts to overthrow them by the Cuban guerrilla method.

Most of the individual components of the political turmoil so evident after 1958 were not new: student demonstrations, revolutionary propaganda, strikes, coup attempts, and exile invasions were part and parcel of the Latin American political scene. But the dramatic intensification of political conflict in the early 1960s propelled many governments toward collapse. Thus in several countries, the political ferment generated by the Cuban Revolution led to preemptive military coups to remove civilian governments considered too sympathetic toward or too ineffectual against *fidelismo*.

In Guatemala, persistent rumors of Cuban-sponsored exile invasions led President Eisenhower to dispatch navy ships to patrol Central American waters in November 1960. Meanwhile, frequent pro-Castro rallies, guerrilla activity, and intermittent government impositions of states of siege underscored popular support for Cuban-style revolution. Eventually, the impeccably credentialed right-wing Guatemalan president, General Miguel Ydígoras Fuentes, was overthrown in May 1963 by even more conservative officers in reaction to the ever-mounting pressure from *fidelistas* and their supporters. Ecuadorean President Carlos Arosemena was overthrown two months later on charges of Communist sympathies after the formation of *fidelista* groups, strikes, land invasions, and guerrilla outbreaks created a climate of unaccustomed turmoil. The military junta that overthrew Arosemena banned the Communist Party and vowed to wipe out "pro-Castro terrorist bands."[6] Similar circumstances led to military coups in Honduras and the Dominican Republic in 1963.

Despite the magnitude of the challenge, the majority of civilian governments weathered the storm of the early 1960s. Governments with the strongest institutional bases, and hence the greatest ability to resolve the conflicts created or exacerbated by the Cuban Revolution, were among the least affected. In traditionally democratic Uruguay, pro- and anti-Castro demonstrations were common, a new *fidelista* party bearing the acronym FIDEL was formed, labor and students grew more militant, and the government cracked down on what it called Communist propaganda from Cuba. Nonetheless, the government's survival was not threatened until late in the 1960s when the Tupamaro guerrillas took up arms. In Chile, another bastion of constitutional democracy, the strongly established political system was able to absorb the initial impact of the Cuban Revolution with relatively little instability. However, the example of the Cuban Revolution—especially land reform—contributed to a leftward movement of the Chilean electorate that brought a reformist government to power in 1964 and culminated with the election of Marxist Salvador Allende in 1970. Costa Rica had experienced a brief civil war in 1948 that led to the abolition of the national army and a new democratic constitution. The country underwent relatively little of the post-1959 turmoil that beset most of Latin America.

Mexico, where the broad-based Institutional Revolutionary Party (Partido Revolucionario Institucional, PRI) had governed for 30 years as heir to the great revolution of 1910, was only mildly affected by the Cuban Revolution. Mexico's rejection of Washington's Cuba policy—Mexico was the only OAS member that did not break relations with Havana—spared the government some of the wrath directed toward those governments that supported U.S. proposals for sanctions against Castro. Nonetheless, President Adolfo López Mateos cracked down on demonstrators following a general increase in student and other leftist activity, especially after the Bay of Pigs invasion. Noteworthy developments in the early years after Castro's victory included the founding of the *fidelista* National Liberation

Movement (Movimiento de Liberación Nacional, MLN) and the establish-ment of a new national peasant movement to compete with the PRI-controlled organization. Significant guerrilla activity did not appear in Mexico until the early 1970s.

The other civilian governments experienced varying degrees of insta-bility in the early 1960s. In Peru, the formation of a revolutionary peasant movement, land invasions, establishment of numerous pro-Castro groups and newspapers, bank robberies to finance revolution, and several out-breaks of guerrilla warfare punctuated the years after Castro came to power. The 1962 military coup that overthrew the conservative civilian government of Manuel Prado was partially motivated by the radicalization of Peruvian politics after 1958.

In Colombia, *fidelismo* exacerbated existing patterns of violence. Colom-bia had a long history of rural conflict, which intensified after the 1948 "Bogotazo" in which popular reformist presidential candidate Jorge Eliécer Gaitán was assassinated. The years following Castro's victory witnessed an increase in both urban and rural violence: rural violence alone was esti-mated to be costing over 200 lives monthly in 1962. The formation of *fidelista*-style fronts channeled the endemic violence into explicitly revolu-tionary movements.

The democratic left AD government of Rómulo Betancourt came to power in Venezuela just six weeks after Castro's victory. What began as a political friendship between Betancourt and Castro soon became a bitter rivalry as the two approaches to change became competitive—Venezuela's with U.S. moral and financial backing. Thus despite a solid record of achievement in reform, including an ambitious agrarian reform program, Betancourt's government not only struggled against Venezuela's long his-tory of dictatorship but also against a *fidelista* campaign of guerrilla warfare, urban sabotage, strikes, coup attempts, and constant agitation. Although he survived and turned the government over to an elected successor in 1964, Betancourt relied heavily on the use of martial law to make reform prevail over revolution in Venezuela.

Fidelismo exacerbated an already tense political climate in Argentina. Fol-lowing the military's removal of Juan Perón in 1955, the powerful Peronist unions and party apparatus continually battled the alternating military and civilian governments to recover their lost political rights. Influenced by the Cuban Revolution, both Peronist and independent leftist groups embraced the armed struggle and launched three brief, easily defeated rural guerrilla insurgencies between 1959 and 1968.

Along with the usual pro-Castro demonstrations and the founding of *fidelista* action groups, a guerrilla movement broke out in Panama in

April 1959. An invasion force of Panamanian exiles from Cuba landed in the same month after the United States, apprised of the plot, sent patrol boats and military supplies to the Panamanian government. To many Panamanians, the U.S.-owned Panama Canal embodied Yankee imperialism; thus the United States rather than the Panamanian government was the target of much of the Cuban-inspired political ferment. In November 1959 the worst anti-American riots in years rocked the country as Panamanians demanded sovereignty over the canal zone. Nationalist sentiment continued to grow through the 1960s and 1970s until the United States agreed in 1977 to surrender ownership of the canal to Panama in 2000.

In Bolivia, where mostly Indian peasants had received land and the vote in the 1952 revolution, *fidelismo* had relatively little impact. It spawned mini-factions, accentuated party competition, and encouraged the left and the tin miners' unions to adopt more aggressive positions until a 1964 coup installed a military government.

Lacking the restraints inherent in democratic governments, Latin America's dictatorships were better prepared than most elected governments to deal with the impact of the Cuban Revolution. Characterized by the proscription of serious opposition, a low level of party and union activity, censorship of news and books, and possessing well-oiled machinery of repression, these governments were usually able to snuff out internal dissent with relative ease. The exception was El Salvador, where progressive officers overthrew the conservative regime of José María Lemus in October 1960. The new government, however, was unable to consolidate power and was replaced after four months by a stridently anti-Castro, military-dominated regime. Although minor uprisings and exile invasions kept the dictatorships in states of alert for several years, the dictators proved resilient: apart from El Salvador's Lemus, only Trujillo in the Dominican Republic fell during the early years of the Cuban Revolution, the victim of an assassination in 1961. The Somoza regime in Nicaragua lasted until 1979, the Duvaliers in Haiti until 1986, and the Stroessner dictatorship in Paraguay until 1989. These were the regimes that Che Guevara, in *Guerrilla Warfare*, assured the world would be the next to fall after Batista.

Taken as a whole, Latin America in the first few years after Castro's victory experienced political turmoil of a level associated only with major crises. Prior to the Cuban Revolution two other waves of political unrest had affected most Latin American countries: that caused by the economic dislocations of World War I, and that set off by the impact of the Great Depression. The level and intensity of the political mobilization following the Cuban Revolution were far greater than those of the first two waves, and the impact of *fidelismo* was more widespread throughout Latin America.

Moreover, the stakes were much higher in 1959: the very economic and social foundations of Latin America were at issue. The titles of journalistic and academic studies of Latin America in the 1960s reflected the prevailing view of a continent in the throes of revolution: *Latin America: Evolution or Explosion?*; *Latin America, the Eleventh Hour*; and *Latin America: World in Revolution.*[7]

Rise of the Agrarian Reform Issue

One of the most far-reaching effects of the Cuban Revolution was to make agrarian reform a pressing political issue in most of Latin America. The example of Cuba's agrarian reform program was the main, but not the only factor influencing Latin American countries to debate, legislate, and in several instances to implement agrarian reform in the 1960s. Castro consistently portrayed his revolution as an agrarian revolution, not only in its results but also in its origins. Minimizing the roles and contributions of the urban resistance and the sugar proletariat in the overthrow of Batista, the official version of the struggle elevated the peasants of the Sierra Maestra to a level second only to that of the guerrillas themselves. Fidel certainly had needed and received peasant support, and late in the campaign, in October 1958, he had decreed the agrarian reform law of the Sierra Maestra to reward the peasants and consolidate their loyalty. Peasant support was thus linked to the success of the Cuban model of rural guerrilla warfare, and such peasant support, as in Cuba, could be won by promises of land. Che Guevara explicitly advised guerrillas to exploit "the age-old hunger of the peasant for the land on which he works or wishes to work" by raising "the banner of . . . agrarian reform."[8] Thus the very existence of Latin America's traditional systems of land tenure, which denied ownership and decent living standards to the vast majority of the rural population, came to be seen as a liability, a condition that the *fidelistas* would exploit.

Agrarian reform, designed to achieve a more equitable distribution of land, improve living conditions for the rural masses, and promote economic development, thus came to be an issue that could not be ignored after 1958. The left promised radical agrarian reform in order to mobilize peasant support for revolution. Reformist parties pushed land redistribution as a means of attacking the power of the large landowners and the national oligarchies, as well as a step toward social justice and economic development. Acknowledging the potency of the issue, even some conservative parties and interest groups embraced token to moderate agrarian reform as a means of preempting the revolutionaries and reformers. The United

States also embraced agrarian reform as a means of countering Cuban influence and made it a centerpiece of the Alliance for Progress.

Agrarian reform was not new to Latin America in 1959. The Mexican Revolution of 1910 had launched an agrarian reform program that continued into the early 1990s. Chile and Colombia had established modest programs of land subdivision in the 1920s and 1930s. Bolivia experienced thorough land redistribution in the wake of its 1952 revolution. The Árbenz administration in Guatemala initiated agrarian reform in the early 1950s; its expropriation of United Fruit Company land was a major cause of U.S. intervention to overthrow the government. Economists in the United Nations' Economic Commission for Latin America (ECLA) had been preaching throughout the 1950s that agrarian reform was essential to the region's economic development. But it was the Cuban Revolution, by linking revolution to land hunger, that brought an unprecedented sense of urgency to the agrarian reform issue throughout Latin America.

Latin America's 1960 population of 208 million was 56 percent rural, defined as living in the countryside or in towns of approximately 2,000 or less. Some 52 percent of Latin America's labor force worked in agriculture. The agricultural population was unevenly spread through the region. In Argentina, the country with the most productive agricultural sector, only 20 percent of the labor force worked in agriculture, in Uruguay 21 percent, and in Chile 30 percent. At the opposite extreme, the labor forces of Haiti, Honduras, and Guatemala were 83, 70, and 67 percent agricultural, respectively.

In general, land tenure in Latin America was skewed into patterns in which a relatively small number of large holdings, or *latifundia*, coexisted with large numbers of tiny plots, or *minifundia*. Representative examples in the mid-1960s include Chile, where the largest 7 percent of the farms occupied 81 percent of the land and the smallest 37 percent of the properties accounted for only 0.2 percent of agricultural surface; Brazil, where 60 percent of the land was held by 5 percent of the owners and 23 percent owned only 0.5 percent of the land; and Guatemala, where 0.1 percent of the owners held 41 percent of the land alongside the 88 percent who owned 14 percent of the land. These statistics describe a land tenure system characterized by large landowners' dominance of the best lands, with smallholders capable of subsistence production or less holding inferior lands; the U.S. or Western European–type family farm was notable by its scarcity in most countries. Land tenure figures do not indicate the great numbers of landless who worked year-round or seasonally on the large estates or squatted on the public domain. The main exceptions to the rule of extremes in land tenure patterns were Mexico and Bolivia, where revolutions had led to the destruction of the traditionally dominant haciendas in many regions, and Costa Rica, which had evolved a reasonably balanced land tenure pattern through its unique historical processes.

Working and living conditions for the landless masses varied greatly among countries and among regions within countries. In settings of modern commercial agriculture, such as Argentina, Uruguay, the Peruvian coast, or the banana districts of Central America's Caribbean coast, wage labor prevailed and some of the work force was unionized; although wages and living conditions were usually inferior to those of urban workers, some of the more onerous and degrading working conditions were absent. By contrast, in highland Ecuador and Peru, the systems of *huasipungueaje* and *pongueaje* were still entrenched: there, resident workers on backward haciendas not only owed most of their working time to the *patrón* in exchange for minimal grazing or cropping rights, but also had personal service obligations in the owner's rural or city houses and no rights of appeal or tenure. These mostly Indian workers, moreover, were often held in virtual slavery through debt peonage. In Guatemala, where racial and linguistic differences shaped landowner–peasant relations as in the Andes, conditions for the Indian peasants were not much better. In Chile the traditional system of *inquilinaje*, although not as brutal as rural labor in the heavily Indian countries, had been tightened since the late 19th century to become much more exploitive.

Landless rural laborers, other than those employed in the modern sector, were the most thoroughly marginalized of Latin America's populations. For the great majority of landless workers and for many subsistence or subsubsistence smallholders who depended on large landowners for seasonal work and credit, political participation was either nonexistent or meaningless. Literacy and property requirements and the simple absence of voter registrars in rural districts disenfranchised great numbers. Where a large conservative vote was important to offset the growing weight of the cities, landowners registered their workers and dependents and dictated their votes. The other potential avenue to political participation was union membership; however, rural unions in most of Latin America were illegal, landowner-dominated (white), or simply repressed by landowners and complicit local authorities.

The continued political marginalization of the rural masses was crucial to the status quo in national politics, as well as to landowners' uncontested control of land and labor. If given a free vote as a result of union pressures or of attaining economic independence of the *patrón* through land acquisition, the rural masses would undermine landowners' disproportionate power in national politics. If the Andean departments of Peru, the northeast states of Brazil, or the Central Valley provinces of Chile did not elect conservative landowners or their surrogates to the national Congress, where they traditionally enjoyed a veto power, or at least the ability to dilute offensive legislation, the more progressive representatives of the cities would prevail, to the peril of landowners' interests.

Thus the situation was a closed circle: lack of access to land and unions kept the rural poor disenfranchised; lack of effective political participation kept them landless, poor, and at the mercy of the landowners. The influence of the Cuban Revolution inspired *fidelistas* and reformers as well as some among the rural masses to try to break this deadlock; this threatened landowners not only with the loss of their land, but also with the loss of their traditional political power based on the exclusion or manipulation of the landless. Landowners' loss of control of the rural vote would lead to the reduction or even the collapse of conservative electoral power at the national level, threatening the interests of the elites in all economic sectors.

Even as the debate over agrarian reform heated up in academic tracts, the press, and national politics, some peasants took matters into their own hands. Latin American history offered ample precedent for the mobilization of the rural poor. The last third of the 19th century was a period of endemic peasant rebellion, especially in the Indian countries of Latin America where landowners used new legislation and the power of the national state to confiscate Indians' communal lands. Recovery of these village lands was the driving force of the peasant movement led by Emiliano Zapata in the Mexican Revolution. In Chile rural strikes, attempts to unionize, and calls for land division appeared sporadically but persistently beginning in 1919. El Salvador experienced a massive peasant uprising against landowners in 1932 which the authorities put down with thousands of deaths; this episode is known simply as "La Matanza" (the slaughter). The Bolivian peasant uprising of 1952 followed nearly two centuries of Indian rebellions in pursuit of land and justice. Overall, few countries had escaped some degree of peasant unrest expressed in land invasions, strikes, unionization efforts, or rebellion against landowners and the authorities.

However, the political awakening of rural Latin America after Castro's victory differed from the agrarian unrest that preceded it in both degree and kind. Whereas earlier outbreaks had been normally local and occasionally regional in scope, the agrarian agitation after 1958 was widely spread through Latin America. Many of the earlier agrarian movements had been politically unsophisticated: sometimes messianic, sometimes primitive *jacqueries*, sometimes localized uprisings based on specific narrow grievances. The situation was different by the 1960s. The transistor radio put illiterate peasants in touch with the outside world for the first time and let them know about Cuba's agrarian reform. The Cuban Revolution, moreover, spurred both Marxists and reformers to proselytize among agricultural workers and smallholders, promising agrarian reform and unionization. As a result, the peasant movements of the 1960s were sometimes national in scope and were often led by non-peasants connected to political parties and labor unions.

In several cases, peasant movements became major forces in national politics. Brazil, where peasant leagues gained wide membership, will be examined separately. In Peru the peasant movement in the remote valley of La Convención became a major factor because of the example it provided for the country's millions of landless Indians. A series of strikes began in 1960 under the leadership of Hugo Blanco, a Trotskyist from nearby Cuzco, and by 1962 the region's approximately 150 peasant unions launched a series of land invasions under their own agrarian reform decree. After sending troops against the thousands of mobilized Indians, the military government declared the valley an agrarian reform zone in an attempt to preempt Blanco and other organizers. Despite these measures, the continuing rise of peasant militancy in Peru produced a wave of land invasions involving some 300,000 people that swept the Andean regions following the 1963 election of President Fernando Belaúnde Terry, who had campaigned on a platform of moderate agrarian reform.

The mobilization of Chilean rural workers after Castro's victory was a major factor in a dramatic leftward shift of national politics. Although rural organizing was not entirely new to Chile, the impact of *fidelismo* heightened peasant demands for land and unleashed a fierce competition between *fidelistas* and non-Marxist reformers over unionization and political recruitment, resulting in an unprecedented rural mobilization. The deterioration of landowners' control of the rural vote was graphically demonstrated in elections beginning in 1961. The left's success in undermining the right's traditional power base opened the way for the elections of Christian Democrat Eduardo Frei in 1964 and Socialist Salvador Allende in 1970.

Elsewhere the combination of rural awakening and urban militants' proselytizing contributed to the climate of agitation and instability sweeping Latin America after 1958. Yet the extent of peasant mobilization should not be exaggerated. Despite their grievances, their heightened political awareness, and the currency of the agrarian reform issue in national politics, many Latin American peasants were held back by conservative attitudes of deference and resignation that had been ingrained over the centuries. The continuance in most countries of the intimidating traditional alliance of landowner and state, with its effective powers of repression, also deterred peasants from action. Conservative attitudes, fear of reprisals, and the

peasants' innate distrust of outsiders often fostered resistance to leftist organizers who ventured out from the cities. And to their dismay, the guerrilla
fighters who took to the hills expecting support from the downtrodden
peasants were usually disappointed. Thus although peasant movements
achieved substantial power in some countries, the specter of bloody peasant revolution did not materialize.

Fidelismo and the Latin American Left

At the time of the Cuban Revolution, the left in Latin America was
divided among Marxist and reformist parties, unions, student federations,
and professional organizations. Marxist groups included the Moscow-
oriented Communist parties, which were subject to the control of the
Communist Party of the Soviet Union. As the Cold War heated up in the
1950s, the United States had pressured Latin American governments to
make these Communist parties illegal; many had done so, but regardless of
their legal status, Communist parties, usually small, existed in every country. Included among the Communists by the 1960s were pro-China parties
and factions. The Marxists also included socialist parties without binding
international connections and small Trotskyite groups. The non-Marxist
left included personalist parties, especially Argentina's Peronists; secular
reformist parties, of which Peru's APRA, Venezuela's AD, and Mexico's PRI
were prototypes; and some of the new Christian Democratic parties, most
notably the Chilean. By 1959 APRA, PRI, and the Peronists were more left
in rhetoric than in conviction; nonetheless, they were historically reformist
and retained mass followings among the poor and the working classes of
their countries.

Although parties, unions, student federations, and other organizations
of the left were found everywhere, their strength was roughly proportion-
ate to a country's level of development. A sizeable industrial workforce and
a significant middle class were prerequisites to the rise of active and influential left parties. Thus the larger countries of South America generally had
more powerful Marxist and moderate left groups than were found in the
less developed countries of Central America and the Caribbean.

The Cuban Revolution had an immediate positive effect on the Latin
American left. The groundswell of demands for change and the radicalization of Latin America's politically participant population invigorated the
left, increasing its electoral appeal and its ability to mobilize the populace
for demonstrations, strikes, and other direct action. Parties and groups
identifying with the Cuban Revolution stood to gain simply by waving the
banner of *fidelismo*. Those of the non-*fidelista* left gained by embracing

the social reforms and the anti-Yankee stance of the Cuban Revolution while rejecting its Communist features.

The left did not merely wait to harvest the additional votes, membership, and support that might accrue from the radicalization of labor, intellectuals, youth, and other elements of the population who already participated in politics; it set out actively to develop followings among the politically marginalized population—especially the peasants. As noted earlier, the impact of *fidelismo* precipitated competition in rural Chile between Marxists and Christian Democrats, resulting in the unionization of thousands of the rural poor and the delivery of their votes to the left. In Brazil's northeast, Christians and *fidelistas* recruited among the politically marginal peasantry, and left cadres penetrated the once-forbidden countryside of several other countries with unprecedented tenacity.

The left also cultivated the growing masses of urban poor. By the 1960s, rural-to-urban migration had created huge rings of slums around Latin America's large cities—Lima's *barriadas*, Santiago's *callampas*, Buenos Aires' *villas miseria*, Rio de Janeiro's *favelas*—whose residents generally belonged to a lumpen proletariat lacking regular work, access to utilities and social services, and even security of tenure for their hovels. These new city dwellers were not as marginal to politics as their rural cousins; they were sometimes courted by paternalistic politicians such as Perón, Odría, and Rojas Pinilla who traded handouts for votes. After the Cuban Revolution heightened the appetite of the unorganized urban poor for change and improvement, Marxists and reformers turned more intensely to proselytizing them through establishing neighborhood organizations, staging protests for the extension of utilities and services to the slums, and directing self-help projects.

Even while boosting the left, the Cuban Revolution also dealt some setbacks to the Marxists and, to a lesser extent, to the moderates. For the Marxists, particularly the Communist parties, Castro's spectacular moves were a challenge to their entrenched modus operandi and to their very conceptions of revolution. Since their founding, the mainline, Moscow-affiliated Communist parties throughout Latin America had followed the lead of the Soviet Communist Party in matters of strategy. With a brief hiatus, the Moscow line after 1935 was to set aside the armed struggle in favor of legal means of action and cooperation with progressive parties. Comintern policy was to build Communist strength over the long run through labor union activity and coalition politics in order to have a vanguard party in place when the "objective conditions" of sufficient economic and political maturity had been reached. Because they were handy scapegoats and thus easy targets for government crackdowns, the Communists often collaborated with dictators such as Batista in exchange for hands-off policies that allowed them to operate.

The mood in Latin America after 1958 was clearly one of impatience with the status quo, of which the orthodox Communist parties were a part. Fearing the loss of the party's vanguard status as a host of new groupings appeared on the left, some Communist militants pushed for a more *fidelista* approach. However, the party apparatus tended to be dominated by older bureaucrats loyal to Moscow, who valued security and adhered to the gradualist strategy that deferred insurrection indefinitely. The dilemma grew worse for the Communist parties after Fidel took his unorthodox revolution into the Communist camp, for his views then enjoyed the patina of Communist legitimacy even when they directly contradicted the word from Moscow.

Despite these pressures, only four Communist parties adopted the insurrectionary line, and then for only a few years. The Venezuelan Communist Party, the most active of these, formally embraced the armed struggle in 1962; it reasserted the primacy of the legal struggle in 1965. In virtually every country, dissidents left the Communist parties, founded *fidelista* groups, and either supported or actively participated in guerrilla warfare and other approaches to overthrowing their governments. One of these dissidents, Carlos Marighela, summarized the *fidelistas'* brief against the established Communist parties in a critique of the Brazilian party: "All its activities consist in holding meetings and publishing policies and information. No action is planned; the struggle has been abandoned."[9] Once split, the Marxists rarely achieved unity on any issue or strategy; rather, the constant squabbling, ideological hair-splitting, and debate over strategy and tactics kept the left divided.

The Sino–Soviet split of 1964 further weakened the Marxists as pro-Chinese factions split from the Moscow-oriented parties in some 10 Latin American countries. The case of Peru demonstrates the extreme of Marxist fragmentation: by 1964 there were Trotskyists, Moscow-oriented Communists, Chinese-oriented Communists, a new party formed by APRA dissidents, and several independent groups, all claiming to have the correct approach to revolution and denouncing the errors of the others' ways. The non-Marxist left parties suffered similar fragmentation under the impact of *fidelismo* as their left wings lost patience with electoral politics. Even where the democratic left held power, as in Venezuela and Chile, frustration at the slow pace of reform, in contrast with the pace of change in Cuba, drove some members out of the parties and into advocacy of immediate revolution: the left broke away from Venezuela's AD in 1960, taking with it most of the AD youth movement and a substantial bloc of congressmen, and the Chilean Christian Democratic Party lost its left wing in 1969, which joined the Allende government in 1970. These defections did not weaken the democratic left to the extent that the Marxist groups were hurt by fragmentation; nonetheless, the cluttering of the political landscape with quarreling mini-parties set back the chances for cooperation in the electoral as well as the guerrilla arena—and cooperation was crucial to the success of either reform or revolution.

Fidelismo and the Brazilian Crisis, 1959–1964

The collapse of Brazil's civilian government and institutions provides a useful case study of the impact of *fidelismo* on Latin American political systems. When it happened in 1964, the military coup was not blamed on Castro's influence or the impact of the Cuban Revolution, but on the threat of a Communist takeover. The semantics, however, should not obscure the fact that the Brazilian Communist Party was not a threat to the government; rather, as elsewhere around Latin America, it was the stimulus of *fidelismo* upon existing, exploitable social, economic, and political conditions that brought on the Brazilian crisis.

In the five-plus years between Castro's victory and the military coup, Brazil exhibited the typical signs of *fidelismo*. The incidence of strikes grew sharply, stimulated by inflation as well as by political activism. Several new *fidelista* political organizations appeared, including an action-oriented spinoff of the Brazilian Communist Party, and preexisting groups such as student federations and labor unions became radicalized. Four competing literacy campaigns were underway by 1963, attempting to enfranchise the poor by qualifying them to meet the literacy requirement for voting. Land invasions grew more widespread during this period, some apparently spontaneous and others organized by the *ligas camponesas*, or peasant leagues.

The peasant leagues of the northeast were perhaps the single most threatening element in the popular mobilization affecting Brazil. Founded in 1955, the leagues initially manifested the messianic traits common to rural movements in the poor northeast and made modest demands, such as decent burials. By 1960, under the leadership of Francisco Julião, the peasant leagues had adopted a more radical stance, demanding land reform and sponsoring strikes, land invasions, and resistance to squatter evictions. This politicization was fueled in part by a combination of drought in the northeast and declining real income for workers on the sugar plantations. It was also driven by the influence of the Cuban Revolution. Julião and 100 peasants visited Cuba in May 1961; after returning, Julião organized a peasant congress whose slogan was "We want land by law or by force."[10]

BRAZIL

In response to the unprecedented rural mobilization, landowners armed themselves and set up or strengthened private security forces.

What was particularly threatening about the peasant leagues and the rural awakening was the very obvious dependence of Brazil's political system on the exclusion of the rural masses. The relatively developed, urbanized, and populous southern states of Rio de Janeiro, São Paulo, Paraná, Santa Catarina, and Rio Grande do Sul accounted for a majority of the country's qualified voters and thus could elect the president. Neutralizing the president, who was likely to be moderate or progressive, was a Congress that reflected Brazil's federal structure. The Senate consisted of three members per state, giving a great preponderance and a veto power to the nineteen rural and poor states over the five urban industrial states of the south.

Thus as in Chile, the prospect of landowners losing control of the rural vote as a result of agrarian reform threatened not only landowners but also urban vested interests. Also frightening to the elites was the prospect of electoral reform: granting the vote to illiterates would affect the outcomes of elections, particularly in the poor, rural states, and threaten the right's veto power in Congress.

The political crisis in Brazil went further than in other countries because in contrast to most of his counterparts, President João Goulart aligned himself with the mobilized forces in Brazil. Goulart had been elected vice president in 1960 and had assumed the presidency in August 1961 upon the surprise resignation of President Jânio Quadros after less than seven months in office. Because of Goulart's pro-labor stance and association with the late dictator Getúlio Vargas, a large faction within the military opposed his accession. A compromise allowed him to take office, but with reduced powers. By a five-to-one margin, a January 1963 plebiscite restored Goulart's full constitutional powers

During the period of his diminished authority, Goulart began to manifest his sympathy for reform. He attended the 1961 peasant congress and in his 1962 May Day speech called for a thorough agrarian reform. After the plebiscite, he sponsored an agrarian reform bill that was easily defeated in Congress; a bill to enfranchise illiterates met the same predictable fate. However, Congress did pass a 1963 law legalizing rural unions and setting minimum wages. Containing many restrictions and obstacles to implementation, the law was intended as window dressing but its effect was to further stimulate the rural mobilization sweeping Brazil.

The standoff between president and Congress on agrarian reform and enfranchisement of illiterates ordinarily would have killed both issues, but Brazil was not experiencing normal times and Goulart was not an ordinary president. Goulart opted to push ahead with his reforms, relying on the state of rural and urban mobilization to intimidate Congress. At a huge rally on March 13, 1964, he issued decrees authorizing a mild version of his agrarian reform bill and nationalizing the oil refineries; he also announced his intention of introducing legislation for a more radical agrarian reform and the enfranchisement of illiterates. With these actions Goulart threw down the gauntlet, for if he could set fundamental national policy by decree, the gates would open to full-scale agrarian reform and enfranchisement of illiterates: in other words, the gates would open to revolution. During Goulart's final months, U.S. personnel on the scene thought "in terms of Brazil as another Cuba."[11]

Goulart capped off his challenge to the Brazilian establishment by granting pardons to 2,000 enlisted sailors and marines who had received military punishment for holding an illegal political meeting. This override of military discipline, which the officer corps saw as an open invitation to sedition, raised worries about insurrection from within the military and the possibility of a fate similar to that of Cuba's professional army after its defeat and dismemberment by Castro. Having alienated conservative and moderate civilians and the military establishment, Goulart had little chance to survive in office. The coup came on March 31, 1964.

The case of Brazil during the high tide of *fidelismo* in Latin America is unique. Whereas the turmoil unleashed by *fidelismo* was usually met with a combination of token reforms and heightened repression, in Brazil the president himself attempted to meet the demands of the mobilized poor and simultaneously to mold them into a broad base of support. Goulart miscalculated in both attempts: Brazil's civilian and military establishments would not tolerate a *fidelista*-style revolution led from above; and despite their state of mobilization, the urban and rural masses were no match for the armed forces, and they knew it. Thus when Goulart called for popular resistance to the coup, his call went unheeded.

The nature of the military-dominated government that replaced Goulart reflected how seriously the conservatives and the officer corps perceived the revolutionary threat in Brazil. The military soon determined that civilians of any political hue could not be trusted to govern until the conditions that had fostered radicalization had been eliminated. This ambitious task brought severe repression and economic hardship for Brazil's masses for many years. The impact of the Cuban Revolution on Brazil gave birth to the first of the new-style, extremely repressive military regimes that dominated much of Latin America in the 1970s and 1980s.

Notes

1. Herbert Matthews, *The Cuban Story* (New York: George Braziller, 1961), 185.

2. Fidel Castro, *The First and Second Declarations of Havana: Manifestos of Revolutionary Struggle in the Americas Adopted by the Cuban People*, ed. Mary-Alice Waters, 3rd ed. (New York: Pathfinder Press, 2007), 72–73.

3. Hal Brands, *Latin America's Cold War* (Cambridge, MA: Harvard University Press, 2010), 27.

4. Che Guevara, *Guerrilla Warfare*, 3rd ed., introduction and case studies by Brian Loveman and Thomas M. Davies, Jr. (Wilmington, DE: Scholarly Resources, 1997), 138.

5. Tad Szulc, *Twilight of the Tyrants* (New York: Henry Holt, 1959).

6. *Current History* 45, no. 265 (September 1963), 186.

7. Mildred Adams, ed., *Latin America: Evolution or Explosion?* (New York: Dodd, Mead, 1963); Gary MacEoin, *Latin America, the Eleventh Hour* (New York: P. J. Kennedy, 1962); and Carleton Beals, *Latin America: World in Revolution* (New York: Abelard-Schuman, 1963).

8. Guevara, *Guerrilla Warfare*, 72.

9. Carlos Marighela, *For the Liberation of Brazil*, trans. John Butt and Rosemary Sheed (Harmondsworth, UK: Penguin Books, 1971), 183.

10. E. Bradford Burns, *A History of Brazil*, 3rd ed. (New York: Columbia University Press, 1993), 439.

11. Morris H. Morley, *Imperial State and Revolution: The United States and Cuba, 1952–1986* (Cambridge: Cambridge University Press, 1987), 171.

CHAPTER FOUR

U.S. Responses to Revolution

The revolution in Cuba was a serious blow to U.S. economic and strategic interests in Latin America. Castro's revolution violated two canons of Washington's Latin American policy. First, in expropriating American property Fidel challenged the doctrine of no expropriation without full and prompt compensation that had been a cardinal rule since the beginning of U.S. economic expansion in the 19th century. Second, Castro crossed the line of acceptable behavior by embracing Communism and aligning Cuba with the Soviet Union in defiance of the U.S. position, previously ratified by the OAS, that Communism was incompatible with the institutions and way of life of the Western Hemisphere. In short, by establishing a socialist economy and an alliance with the Soviet Union, Castro for the first time created a breach in U.S. hegemony over the Western Hemisphere and opened a new theater in the Cold War.

As challenging as the Cuban Revolution was to the United States, a far greater threat was the potential spread of Cuban-style revolution throughout Latin America. While the United States could survive the economic and strategic loss of a single island, it feared the exportation of the Cuban model of revolution to other countries. The rise of *fidelismo* throughout Latin America made it clear that the United States faced the urgent task of developing new strategies for dealing with a completely unprecedented situation—a hemisphere that appeared to be on the verge of revolution.

Elimination of Revolution at the Source

The initial U.S. response to Castro was to quell the revolution in Cuba itself, thereby not only eliminating revolution at its source, but also in the process preventing its spread. This strategy ran the gamut from pressuring Castro toward moderation—a difficult challenge—to attempting to eliminate him through military intervention, insurrection, and assassination.

U.S. efforts to influence Fidel toward moderation basically consisted of the use of escalating economic leverage over the very dependent and vulnerable Cuban economy. The United States responded to Castro's nationalistic economic measures, beginning with the May 1959 agrarian reform law, by threatening or implementing economic sanctions to slow or halt the leftward movement of the revolution. The main U.S. weapon was the sugar quota, which Eisenhower suspended in July 1960. In taking this and other measures, the Eisenhower administration, failing to gauge the full extent of Castro's commitment to ridding Cuba of U.S. economic dominance, was employing the standard tools for a conventional situation. Castro was not intimidated. Every American step elicited a progressively more radical countermeasure, as when Fidel responded to the U.S. oil refineries' refusal to refine Soviet crude by confiscating the facilities.

By late 1960, with all American investments nationalized and the sugar quota cancelled, Washington escalated the economic pressure on Cuba by applying a trade embargo. On October 19 the Eisenhower administration prohibited all exports to Cuba except medicines and nonsubsidized foodstuffs; these exceptions were soon eliminated. President Kennedy further tightened the pressure on Castro in February 1962 by issuing Proclamation 3447, which forbade all trade between the United States and Cuba. The embargo was designed simultaneously to cause such economic hardship as to provoke an uprising against Castro and to serve as a warning to other Latin American governments about the consequences of straying from the fold.

U.S. economic sanctions were a primary cause of the economic problems that plagued Cuba in the 1960s. Closing the U.S. sugar market was not particularly successful, as Cuba had already begun exporting to the Soviet Union and subsequently expanded its markets there and in Eastern Europe. But the general trade embargo caused serious dislocations: given the preponderance of American equipment throughout the Cuban economic infrastructure, the withholding of spare parts alone was a major blow, requiring replacement of complete plants in some cases. The reorientation of Cuban trade raised transportation costs substantially, and U.S. pressure gradually brought most of the European allies to cut back or suspend their dealings with Castro. A notable exception, illustrating the color blindness of money, was the significant growth of trade between Castro's Cuba and Franco's Spain. U.S. pressure on the Latin American countries to suspend trade was largely symbolic, given that only a small fraction of

Cuba's trade was with Latin America. Although the embargo inflicted substantial economic damage, it was a complete failure in its primary purpose of causing popular discontent leading to an insurrection against Castro; on the contrary, the embargo gave Castro a rallying cry against Yankee aggression that served him for half a century.

The Bay of Pigs invasion was a dismal failure, and other U.S. actions to eliminate Castro were no more successful. The Eisenhower, Kennedy, and Johnson administrations resorted to CIA- and Mafia-executed assassination plots against Castro, employing poison pens, poisoned cigars, and a plan to substitute a lethally contaminated diving suit for the one Fidel normally wore on his frequent diving excursions. Seeking to provoke an uprising against Castro, the United States trained, armed, and sustained exile raiding parties, underground opposition, sabotage units, and, for a time, guerrilla operations in the Sierra de Escambray and Oriente province. It also beamed anti-Castro propaganda to the island via radio. Following the Bay of Pigs, Washington launched "Operation Mongoose" to coordinate and intensify the internal subversion activities. One of the more bizarre Mongoose plots involved alerting Cubans to the impending second coming of Christ. On the day of Christ's announced return, a U.S. submarine would surface and set off fireworks along the coast, prompting a rebellion against the anti-Christ, Castro. One CIA agent called this "elimination by illumination."[1] By 1964, however, the United States largely abandoned its efforts to incite uprisings in the face of convincing evidence of Castro's popularity, his tight control over potential dissidents, and the difficulty of sustaining resistance groups without the physical presence of an embassy.

Diplomatic Isolation of Cuba

In concert with its attempts to eliminate Castro, the United States also sought to limit Cuba's ability to influence Latin America by terminating formal contacts between the island and the rest of the hemisphere. This approach to containment was designed to prevent Castro's using Cuban embassies for intelligence gathering and political recruitment and diplomatic pouches for transporting propaganda, money, and even arms for *fidelista* groups. Castro's ability to show off the accomplishments of the revolution and offer indoctrination and guerrilla training also depended on the freedom of Latin Americans to travel to the island. Thus in pressuring the hemispheric countries to break diplomatic relations with Cuba, the United States was attempting to limit Castro's ability to create and support revolutionary movements in those countries.

From the beginning of its effort to impose collective diplomatic sanctions on Cuba, the United States relied on a Cold War corollary of the Monroe Doctrine. The 1954 Declaration of Caracas was a statement of anticommunist principles that the Eisenhower administration had rammed through the OAS as justification for the overthrow of the Árbenz government in Guatemala: "The domination or control of the political institutions of any American state by the international communist movement . . . would constitute a threat to the sovereignty and political independence of the American states, endangering the peace of America."[2] With Castro moving ever closer to the PSP and the Soviet Union, the Eisenhower administration tested Latin American sentiment toward Cuba at an August 1960 OAS foreign ministers' meeting. However, the United States was unable to persuade the gathering to condemn Cuba; it got only a mild statement on totalitarianism and nonintervention—the latter potentially applying to the United States as well as Cuba.

Although the dictatorships and a number of the more conservative governments voluntarily broke relations with Cuba, the ultimate success of the U.S. drive for hemispheric diplomatic isolation of Castro depended on a significant change in the attitudes of the more liberal Latin American governments. Those governments initially tended to view Castro as a bilateral problem between the United States and Cuba in which the OAS should not take sides. Over the next four years, however, the impact of *fidelismo* on their own countries, combined with continuing U.S. pressure, drove the majority of OAS members—eventually, all but four—to agree that Cuba was a menace that had to be contained. These countries broke their own relations with Cuba and then came around to voting with the United States to require all OAS member states to implement collective sanctions.

The first step was the expulsion of Cuba from the OAS. Meeting in Punta del Este, Uruguay, in January 1962, the OAS foreign ministers agreed to the expulsion, with Mexico opposed and Brazil, Argentina, Chile, Bolivia, and Ecuador abstaining. The United States had wanted stronger measures but could not even get the support of the largest and most powerful of the Latin American countries for the relatively mild step of expulsion from the principal hemispheric organization. By July 1964, however, the required two-thirds of member states were ready to back the United States in its quest to isolate Cuba. By this time the elected governments of Argentina, Ecuador, and Brazil had been replaced by military regimes; only Mexico, Chile, Bolivia, and Uruguay voted against Washington, and Argentina abstained. The agreement required all OAS members to suspend diplomatic relations, trade, air and maritime transport, and travel to and from Cuba.

All member states complied except Mexico, which followed it
nationalistic course of rejecting Washington's lead in foreign
the exception of Mexico, the OAS sanctions remained firm ui
ean government of Salvador Allende reestablished relations with Cuba in
1970.

The diplomatic isolation of Cuba was successful in reducing Castro's
ability to aid Latin American revolutionaries. Cuba lost the convenience
of a physical presence in other countries and of diplomatic immunity, and
the prohibition of travel to Cuba discouraged all but the most committed
from risking the trip; those who did often faced the expense of traveling
through Eastern Europe to reach Cuba. Although the disruption of con-
tact between Cuba and the rest of Latin America succeeded in impeding
Castro's intervention in those countries, it did little to reduce the most
important influence that the Cuban Revolution exercised in the hemisphere: the power of its example.

The Alliance for Progress

The Alliance for Progress was the United States' most highly publicized
response to the Cuban Revolution. In contrast to the economic, diplomatic,
and military measures against Cuba, which were premised on the notion
that Castro's actions to export revolution were responsible for radicalizing
the Latin American political climate in the early 1960s, the Alliance was
anchored in the acknowledgment that the real threat from Cuba was the
power of its example to incite demands for change. Announced by President John F. Kennedy in March 1961 and formally established five months
later at Punta del Este, Uruguay, the Alliance for Progress was designed to
preempt the revolutionaries by attacking the conditions that made revolution appealing to the masses. Specifically, it called for a range of social
reforms to create more just societies, economic development to eliminate
poverty, and the strengthening of democracy across the region. Overall,
according to the document that created it, the Alliance for Progress was to
be "a vast effort to bring a better life to all the peoples of the continent."[3]

The Alliance for Progress grew out of a mounting awareness in the
United States that the condition of Latin America was a source of anti-
Americanism and of potential revolution. After crowds greeted Vice President Richard Nixon with tomatoes and riots on his 1958 Latin American
tour, the Eisenhower administration appointed the Rockefeller Commission to study the causes of such hostility toward the United States. In a
December 1958 speech, then-Senator Kennedy called in general terms for
a special aid program for Latin American development. A cadre of academic

specialists and diplomats also lobbied persuasively for a program of development aid tied to reform.

Latin Americans themselves had urged the United States to underwrite a program similar to the Marshall Plan to fund rapid economic development. Among them, Brazilian President Jascelino Kubitschek called in 1958 for an "Operation Pan-America," and Fidel Castro, at a 1959 meeting of Latin American governments in Buenos Aires, called on the United States to invest $30 billion in Latin America's development in the coming decade. But it was the radicalization of the Cuban Revolution and the impact of *fidelismo* upon the hemisphere that prompted action, which began with Eisenhower's "Act of Bogotá" of September 1960 committing $500 million for social and economic development. During his presidential campaign, Kennedy elaborated upon his earlier idea and appointed a Latin American Task Force under the leadership of Adolf Berle to formulate plans for a cooperative hemispheric venture.

The Alliance for Progress was an inter-American agreement based on U.S. funding of a major part of $20 billion in development aid over the next decade and on the commitment of the Latin American countries to undertake reforms and invest more of their own resources in social and economic development. The Charter of Punta del Este spelled out ambitious goals, including a minimum annual per capita economic growth rate of 2.5 percent, more equitable distribution of national income, tax reform, comprehensive agrarian reform, elimination of adult illiteracy, a minimum of six years' schooling for all children, public health measures to raise life expectancy, and increased low-cost housing and public services. In relation to the promotion of democracy, Kennedy called the Alliance "a plan to transform the 1960s into an historic decade of democratic progress."[4] In order to receive funding, all countries were required to formulate long-range economic and social development plans, preferably within 18 months of the signing of the charter.

Launched with great fanfare and lauded as a new Marshall Plan, the Alliance for Progress proved far less successful than its European predecessor. To be sure, some noteworthy accomplishments came from the Alliance during the 1960s. Between 1961 and 1968, the United States and its European allies committed an average of $2 billion per year in development aid, primarily in loans; however, actual disbursements under the Alliance were $1.1 billion per year, and factoring in debt service, the net annual inflow of development capital was $638 million. Although substantially less than projected, this amount made a difference, as evidenced in potable water projects, housing developments, health clinics, and roads throughout Latin America, funded by the Alliance, dedicated with appropriate ceremonies, and marked with plaques bearing the Alliance emblem. Supplementing the Alliance proper, the Peace Corps, established by Kennedy in 1961, sent some 16,000 volunteers to Latin America during its first decade.

Two countries stand out during the 1960s as showcases for the Alliance for Progress approach. Venezuela under the AD administrations of Rómulo Betancourt (1959–1964) and Raúl Leoni (1964–1969) and Chile under Christian Democrat Eduardo Frei (1964–1970) came reasonably close to the model set forth in the Punta del Este Charter for social reform and economic development within a democratic framework. Both countries carried out structural agrarian reform that attacked the predominance of the traditional hacienda while distributing land to tens of thousands of rural workers; both invested heavily in social services in the countryside and in city slums; and through tax reform, minimum wages, and supportive labor legislation, both made serious attempts at income redistribution. In both countries, political participation was expanded by the incorporation of previously disenfranchised peasants and urban marginals. In sum, although not meeting every one of the Alliance's goals, Venezuela and Chile made sufficient progress so as to provide two credible models of a reformist alternative to the Cuban Revolution.

Venezuela and Chile were notable exceptions to the general rule of failure. Across Latin America, the 1961–1968 period witnessed an annual per capita income growth rate of 1.8 percent—well below the minimum goal of 2.5 percent. Income redistribution in most countries favored the wealthy few at the expense of the multitudes of poor. Most countries made a mockery of agrarian reform—the most emotion-laden social and political issue of the 1960s. In order to receive Alliance funds, they drew up plans, established agrarian reform bureaucracies, and sometimes set up pilot projects or colonization zones in marginal areas; outside of Chile and Venezuela, however, efforts to meet the Alliance goal of "effective transformation . . . of unjust structures and systems of land tenure" were textbook cases of tokenism.[5] The strengthening of democracy also proved illusory. In contrast to the high point of civilian constitutional governments when the Alliance for Progress was announced in 1961, Latin America a dozen years later was dominated by men in uniform as at no time since the Great Depression triggered coups throughout the region.

Beyond failing in its objectives, in its early years the Alliance for Progress actually tended to work against U.S. purposes. The massive propaganda attached to the launching of the Alliance and the very attractiveness of its goals undoubtedly contributed to the growth of expectations underlying the turmoil of the early 1960s. The visibility of the Alliance in political rhetoric, ceremonial dedications, and new government departments and initiatives was a constant reminder that the United States itself was publicly committed to change and betterment for the masses. Thus although intended to counter the Cuban Revolution, the Alliance initially added its own fuel to the destabilizing influence of *fidelismo* by contributing to a revolution of rising but unfulfilled expectations.

Underlying the failure of the Alliance was a condition deeply embedded in Latin American reality. Despite the Kennedy administration's efforts and the financial incentives offered, no Latin American government could be persuaded to take the goals of the Alliance for Progress seriously. Dictators were not interested in stepping aside to watch democracy take root and flower; oligarchs were not anxious to share power with slum dwellers; the wealthy did not rush forward to reduce their share of the national income; landowners did not push legislation to dismantle the land tenure system they controlled. Nor were the Chilean and Venezuelan governments, which carried out progressive reform programs, persuaded primarily by the Alliance for Progress; AD and Chile's Christian Democrats were genuinely reformist parties whose principles and programs antedated the Cuban Revolution and the Alliance for Progress. As for the other countries, rather than reform themselves out of existence, the elites turned to another remedy for the threat of revolution: the military solution.

The Military Response

Concurrently with its other efforts to prevent the spread of revolution beyond Cuba, the United States readied a military response to that threat as part of a general reordering of Washington's global military strategy. In the early post–World War II years the United States had relied on its nuclear arsenal and the doctrine of massive retaliation, combined with military and economic aid to friendly governments, to contain revolutionary movements in underdeveloped parts of the world. The strategy of massive retaliation was premised on the assumption that Moscow controlled all dangerous political movements throughout the world and, under threat of nuclear strikes against the Soviet Union, would rein them in upon demand. By the latter years of the Eisenhower administration, critics of U.S. military posture had begun to point out that although the country's nuclear strategy might work against the Soviet Union, it had no deterrent effect on the unconventional wars of national liberation that had broken out in the colonial world of Africa and Southeast Asia and the type of guerrilla war that Castro had employed in Cuba.

Faced with threatening situations in Southeast Asia and Latin America and with potential dangers throughout the Third World, shortly after taking office the Kennedy administration turned its attention to developing strategies to deal with unconventional warfare. A major component of the Kennedy doctrine of "flexible response" was counterinsurgency. The president took a keen personal interest in the topic. He read Mao Zedong and Che Guevara on guerrilla warfare, ordered the creation of special courses on counterinsurgency for diplomatic and military officers posted in Third World countries, and set up a "Special Group for Counterinsurgency" to formulate policy.

U.S. military policy toward Latin America after World War II, formalized in the Rio de Janeiro Treaty of 1947, had been based on the concept of collective hemispheric security against external aggression by the Soviet Union. Given the remoteness of Latin America from anticipated theaters of war and the obvious impossibility of outfitting 20 republics' armed forces for nuclear war, Latin America was of minor importance to the U.S. global military strategy. Thus U.S. military assistance consisted primarily of maintaining small missions in each country, training Latin American officers in techniques of conventional warfare at the service schools in the United States and the Panama Canal Zone, and providing equipment—much of it obsolete. By law, the equipment sent to the Latin American militaries could serve only external defense purposes unless the White House determined that internal security considerations warranted an exception.

In response to the alleged Communist threat to Guatemala under the Árbenz administration (1951–1954), the United States had begun to reconsider its military strategy in Latin America. The 1954 Declaration of Caracas, which equated internal subversion with international Communist penetration, began to blur the line between internal security and external defense. When the Cuban Revolution raised the prospect of guerrilla warfare and general insurgency in the hemisphere, the United States quickly forgot the potential Soviet military threat to Latin America. In the words of Kennedy's secretary of defense, Robert McNamara, the new U.S. objective was "to guard against external covert intrusion and internal subversion designed to create dissidence and insurrection."[6] Public Law 87-135 of September 1961 translated the Kennedy administration's thinking into legislation directing U.S. military aid toward fighting the spread of revolution.

Although the United States moved rapidly to develop its own counterinsurgency capabilities featuring the Army's Special Forces or Green Berets, the guiding premise of Washington's counterinsurgency concept for the hemisphere was that each country should be prepared to deal with subversion within its borders. Thus the Military Assistance Program for Latin America emphasized training and equipping the hemisphere's armed forces for their newly important internal security role. Preparation of the Latin American militaries involved both new strategies and hardware; innovation in both accelerated as U.S. involvement in Vietnam deepened. Army troops had to be taught to emulate the guerrillas' ability to live in and off of the jungle, to set traps and ambushes, and to use all types of personal combat in addition to weapons. Sophisticated lightweight weapons and communications equipment were developed to enhance the troops' mobility on the ground, and, as in Vietnam, helicopters were to provide rapid deployment to the guerrilla zones and supplemental fire power. One of the most useful new technologies for Latin America was infrared aerial photography, which could detect even a small band of guerrillas in areas too rugged or remote for effective reconnaissance by normal methods. The counterinsurgency units developed in Latin America, like the Green Berets who trained them, were instilled with a strong sense of mission and an *esprit de corps* appropriate to an elite group within the armed forces.

Civic action, used extensively in Vietnam, was the preventive aspect of the military response. Civic action was designed to secure the loyalty of the peasantry—on whom the insurgents depended for support—to the government. Citing the U.S. Army Corps of Engineers as an example of military involvement in projects for civilian benefit, the United States promoted the use of troops to build or improve roads, schools, clinics, water systems, and other public works in remote areas lacking a strong government presence and suitable for guerrilla operations. Civic Action Mobile Training Teams consisting of specialists in engineering, agriculture, education, and public health were dispatched in 1961 and had done training in most Latin American countries by 1965. Although civic action was widely employed, some officers, feeling that manual labor demeaned military honor, resisted the imported concept. Critics pointed out that no correlation could be established between civic action programs and living standards or degree of loyalty to government; others noted that in some countries civic action tended to focus disproportionately on road building to facilitate military access to potential insurgency zones.

Complementing the training and equipping of the Latin American militaries for counterinsurgency was a parallel program for the police. This approach to internal security recognized the primary role of police in day-to-day enforcement of order, the importance of effective crowd control and riot prevention, and the potentially greater role the police could play in gathering intelligence on subversive groups. Training and equipping police was also far more economical than providing the expensive hardware needed for military counterinsurgency. Accordingly, President Kennedy expanded the small program of assistance to foreign police and placed it in the U.S. Agency for International Development's (USAID) Office of Public Safety, which trained police in most hemispheric countries and at the Inter-American Police Academy in the Panama Canal Zone and the International Police Academy in Washington. The advent of urban guerrilla warfare in the late 1960s highlighted the importance of police counterinsurgency training, but instruction in interrogation techniques, widely denounced as torture, also gave the left a useful propaganda weapon.

Latin American officers received regular and counterinsurgency training in the Panama Canal Zone and at over 100 service schools in the United States, while officers and enlisted men alike were trained in their own countries. Special counterinsurgency curricula were established at Fort Bragg, North Carolina; Fort Gordon, Georgia; and at the Southern Command's Fort Gulick in the Canal Zone—known by its critics as the "school of assassins" because of the large number of officers trained there who carried out coups and repression in their countries. Over 20,000 Latin American officers underwent training in Panama alone during the 1960s. A 1,000-man unit of the Special Forces, assigned to Fort Gulick, formed the Mobile Training Teams sent to the Latin American countries to provide antiguerrilla training. In addition to scheduled training missions, the Green Berets were ready for emergency training and advising of counterinsurgency units such as those created in Bolivia in 1967 to fight Che Guevara. The Inter-American Defense College, founded in 1962 at Fort McNair in Washington, D.C., offered annual 10-month courses on social, economic, and political problems of the Americas as well as military matters for 40 to 60 officers of colonel rank and above. Periodic service chiefs' conferences and frequent joint tactical exercises such as the Unitas naval operations further refined the training for military operations. The United States also expanded its resident military missions in Latin America in the 1960s.

An explicit goal in both the conventional and counterinsurgency training of officers was to draw U.S. and Latin American military personnel closer together, both personally and ideologically. In arguing for the creation of the Inter-American Defense College, DeLesseps Morrison, Kennedy's ambassador to the OAS, said that the school would be "both a weapon in the struggle against Castro and a means for indoctrinating key Latin American officers in the political and social mores of the United States"—in other words, in the anti-leftist, anti-Communist National

Security Doctrine, a concept that reoriented military thinking away from external defense toward fighting the enemy within.[7] This enemy was not just the guerrillas, but a broad category of "subversives." Officers were taught that Marxists and *fidelistas* infiltrated society and operated inside political parties, schools, labor unions, the mass media, and the professions. As portrayed during the McCarthy era in the United States, these subversives were not only disloyal to their country but were clever, amoral, devious, and capable of taking over existing organizations for their own nefarious purposes. An Argentine army report from the early 1960s reflected this thinking: "The enemy is tremendously dangerous. We are not attacked from outside but subtly undermined through all channels of the social fabric."[8] Indoctrination in National Security Doctrine would culminate in the state terrorist regimes of the 1970s and 1980s.

A new Foreign Area Specialist Program, established in 1961, gave selected U.S. officers two and a half years of graduate training in language and area studies to enhance their effectiveness at building bonds with their southern counterparts. Expanded in-country missions were particularly useful in building close personal and professional relationships and thus in developing strong influence over the Latin American officers. A former member of the mission in the Dominican Republic reported that the Dominican military "is clearly sitting around waiting for the MAAG (Military Assistance Advisory Group) to tell it what to do. And it is also clear that the president [of the Dominican Republic] has less power over the Dominican military than the MAAG does. The 65-man MAAG mission lives, eats, sleeps with those guys."[9] A related function of the buildup of training and material aid was to bind the Latin American militaries more closely to U.S. weaponry, serving not only the interests of the American weapons industry, but also making it difficult to switch to alternative sources of supply and hence alternative political influences.

In responding to the buildup of revolutionary threats in the hemisphere, the United States doubled its annual military assistance budgets for Latin America from an average of $58 million from 1953 through 1961 to $129 million from 1962 through 1965. These figures do not include the cost of USAID's police training program and some other military expenses. Yet the Military Assistance Program and USAID budgets do not tell the entire story of the U.S. military response to the Cuban Revolution. The military options also included sponsorship of insurgency against established governments, including those of Salvador Allende in Chile and the Sandinistas in Nicaragua. The assiduous cultivation of the Latin American officer corps provided a safety net, an assurance that the ultimate arbiter of power in each country would be pro–United States and opposed to revolution—with the single exception of the Peruvian military between 1968 and 1975.

Although the general policy was to prepare the Latin American armed forces to handle their own insurgencies, Washington was ready to use U.S. forces when national forces appeared incapable of doing the job alone. Thus in addition to their training functions, Green Berets conducted clandestine missions in several countries during the 1960s; several died in counterinsurgency operations in Guatemala. The overt use of U.S. troops was a last resort, but the invasions of the Dominican Republic in 1965 and Grenada in 1983 removed any doubt that the United States would go to war if necessary to defend its hegemony in the hemisphere.

Repression over Reform

The U.S. military response to the threat of revolution was ultimately incompatible with the objectives of the Alliance for Progress. The historic U.S. suspicion of Latin American reformers and revolutionaries was exacerbated by the advent of the Cold War and the threat of the spread of Communism beyond Cuba. Thus when confronted with a choice between placing its faith in the anticipated but unproven long-term results of reform promised by the Alliance for Progress versus the short-term security of a military government willing to crack down on subversives, the United States invariably opted for the latter. The incompatibility between military governments and the Alliance for Progress was explicit in the Alliance's goal of strengthening democracy; the incompatibility was implicit in the area of social reform, which the armed forces usually viewed as closely akin to Communism. During his truncated administration, President Kennedy faced the dilemma of dealing with six military coups that overthrew elected governments in Argentina, Peru, Guatemala, Ecuador, the Dominican Republic, and Honduras. Although some of the overthrown governments, most notably those of Guatemala and Peru, were anything but progressive, the extension of diplomatic recognition and aid to the new military governments called into question the seriousness of Kennedy's commitment to promoting democracy. And the termination of the Ecuadorian administration of Carlos Arosemena, and especially the Honduran regime of Ramón Villeda Morales and the Dominican government of Juan Bosch, were clear setbacks to the process of social reform.

Kennedy's responses to the resurgence of military rule were inconsistent. He routinely spoke out against militarism and denounced coups when they occurred. He lamented the overthrow of Peru's government, saying that "This hemisphere can only be secure and free with democratic governments." The State Department chastised the Ecuadorian officers by proclaiming that "[m]ilitary seizures of power should not become an acceptable substitute for constitutional procedures."[10] U.S. actions varied from immediate recognition of the junta that ousted Argentine President Arturo Frondizi to the withholding of diplomatic recognition and aid to the juntas that overthrew Bosch and Villeda Morales for 11 and a half and 10 and a half weeks, respectively. Kennedy's assassination during the suspension of relations with Honduras and the Dominican Republic prohibits solid conclusions as to his final disposition toward military regimes. On the one hand, he extracted at least vague assurances of future elections before recognizing the juntas in Peru, Guatemala, and Ecuador, thus keeping alive at least a rhetorical commitment to constitutionalism. On the other hand, his failure to marshal all available resources to prevent coups—especially evident in the Dominican Republic case—made it appear that Washington's traditional anti-leftism outweighed Kennedy's commitment to strengthening political democracy, thereby compromising the credibility of the Alliance for Progress.

Kennedy's inconsistent attitude toward military governments was followed by the Johnson administration's explicit policy of recognizing and supporting any military regimes that served the purposes of the U.S. government. The Mann Doctrine was authored by Assistant Secretary of State for Latin America Thomas Mann in March 1964, on the eve of the U.S.-supported coup in Brazil. It held that U.S. diplomatic recognition and offers of assistance would not be based on a regime's origin; elected governments and military regimes would be judged on their merits, not their provenance. The Mann Doctrine amputated one of the three legs on which the Alliance rested, and given the predominantly conservative outlook of the Latin American military, it implied that the United States had lost interest in the social reform goals of the Alliance as well. With two of its three goals contravened by the Mann Doctrine, the tottering Alliance for Progress expired as a coherent policy a few months into the Johnson administration, although it continued to be funded and to finance development projects through the 1960s.

Two of President Johnson's actions telegraphed the message that the United States would not tolerate suspect governments, no matter how closely their goals and policies matched the objectives of the Alliance for Progress. First was U.S. involvement in the overthrow of the Goulart government in Brazil. Washington had been wary of Goulart since his accession to the presidency in 1961 because of his association with leftists, his calls for Alliance for Progress–style reforms, expropriations of some American holdings, a law limiting remittances on foreign investments, and

Goulart's resistance to breaking relations with Cuba. Supplementing U.S. economic and diplomatic pressure, the CIA had carried out a covert campaign since 1962, first to moderate Goulart and later to weaken him in preparation for an overthrow. Encouraged by the announcement of the Mann Doctrine, the Brazilian military wasted no time and, with the full knowledge and support of the Johnson administration, overthrew Goulart on March 31 while a U.S. carrier task force stood offshore to lend assistance if requested. Johnson congratulated the officers within four hours of their seizure of power, and Ambassador Lincoln Gordon declared the coup "the single most decisive victory for freedom in the mid-twentieth century."[11] The military regime immediately broke relations with Cuba and welcomed new foreign investment; in response, the aid pipeline resumed its flow and American largesse poured in to support what its perpetrators called the Brazilian "revolution."

In April 1965, Johnson emphatically revealed the true face of U.S. policy for containment of the Cuban Revolution when he ordered American troops to the Dominican Republic to prevent the overthrow of the conservative government of Donald Reid Cabral by supporters of former President Juan Bosch. The first president elected after Trujillo's assassination, Bosch had won 62 percent of the vote in the 1962 election with promises of Alliance for Progress–style reforms. When he set out to implement agrarian reform and build up the weak labor movement, Bosch encountered resistance from the Dominican right and military, from U.S. economic interests on the island, and from Ambassador John Bartlow Martin, who accused the president of being soft on "Castro/Communists [sic]."[12] Facing the choice between Bosch's attempts to build a democratic society on the ruins of Trujillo's three decades of dictatorship and the short-term security of a military-conservative coalition certain to protect American investments and act against suspected revolutionaries, Kennedy vacillated. After weakening Bosch's government by reducing aid and discouraging his reforms, the Kennedy administration stood by in September 1963 when the military overthrew him, then denounced the coup and suspended diplomatic recognition and aid. This "hands-off" stance contrasted sharply with the overt U.S. intervention in Dominican politics during the previous three years, when Washington had used economic and diplomatic pressure and threats of military intervention to eliminate Trujillo and shape an acceptable post-Trujillo regime.

The events that led to U.S. military intervention began on April 24, 1965, when a group of military officers rebelled to restore Bosch to the presidency. The fighting quickly spread to the civilian population, and after four days the rebels appeared to be gaining the upper hand. At this juncture,

President Johnson ordered the landing of American troops under the pretext of assuring the safety of U.S. nationals. A few days later, Johnson declared that the action had been taken to prevent "the establishment of another Communist government in the Western Hemisphere."[13] The Communists that U.S. sources had detected were a small minority of the civilians involved in the revolt, whereas the leadership of the pro-Bosch movement was noncommunist or anticommunist. The allegation of large-scale Communist participation in the uprising and hence the likely Communist control of the restored Bosch regime was not consistent with the facts as established in subsequent U.S. congressional hearings.

After the invasion, the United States pressured the OAS into an ex post facto endorsement of the intervention and persuaded Brazil, Paraguay, Nicaragua, Honduras, El Salvador, and Costa Rica to send token contingents of personnel to join the 22,000 American soldiers in a "collective" OAS peace-keeping exercise. The United States withdrew its forces after restoring order and arranging for a caretaker government and subsequent elections. The Dominican invasion made it clear that when challenged by a potentially threatening situation, repression would prevail over reform, rendering the Alliance for Progress mere window dressing.

Notes

1. Jim Rasenberger, *The Brilliant Disaster: JFK, Castro, and America's Doomed Invasion of Cuba's Bay of Pigs* (New York: Scribner, 2011), 360.

2. Avalon.law.yale.edu/20th_century/intam11.asp.

3. Mark Eric Williams, *Understanding U.S.-Latin American Relations: Theory and History* (New York: Routledge, 2012), 191.

4. *Department of State Bulletin* 44, no. 1136 (April 3, 1961), 472.

5. "Declaration to the Peoples of America," *Department of State Bulletin* 45, no. 1159 (September 11, 1961), 462.

6. Quoted in Che Guevara, *Guerrilla Warfare*, 3rd ed., introduction and case studies by Brian Loveman and Thomas M. Davies, Jr. (Wilmington, DE: Scholarly Resources, 1997), 26.

7. John Child, *Unequal Alliance: The Inter-American Military System, 1938–1978* (Boulder, CO: Westview Press, 1980), 75.

8. Martin Edwin Andersen, *Dossier Secreto: Argentina's Desaparecidos and the Myth of the "Dirty War"* (Boulder, CO: Westview Press, 1993), 44.

9. Michael T. Klare, *War without End: American Planning for the Next Vietnams* (New York: Vintage Books, 1972), 75.

10. *Historical Study: U.S. Policy toward Latin America: Recognition and Non-Recognition of Governments and Interruptions in Diplomatic Relations, 1933–1974*

(Washington, D.C.: Department of State, Bureau of Public Affairs, June 1975), 81, 86.

11. E. Bradford Burns, *A History of Brazil*, 3rd ed. (New York: Columbia University Press, 1993), 444.

12. Abraham F. Lowenthal, *The Dominican Intervention* (Cambridge, MA: Harvard University Press, 1972), 27.

13. Howard Jones, *Crucible of Power: A History of American Foreign Relations from 1945* (Lanham, MD: Rowman & Littlefield, 2009), 151.

PART 3

Guerrilla Warfare

CHAPTER FIVE

Che's Way: Rural Guerrilla Warfare

Guerrilla warfare takes its name from the response to Napoleon's 1808 invasion of Spain when, after the defeat of the Spanish army, irregular forces harassed and skirmished with the Napoleonic army for several years. "Little war" (*guerra*, the Spanish term for war, modified by the diminutive) was not new in 1808: it was a strategy as old as the earliest, unrecorded use of unorthodox methods of fighting by weaker groups against a regular army. Wars of irregular forces against regular armies were certainly known in Latin America prior to Castro's defeat of Batista. The early 19th-century wars of independence, Cuba's independence wars, and the Mexican Revolution of 1910, for example, involved guerrilla actions, as did Augusto C. Sandino's 1927–1933 fight against the U.S. Marines occupying Nicaragua. But it was not until the Cuban Revolution that guerrilla warfare became the preferred method of insurrection in Latin America.

Castro's victory over Batista was cast as the work of the guerrillas in the Sierra Maestra, and following the failure of the April 1958 general strike, their vanguard role in the final stages of the protracted struggle against Batista appeared to validate the "heroic guerrilla" thesis. The significance of Castro's successful rebellion was momentous: since the professionalization of Latin America's armed forces in the late 19th and early 20th centuries, the national armies, with their advanced training and superior materiel, had been able to thwart virtually all attempts to overthrow governments by insurrection. Indeed, in the 20th century the primary nonelectoral method of changing governments was the coup carried out by the armed forces themselves. Against this backdrop, Castro's defeat of the professional Cuban army appeared to open a new path to power for those inspired by the Cuban Revolution.

Che Guevara on Guerrilla Warfare

Having overall responsibility for carrying out the revolution in Cuba, Fidel left the field of guerrilla warfare to Che Guevara, whose first loyalty was to the cause of revolution rather than to his adopted island nation. While always acknowledging Fidel's preeminent role in the Cuban guerrilla war, with the publication of his *Guerrilla Warfare* in 1960, Che assumed the mantle of spokesman for the Cuban Revolution in matters of insurrection. Che's book can hardly be called a major theoretical contribution to the study of guerrilla warfare. In the areas of strategy and tactics, he adds little to the insights of Mao Zedong and Vietnamese General Vo Nguyen Giap, who wrote about rural-based guerrilla warfare from their experiences. The book is primarily a "how-to" manual based on the Cuban case, describing the organization, training, supply, and operation of a guerrilla *foco*—the guerrilla force itself. *Guerrilla Warfare* is replete with homilies on the spiritual and physical requirements for guerrilla fighters; advice on selecting knapsacks, shoes, and weapons; instructions on tactics for fighting the army; and descriptions of the various stages through which the successful *foco* develops.

The real importance of *Guerrilla Warfare* is its validation of rural guerrilla warfare as the model for insurrection in Latin American. Building upon the official story of guerrilla preeminence in the fight against Batista, Che's work reduced the lessons of the Cuban Revolution to axioms: "1) Popular forces can win a war against the army; 2) It is not necessary to wait until all conditions for revolution exist; the insurrection can create them; 3) In underdeveloped America the countryside is the basic area for armed fighting."[1] This message, offered in authoritative fashion by a protagonist and with Fidel's blessing, added the patina of intellectual legitimacy to the multiple signals coming from Cuba that Castro's exploit could be replicated. In Che's words, apparently directed at the Communists, "Of these three propositions the first two contradict the defeatist attitude of revolutionaries or pseudo-revolutionaries who remain inactive and take refuge in the pretext that against a professional army nothing can be done, who sit down to wait until in some mechanical way all necessary objective conditions are given without working to accelerate them."[2]

While goading the Latin American left to take action, *Guerrilla Warfare* placed strict limitations on the applicability of the Cuban model. In a crucial caveat, Che qualified the ability of the insurrection to create conditions necessary for revolution: "Where a government has come into power through some form of popular vote, fraudulent or not, and maintains at least an appearance of constitutional legality, the guerrilla outbreak cannot be promoted, since the possibilities of peaceful struggle have not yet been exhausted."[3] Given the unusually large number of elected civilian governments in power in the early 1960s, guerrilla war would have had little application outside the dictatorships of Trujillo, Duvalier, Somoza, Stroessner, and the Salvadoran military. But a year after the publication of *Guerrilla Warfare*, Che began to modify his position on the ability of the insurrection to create the conditions for revolution by declaring that the objective conditions—things such as poverty, oppression, class conflict—were in place throughout Latin America. Glossing over the problem of constitutional governments and the existence of possibilities for peaceful struggle, Che now declared that the subjective conditions—the belief that revolution could occur and the will to undertake it—could be created by the insurrectional *foco*.

By 1963 Che finished his theoretical formulation of the guerrilla's role in sparking revolution. In "Guerrilla Warfare: A Method" he attacked head on the problem of how to proceed in those countries with elected and potentially responsive governments. Reflecting a firming-up of his Marxist theoretical underpinnings, he now identified this type of constitutional government as "the dictatorship of the exploiting classes."[4] Propped up by U.S. imperialism, those governments had no more real legitimacy than did the Caribbean-style dictatorships. The function of the guerrilla *foco* was to drive the bourgeois-landowner state into the use of force, unmasking the true face of the oligarchic regime. Thus the *foco* itself would start the revolutionary process by turning the constitutional government into a repressive dictatorship against which popular opposition could be generated. By elaborating the concept of *foquismo*, or the primacy of the guerrilla *foco* itself in the revolutionary process, Che was able to apply his version of the Cuban model to virtually any Latin American country.

Che gave fair warning that the guerrilla struggle would be long and hard. In his 1967 "Message to the Tricontinental," Che predicted that "many shall perish" in the cause of the Latin American revolution.[5] Besides the obvious difficulties of launching and sustaining a *foco*, Che admitted the importance to the Cuban Revolution of that "telluric force called Fidel Castro."[6] He also pointed out the great advantage to Cuba of being the first contemporary Latin American guerrilla war to succeed: it had had the support of some of the bourgeoisie, and not understanding the full implications of Castro's insurrection, the United States had been disoriented.

Despite these warnings, Che was not entirely candid in laying out the difficulties facing guerrilla fighters. Explicit in *Guerrilla Warfare* and other writings is the official version of the struggle against Batista, the myth of the heroic guerrilla. Accordingly, despite repeated assertions that his analysis was based on the Cuban experience, Che focused on the guerrilla *foco* itself, to the virtual exclusion of the broader anti-Batista struggle. After stating that "The struggles of the city masses of organized workers should not be underrated," *Guerrilla Warfare* devotes no more than 2 percent of its text to the "external front," or the urban resistance, which, it adds, must be subordinate to the "central command."[7] Because of the extreme popularity of the Cuban Revolution and the stature of Che Guevara, millions of Latin Americans took his words as gospel. Thus, in portraying the myth of the heroic guerrilla as fact, Che was not only distorting Cuban history, he was presenting a flawed model to the revolutionaries of Latin America— one that would lead many to their deaths.

Guerrilla Movements of the 1960s

The first couple of years after the fall of Batista witnessed a rash of guerrilla outbreaks throughout Latin America. Inspired by Castro's success, armed bands in many countries took to the mountains and jungles in emulation of the Cubans. These quixotic ventures usually collapsed as the would-be revolutionaries encountered the reality of hunger, the elements, peasant indifference or hostility, and, if these were not enough to make them abandon their quest, army bullets. While exacerbating the general climate of instability that *fidelismo* created, the first, naive wave of guerrilla warfare did not seriously threaten any established government.

The failed naive phase of guerrilla warfare was followed by a different kind of guerrilla movement in the early and mid-1960s. The new movements were less impulsive in their origins, better prepared, and more committed to the hard work and time necessary to overthrow a government. The guerrillas in Guatemala, Venezuela, Colombia, Peru, and Nicaragua were powerful enough to require major governmental commitments of force and resources to combat them.

The first of these more mature rural guerrilla movements was the Nicaraguan Sandinista National Liberation Front (Frente Sandinista de Liberación Nacional, FSLN), founded in 1961. It was also the least visible during the 1960s, as the Somoza dictatorship kept it bottled up in the northern Nicaraguan highlands and across the border in Honduras, where it gradually built its strength. After 18 years, the FSLN finally defeated the Somoza regime in the only successful guerrilla insurrection after Castro's.

Guatemala offered generally good conditions for guerrilla warfare in the early 1960s. It had appropriate terrain, oppressive rural social and land tenure systems, and a government that, although elected, was headed by a conservative general and closely overseen by the military. Between 1944 and 1954, the reform governments of Juan José Arévalo and Jacobo Árbenz had introduced far-reaching reforms that challenged the heretofore untouched hegemony of landowners and foreign capital. After organizing some 200,000 urban and rural workers and expropriating 600,000 hectares of land for redistribution—some of it belonging to the United Fruit Company—Árbenz was overthrown in 1954 by a surrogate CIA invasion force headed by Colonel Carlos Castillo Armas. Castillo Armas quickly restored the status quo ante through violent repression. Having experienced the beginnings of reform, some workers, intellectuals, and peasants were predisposed to a resumption of the struggle under the influence of *fidelismo*, whereas a majority had been chastened by the repression.

The Guatemalan guerrilla movement developed out of a failed November 1960 coup attempt by young nationalist army officers. Coup leaders Marco Antonio Yon Sosa and Luis Turcios Lima returned from exile in 1962 to establish the Rebel Armed Forces (Fuerzas Armadas Rebeldes, FAR). The FAR was able to win some skirmishes and was a contributing factor to the overthrow of President Ydígoras Fuentes in 1963. Yet in the next few years the FAR and other guerrilla groups encountered serious obstacles in the form of peasant indifference, troops trained in counterinsurgency, contingents of U.S. Green Berets in combat, and disunity within their own ranks. Severe government repression against all potential collaborators also hampered the guerrillas' efforts. Stymied in their attempt to establish a secure zone of operations, the guerrillas sustained their visibility by killing Green Berets, kidnapping officials, and killing U.S. ambassador John Gordon Mein during a kidnap attempt in 1968. By the end of the 1960s, a pattern of limited guerrilla activity and heavy government repression became the norm in Guatemala.

Guerrilla activity in Venezuela developed in a very different political context. After living under military dictatorships during most of its republican history, Venezuela had established a civilian government under AD leader Rómulo Betancourt in February 1959, just six weeks after Castro's victory over Batista. AD was committed to a broad program of reforms, including agrarian reform. Its ambitious goals frightened the right, whereas for the *fidelistas* AD's agenda was too conservative and its pace too slow. Moreover, after a friendly beginning of their relationship as Latin America's newest reformers and as sworn enemies of the Trujillo dictatorship in the Dominican Republic, Castro and Betancourt soon parted ways over their differing attitudes toward reforms and elections. After the falling out, Fidel actively supported the overthrow of Betancourt in a concerted attempt to derail the leading reformist alternative of the early 1960s to his style of revolution.

Venezuela's guerrillas were a heterogeneous grouping of university students, former AD members, ex-Communists, and dissident military officers. Between 1962 and 1965 the Venezuelan Communist Party embraced the armed struggle as well. The attack on AD began with urban actions that included street demonstrations, strikes, sabotage, and assassinations. Guerrilla *focos* were operating in the Andean terrain of nine states by 1961, but until the founding of the Armed Forces of National Liberation (Fuerzas Armadas de Liberación Nacional, FALN) in 1963, cooperation among the groups was haphazard. Despite the improved coordination that followed, counterinsurgency tactics, peasant support of AD, and the government's agrarian reform program worked against the guerrillas' attempts to establish a liberated zone.

The *focos* and their urban counterparts suffered a severe setback when, ignoring the guerrillas' assassination threats, over 90 percent of eligible voters turned out in the 1963 presidential elections won by AD's Raúl Leoni. Leoni's offer of amnesty further undermined the guerrillas, as did the Venezuelan Communist Party's abandonment of the *fidelista* line in 1965. These developments isolated FALN leader Douglas Bravo and his collaborators, reducing the guerrilla movement to a nuisance. Nonetheless, periodic skirmishes continued until 1969, when the new Christian Democratic (COPEI) government of Rafael Caldera offered another amnesty that further thinned guerrilla ranks. This action, combined with the disheartening death of Che Guevara in 1967, spelled the end of the Venezuelan guerrillas as an effective force.

Guerrilla warfare in Colombia, a complex phenomenon with unique characteristics, antedated the Cuban Revolution. Rural violence between supporters of the dominant Liberal and Conservative Parties had a long tradition in Colombia, with roots in the 19th century. The assassination of populist leader Jorge Eliécer Gaitán in 1948 touched off severe urban rioting which spread to rural areas, exacerbating the endemic violence and ushering in an era known straightforwardly as "La Violencia." Despite strenuous efforts and some success, the weak Colombian state proved incapable of quelling the violence.

By the time of the Cuban Revolution, then, Colombia had been in the grip of La Violencia for a decade. When they appeared, *fidelista* groups promoted several minor *focos*, but it was not until 1964 that the first significant, expressly revolutionary guerrilla organization, the Army of National Liberation (Ejército de Liberación Nacional, ELN), emerged from an amalgamation of existing guerrillas with revolutionaries from the cities. The same year, a Communist faction founded the Revolutionary Armed Forces of Colombia (Fuerzas Armadas Revolucionarias de Colombia, FARC) on the basis of the independent peasant republic of Marquetalia, and Maoists established the Popular Liberation Army (Ejército Popular de Liberación, EPL) two years later. Father Camilo Torres, Latin America's best-known guerrilla priest, fought briefly with ELN before falling in action in 1966.

While the Liberal and Conservative governments that alternated in power through the 1960s were unresponsive to demands for reform, the intermittent surfacing of populist leaders demonstrated that the legal struggle was not exhausted in Colombia. Partially offsetting the socially retrograde land tenure system were extensive vacant lands and government colonization programs in the hinterlands, which relieved some pressure for agrarian reform. Although not seriously threatened by the guerrillas through the 1960s, the Colombian government was unable to defeat them with concerted military campaigns. The FARC and ELN gained strength and momentum in the late 1990s, and guerrilla warfare in Colombia continued well into the 21st century.

Peru also experienced significant guerrilla activity in the 1960s. Peru offered good terrain in the Andes and the upper Amazonian jungle for Che's version of guerrilla war. It had an impoverished, largely Indian rural population; an extremely skewed land tenure pattern; and a labor system on traditional Andean haciendas that resembled serfdom. Peru also had a history of rural uprisings against landowners and government authorities. Still, when the major *focos* were launched, Peru had a relatively popular elected president in Fernando Belaúnde Terry, a moderate reformer who favored moderate agrarian reform.

Dissident Communists and former APRA members organized most of the guerrilla activity. Héctor Béjar, a former Communist, founded the National Liberation Army (Ejército de Liberación Nacional, ELN) in 1963. It went into action in May of that year, crossing into Peru from Bolivia in an attempt to link up with Hugo Blanco's peasant movement in the Valley of La Convención. Army troops defeated the ELN near Puerto Maldonado and killed or dispersed its fighters. The ELN carried out another short-lived guerrilla action in 1965 in the Ayacucho region.

After several trips to Cuba, former APRA member and leader of the Movement of the Revolutionary Left (Movimiento de Izquierda Revolucionaria, MIR), Luis de la Puente Uceda, went underground in 1964 to prepare for a guerrilla war. The MIR created three separate units in different parts of the Andes in 1965. One located on the border with Ecuador did not take action. Another *foco* at Mesa Pelado near La Convención lasted two months in the face of the Peruvian army's elite counterinsurgency troops, trained and advised by U.S. Green Berets. The third MIR *foco*, near the jungle town of Satipo, achieved some minor victories and survived seven months before the army destroyed it. The strategy of multiple *focos* failed to take root in Peru.

The outcomes of these guerrilla movements of the 1960s demonstrated that successful insurrection was not as easy as Che and Fidel had proclaimed. Compared with Castro's guerrilla movement, the *focos* of the 1960s faced greater obstacles to success. First, after the enormous publicity about Cuba's guerrillas, combined with Fidel's and Che's open calls for insurrection, the appearance of *focos* in any country was no surprise. Except in Venezuela, those *focos* lacked solid urban support to form resistance units, carry out propaganda, and provide supplies and recruits for the guerrillas. Moreover, the 1960s guerrillas faced counterinsurgency forces whose training and equipment benefited from the U.S. experience in Vietnam. And ignoring Che's caveat in *Guerrilla Warfare*, all except the Nicaraguan guerrillas sought to overthrow elected governments, two of which—Betancourt's in Venezuela and Belaúnde's in Peru—were reformist and popular.

Che in Bolivia

Che Guevara was a highly visible figure in revolutionary Cuba. He was a member of Fidel's inner circle and the most powerful man in Cuba after Fidel and Raúl Castro. He was president of the National Bank of Cuba from November 1959 to February 1961, minister of industries from then to April 1965, a member of the executive committee of the ruling party, and a colorful and charismatic leader in his own right. Che's intractable radicalism, expressed in his establishment of moral incentives for labor and his strident criticism of the Soviet Union's relations with the Third World, eventually proved counterproductive to economic development and damaging to Cuban–Soviet relations. With Fidel's blessing, Che left Cuba in April 1965 to pursue his true vocation of transnational revolutionary. After spending a few frustrating months with a guerrilla group in the Congo, he returned to Cuba in March 1966 to develop his plans for promoting the Latin American revolution.

Che's guerrilla war in Bolivia was the centerpiece of a bold Cuban plan to reinvigorate the flagging momentum of revolution in Latin America. Despite Castro's untiring efforts to support the insurrectionary movements that his revolution had inspired, little had been accomplished in the seven years since his triumph, and prospects for revolution seemed to be dimming. Of the numerous guerrilla movements that developed in the region, only a few became credible *focos*, and none of these achieved appreciable success in the 1960s. Complicating the picture was the further fragmentation of the Marxist left, not only among Communists, Trotskyists, and *fidelistas*, but also, by 1966, the pro-Chinese Communists and a plethora of splinter groups that formed to fill the leftover theoretical interstices. Rounding out the bleak panorama facing Fidel and Che was the strident determination of the United States to stop revolution, demonstrated by U.S. support of the 1964 Brazilian coup, the 1965 invasion of the Dominican Republic, and the Pentagon's extensive and effective counterinsurgency program.

True to his character and consistent with his past behavior, Fidel responded to adversity by setting higher goals—in this case, continent-wide, even worldwide revolution. Given the growing U.S. involvement in Vietnam, Che and Fidel reasoned that the outbreak of revolutionary movements around the world might tie down American military forces and ultimately stretch them to the breaking point, dealing a death blow to U.S. imperialism. In Che's words, the world's exploited masses could anticipate "a bright future should two, three, many Vietnams flourish throughout the world with their share of deaths and their immense tragedies, their everyday heroism and their repeated blows against imperialism, impelled to disperse its forces under the sudden attack and the increasing hatred of all peoples of the world."[8] To generate enthusiasm and organizational support for the emerging concept of coordinated anti-imperialist insurrection, Fidel held two important congresses in Havana within 18 months. The Tricontinental Conference, meeting in January 1966, brought together progressive governments and movements from throughout the Third World to promote anti-U.S. action. OLAS, convened in July 1967, was designed to cement the support of Latin America's revolutionary groups for the continental revolution.

Fidel and Che also put out a renewed call for revolution through French philosopher Régis Debray, who published *Revolution in the Revolution?* in 1967. Debray's message was simple: the failure of attempts at revolution since 1959 was due to deviations from the Cuban model—heresies such as "armed self-defense," "armed propaganda," and the subjection of the guerrilla *foco* to a political party. He vigorously attacked the thesis of "Cuban exceptionalism"—the notion that the Cuban Revolution was a unique phenomenon that could not be repeated elsewhere in Latin America.[9] Debray assured his readers that the correct application of Che's *foco* principle would yield results. He implored revolutionaries to rise above the ideological and strategic hair-splitting that divided the left and take action in a continental insurrection against the United States and its puppets.

In order to implement the renewed push for revolution and the continental strategy, Fidel and Che devised a plan based on the Cuban experience of the initial *foco* spawning a second and then multiple fronts. Initially, a single *foco*, led by Che himself with veteran Cuban guerrillas and Fidel's material and moral support, would serve as a training school for fighters from around the hemisphere. They in turn would establish new fronts in their own countries as conditions permitted until all of Latin America would be aflame with insurrection. Che initially looked to his Argentine homeland as the location of his *foco*/training school, but Fidel and others persuaded him to look elsewhere, and eventually he chose Bolivia. Cuban agents contacted Mario Monje, leader of the Bolivian Communist Party, in early 1966 and scouted the country for a base of operations.

Analysis of the failure of Che's Bolivian *foco* and hence of his ambitious continental strategy must begin with the question of his choice of Bolivia. Bolivia was suited in some ways to Che's purposes: it was extremely poor, heavily rural, and Indian, and it had been ruled since November 1964 by a general. The tin miners, the largest sector of the industrial labor force, were well organized and militantly leftist. Situated in the heart of the Andes and bordering five South American countries, Bolivia was especially appealing as the nerve center for the continental revolution. Although Bolivia's excellent terrain was remote from the bulk of the population living on the *altiplano*, the country appeared suitable for purposes of launching multiple *focos* in several countries.

Bolivia's recent history, on the other hand, militated against Che's choice. As a result of the 1952 revolution and the subsequent thorough agrarian reform, Bolivia had no significant land problem. Despite the prevailing rural poverty, the peasantry had become essentially conservative in defense of its newly won land. Che may also have underestimated the popularity of the government of General René Barrientos; although by 1966 Che had embraced *foquismo*, or a belief in the ability of the *foco* to create conditions for revolution irrespective of the type of government in power, he may have interpreted Barrientos' government as a Caribbean-type reactionary regime which might be more vulnerable than an elected government to insurrection. Although he had overthrown a constitutional government in 1964, Barrientos had been elected president in 1966 with 62 percent of the vote. He was something of a populist who spoke Quechua and constantly visited remote Indian settlements to cultivate support among the rural population.

In launching his *foco*, Che faced two challenges common to most guerrilla movements of the 1960s, but exacerbated by time and place. The United States had developed its counterinsurgency forces beginning in 1961, and by the time they were needed in Bolivia, the Americans were highly skilled at the rapid creation and subsequent advising of counterinsurgency units as the result of their experience in Latin America and Vietnam. The universal problem of urban support was exacerbated in Bolivia by two factors. First, the *foco* was a Cuban operation, directed by Che; although he expected to recruit Bolivian cadres for work in the "external front" as well as the *foco*, his insistence on controlling the operation discouraged recruitment efforts by Bolivian Marxist groups. Second, the fragmentation typical of the Latin American left was extreme in Bolivia. Although Che's agents initially dealt with Monje of the Bolivian Communist Party, they found his party caught in the common vacillation between legal and armed struggle; thus Monje's promises of fighters and urban cadres were inflated. Yet when the Cubans tried to deal with more committed *fidelistas* such as Moisés Guevara, the Communists threatened complete withdrawal. Advance man Pombo recorded the Cubans' frustration in his diary: "We asked them what they had done to date; they replied, 'Nothing.' We told them we could not sit around 20 years waiting for them."[10] On balance, the Cubans' belief in Bolivia's strategic value to the continental revolution outweighed the obvious problems of establishing a *foco* in that country.

Che entered the country disguised as a Uruguayan businessman in the first week of November 1966, four months after his advance party had arrived. Within days the Cubans proceeded to the large farm purchased in the rugged hills of Santa Cruz province where training was to start. The farm at Ñancahuazú met the basic requirements for a training camp: it was sprawling, relatively isolated, and contiguous to the zone selected for the *foco*. After the first month of secret training, however, the seemingly routine beginning disintegrated into a nightmare culminating in defeat and death. Read in juxtaposition to Che's *Guerrilla Warfare*, the diaries of Che and three Cuban companions, Rolando, Pombo, and Braulio, tell a tale of serious miscalculation and disregard for the rules; as the story unfolded, it was as though the master had not read his own guidebook.

A fundamental part of the problem was the terrain. It was remote and hilly, and its vegetation was thick and spiny enough to require constant use of machetes for passage, but not sufficiently tall and dense to provide good cover for a guerrilla party. Nor were there prominent peaks for orienting Che's group. The dominant feature of the Ñancahuazú region was the Río Grande and its tributaries, which flowed between high banks, forming steep canyons filled ordinarily from bank to bank with water. The scarcity of fords often necessitated the building of rafts for crossings, and incoming streams made travel along the rivers' banks difficult. The rivers took their toll in drowned men and lost supplies, and they turned out to be traps for the party—guerrillas or army—that found itself pursued into the canyons.

Che's *Guerrilla Warfare* describes *foco* operations in favorable and unfavorable terrain. The Ñancahuazú area is closer to the second category, raising doubts as to its selection as the launching pad for the continental revolution. Although Che prescribes tactics for successful operations in unfavorable terrain, it would seem that the choice of the Beni region, a jungle and mountain zone east of La Paz originally favored by the Cuban advance party, would have offered greater possibilities for establishment of a liberated zone—a requisite to the *foco's* ultimate success. However, after initially offering some cooperation, Communist chief Monje apparently turned against Che's venture and influenced the decision to move the operation to the southeast, perhaps hoping to rid himself of the Cuban scheme. On the other hand, southeastern Bolivia offered far better access to neighboring countries, particularly to Argentina, than did the remote Beni, and thus it fit better into the strategy of continental revolution.

The difficulty of the terrain and the guerrillas' ignorance of regional geography became manifest in February 1967, when the small group set out on a training and reconnaissance exercise. Designed for 25 days, the exercise lasted 48—twice as long as scheduled. The training march revealed two critical weaknesses in the *foco*, even before it planned to go into combat. In *Guerrilla Warfare*, Che posits that to compensate for the more open countryside and greater presence of roads in unfavorable terrain, "the mobility of this type of guerrilla should be extraordinary."[11] Frequently lost and slowed by the difficult riverine terrain, the *foco* at this early stage was anything but mobile; although *Guerrilla Warfare* suggests that a *foco* should be able to march 30 to 50 kilometers (18 to 30 miles) per day in unfavorable terrain, Che's band covered just a few kilometers on good days and almost nothing on bad days. The exercise also cost two men drowned and the loss of considerable equipment swept away by the currents.

Guerrilla Warfare also admonishes that "work on the masses . . . is even more important in the unfavorable zones."[12] The seven-week march was not the definitive test, but it was discouraging that not a single peasant joined the *foco*. Reflecting the demoralizing turn of events during the training exercise, Che's diary is full of pessimism: "A black day for me; I made it by sheer guts, for I am very exhausted" (February 23); "The men are getting increasingly discouraged at seeing the approaching end of the provisions but not of the distance to be covered" (March 7); "The morale of the men is low; Miguel has swollen feet, and there are several others in that condition" (March 15).[13] A new arrival at the farm described Che upon his return from the exercise: "His clothes were torn to shreds . . . He was wearing the clothes of universal misery, threadbare and filthy."[14]

Upon returning to the farm, tired and discouraged, the *foco* learned that the Bolivian army, informed by two deserters, had discovered and raided the training base. In response, Che decided to begin combat immediately, before the army could organize an effective campaign against him. On March 23, the guerrillas ambushed a 32-man army patrol, killing or wounding 13 and capturing large amounts of arms and ammunition. Although the victory was good for guerrilla morale, fellow Argentine guerrilla Ciro Bustos wrote, "The strategic initiative of the foco could not be implemented. Che was on the defensive before he had even finished drawing up his plans."[15]

A second successful engagement, in which the army suffered some 15 casualties, took place on April 10. In response, the government declared four southeastern provinces an "emergency zone." A week later the *foco* accidentally split; despite weeks of searching for each other, wasting time, energy, and supplies needed for warfare, the band led by the Cuban Joaquín and the larger one under Che's command never linked up. During May and June a series of small, indecisive encounters took place as Che's band moved north without apparent plan. The military high point for Che came on July 6, when his group captured the small town of Samaipata on the highway linking the major cities of Cochabamba and Santa Cruz. After holding it for a few hours and acquiring some supplies, the guerrillas moved on. However, the capture of such a strategically important locale by the redoubtable Che Guevara, whose presence in Bolivia had just been announced, received worldwide news coverage. It also spurred the Bolivian command to commit two field divisions to the antiguerrilla campaign.

From this point onward, Che's diary reflects growing despair and a monotonous litany of problems: food and water shortages, exhaustion, sickness, loss of essential equipment, desertions, low morale, breaches of discipline, quarrels between Cubans and Bolivians, and a virtually total lack of support from peasants and urban cadres. All communication with Havana was lost. Three and a half months after entering combat, rather than preparing a second front, the *foco* was reduced to a daily struggle for survival.

Central to the problems of the *foco* was the failure to gain the support of the area's peasantry. Che states unequivocally in *Guerrilla Warfare*, "The guerrilla fighter needs full help from the people of the area"; he continues, "While [the enemy] must operate in regions that are absolutely hostile, finding sullen silence on the part of the peasants, the rebels have in nearly every house a friend or even a relative."[16] In the case of Che's Bolivian operation, the prescribed roles of army and guerrillas were reversed. Throughout the 11 months of its operation, not a single inhabitant of the area joined the *foco*; some were indifferent, others were hostile to the guerrillas and cooperative with the army, which had been carrying out civic action projects in the zone. Near the end of his venture, Che complained, "The peasants do not give us any help and are turning into informers."[17] One of the most telling miscalculations was the language problem. Rather than Quechua, a widely spoken Indian language that most the Bolivian guerrillas knew and the Cubans studied, the *lingua franca* of the zone was Guaraní, which no one in the *foco* spoke. In addition, the banner of agrarian reform was useless in the war zone, where land was unusually abundant.

Another critical weakness of Che's *foco* was the lack of reliabl[e] the Bolivian left. Given the failure of peasant recruitment, it wa[s] have recruits from the Bolivian cities to augment the core or Cuban veterans sent with Che. At the *foco's* maximum strength of 51, reached in March, 29 were Bolivians and the majority of the rest Cubans; of the 29 Bolivians, Che felt that many were uncommitted and unreliable. The presence of so many Cubans made it easy for the Bolivian government to depict the *foco* as a foreign invasion force, and the Cubans' beards, long hair, and speech confirmed the government's allegations to the peasantry of the zone. President Barrientos cleverly used the foreign invasion argument to firm up support at the national level, persuading leaders of the powerful peasant militias to sign a "Peasant-Military Pact" against subversion in July 1967. Despite the excellent credentials and high rank of the Cubans sent to Bolivia—all were Sierra Maestra veterans and officers in the Cuban army, and four were members of the Communist Party's central committee—they could not build a successful *foco* without help from the Bolivian left and the peasantry.

Guerrilla Warfare insists that "A good supply system is of basic importance to the guerrilla band" and dwells on the need for proper equipment, clothing, and medicines.[18] The failure of supply during the final three months of Che's *foco* took a greater toll than the army did. Food was a constant problem. Because local support was not forthcoming, the diet was what the guerrillas could kill or pick. Che's entry for August 24 reveals the situation: "At dusk the macheteros returned with the traps, they caught a condor and a rotten cat. Everything was eaten together with the last piece of anteater meat."[19] Che's asthma medicine had been lost for some time, and as his attacks became more debilitating he had to resort to riding the horses and mules that were not eaten. Weapons and ammunition were in short supply as well.

In the monthly summaries that Che entered in his diary, he regularly noted the low quality of the army units sent against his *foco*. His analysis for September—"now the Army appears to be more effective in its actions"— reflected the integration of newly trained counterinsurgency ranger units into the forces arrayed against Che.[20] The United States had been involved in the fight against Che since the first reports of guerrilla activity, when the Pentagon had commissioned an infrared aerial reconnaissance of southeastern Bolivia that helped to locate the *foco*. In April 1967, a Special Forces Mobile Training Team from the Panama Canal Zone under the command of Major Ralph W. "Pappy" Shelton arrived to create counterinsurgency units. Some 650 Rangers were in place by mid-August, and Che quickly detected the difference that they made. As his diary so poignantly reveals, Che was defeated by his own mistakes and miscalculations; but the Pentagon's counterinsurgency program clearly hastened his demise.

The end came for Che's guerrillas in two engagements when the army's noose finally closed on the *foco*. Both battles underscored the deadly potential of the rivers for trapping retreating units in inescapable gorges. Joaquín and his band were destroyed in the Vado del Yeso on August 31. After another five weeks of pursuit and skirmishes, the army pinned down Che's group in the Quebrada del Yuro on October 8, killing six and capturing Che. He was executed the next day by Bolivian officers in the presence of U.S. personnel.

Rural Guerrilla Warfare After Che

Che's death transcended the eradication of a small *foco* in southeastern Bolivia; it meant the burial of his and Castro's plan for continental revolution. The death of the master at his own game, following the failures of dozens of lesser-known guerrilla movements, forced a reexamination of the *foco* thesis and of the validity of rural guerrilla warfare itself. Yet while the U.S. authorities and their Latin American allies celebrated Che's demise, the defeat in Bolivia did not spell the end of rural guerrilla warfare in Latin America.

During the decade after 1967, few new rural *focos* appeared. The surviving guerrilla movements in Guatemala, Colombia, and Nicaragua fought on; the first two gained little or no ground during the 1970s, while the Nicaraguan guerrillas succeeded in taking power at the decade's end. The two most important new rural guerrilla movements to surface after Che's death became major threats to their countries' governments in the 1980s. The insurgency in El Salvador is examined in Chapter 11. The other major rural guerrilla war developed in Peru.

Peru experienced the most violent guerrilla insurgency in Latin America, the only one that institutionalized terrorism against authorities and civilians alike. The Communist Party of Peru in the Shining Path of Mariátegui (Partido Comunista del Perú en el Sendero Luminoso de Mariátegui, or Sendero Luminoso) was founded in 1970, during the 1968–1975 Peruvian military revolution. Despite carrying out a thorough agrarian reform, the government led by General Juan Velasco Alvarado was unable to satisfy demands for land in the heavily populated south-central Andes where agricultural and grazing lands were limited. This is precisely where Abimael Guzmán, a philosophy professor at the University of Huamanga in Ayacucho, founded the Sendero Luminoso. The university's mission was to promote development in the heavily Quechua Indian region by training specialists in agronomy and public health and returning them to their villages to work. This provided Guzmán, the self-proclaimed "Fourth Sword of Marxism," an ideal means of disseminating his doctrine and building a following. His disciples revered him as a demi-god, took his word as gospel, and executed his directives unquestioningly.

The Sendero Luminoso embraced a radical ideology derived largely from Mao Zedong and Peru's own progressive thinker of the 1920s, José Carlos Mariátegui. The Maoist influence was evident in Sendero's rejection of the *foco* approach in favor of long-term cultivation of support among the rural masses prior to launching armed action—a phase that lasted ten years. Mariátegui's call for the abolition of the existing land tenure system and a return to a hypothetical pure native Andean Communism rooted in the communal village, or *ayllu*, was at the core of Guzmán's ideology. Following the lengthy period of building support, the Sendero plan involved a five-stage insurgency designed to culminate in the siege and fall of Lima, Peru's capital. At that point all traces of capitalism would be quickly eradicated; anyone resisting would be killed.

Initiating armed action in 1980, the Sendero Luminoso quickly overran most of Ayacucho Department and adjacent areas, winning new converts, particularly among Indian youth through the promise of ending the exploitive capitalist order and establishing a just, egalitarian society. Initially, even the more skeptical peasants acquiesced in the Sendero presence as the movement appeared unstoppable. Optimistic about the movement's prospects, Guzmán publicly introduced the Sendero Luminoso in a January 1981 call to arms: "Peruvian people! Today, after twelve years of false revolution and the true reinforcement of your chains under the fascist military regime . . . a new government commands behind the decrepit reactionary bulk of so-called 'representative democracy' . . . Your history is the heroic and enduring struggle of the masses . . . to create and forge with weapons in hand a new world for your children."[21]

As early as 1982, the Sendero's actions began to produce resistance. First, Sendero's millenarian ideology included the notion of cleansing through violence. Guzmán called for a "blood bath" and in 1981 instructed his followers "to intensify radically the violence," unleashing what an observer called a "colossal campaign of horror" that included massacres in numerous villages.[22] In the areas it controlled, the Sendero implemented a puritanical reign of terror with strict rules, including the prohibition of traditional village fiestas, drinking, and the use of coca. Violators such as cattle thieves, wife beaters, drunkards, and alleged petty exploiters received barbaric punishments, including amputation of limbs and death by stoning, hacking, dynamiting, and boiling alive. In taking charge of villages, moreover, the militants overturned the Andean tradition of rule by elders that predated the Spanish conquest, replacing them with Sendero cadres, usually young outsiders. Between the brutal terrorism and the upending of traditional villages' practices and values, the Sendero began to alienate the very population it counted on to help it establish what it called the "new power."

Alienation turned to resistance when, by late 1982, a few communities began forming "*rondas campesinas*," or self-defense patrols, to protect themselves from the Sendero. At the same time the authorities decided that the national police were incapable of stopping the Sendero and sent the military to the war zone. As Sendero militants wore no uniforms, they were indistinguishable to outsiders from ordinary villagers, making it difficult for the army to identify its enemy. Assuming that all villagers were members or supporters of Sendero, the military initially carried out scorched earth tactics, killing many and driving thousands out of the countryside to provincial towns. However, military authorities soon came to realize that the *rondas* were potentially valuable allies and began encouraging their formation, providing minimal training and arms. The *rondas* then became the targets of brutal Sendero reprisals, resulting in even more carnage in the highlands. By 1991, some 1,200 villages had established *rondas* and the Sendero had lost control of much of the territory and population that it initially held.

The final stage envisioned in the five-step Sendero strategy for victory was to encircle and lay siege to Lima until it fell. Despite setbacks in the Andes, Guzmán sought to take advantage of a severe economic and political crisis afflicting the country to complete the conquest of Peru. Thus in 1988 he directed his cadres to intensify the pressure on Lima, home to a third of the Peruvian population and flanked by the *barriadas*, huge slums created by migrants from the Andes, some of whom had fled Sendero violence. All the main transportation arteries into Lima passed through the *barriadas*, so controlling the slums offered the prospect of starving the city of sustenance and achieving victory. As the Sendero threat loomed ever larger, Peruvians elected Alberto Fujimori president in 1990. Fujimori escalated the government offensive, targeting real and potential civilian supporters and sympathizers as well as Sendero militants, and the death toll mounted.

Despite alienating many slum dwellers through its indiscriminate violence, as it had earlier the Andean peasantry, the Sendero was firmly established in the *barriadas* by 1991; in May of that year Guzmán declared that Sendero had reached "strategic equilibrium" with the government forces. But before Peru reached the tipping point, discarded tubes of psoriasis medicine and Marlboro cigarette packets led police in September 1992 to the Lima apartment from which Guzmán directed his movement.

With its revered leader captured, the insurgency flagged, but not before exacting a huge toll in human suffering. In addition to displacing hundreds of thousands of Indian peasants, the conflict, according to a 2003 Truth Commission report, cost over 69,000 lives. Of those, 85 percent lived in the primary war zone in the south-central Andes, 79 percent were rural, and 75 percent were speakers of Quechua or another indigenous language. The commission found the Sendero Luminoso responsible for 54 percent of the deaths and government forces for most of the rest.

Notes

1. Che Guevara, *Guerrilla Warfare*, 3rd ed., introduction and case studies by Brian Loveman and Thomas M. Davies, Jr. (Wilmington, DE: Scholarly Resources, 1997), 50.

2. Guevara, *Guerrilla Warfare*, 50.

3. Guevara, *Guerrilla Warfare*, 51.

4. Guevara, "Guerrilla Warfare: A Method," in *Guerrilla Warfare*, 152.

5. Guevara, "Message to the Tricontinental," in *Guerrilla Warfare*, 172.

6. Daniel James, *Che Guevara: A Biography*, 1st Cooper Square Press ed. (New York: Cooper Square Press, 2001), 128.

7. Guevara, *Guerrilla Warfare*, 51, 110.

8. Jon Lee Anderson, *Che Guevara: A Revolutionary Life*, rev. ed. (New York: Grove Press, 2010), 687.

9. Régis Debray, *Revolution in the Revolution? Armed Struggle and Political Struggle in Latin America*, trans. Bobbye Ortiz (New York: Grove Press, 1967).

10. Pombo's diary, September 24, 1966, in Daniel James, ed., *The Complete Bolivian Diaries of Che Guevara and Other Captured Documents*, 1st Cooper Square Press ed. (New York: Cooper Square Press, 2000), 274.

11. Guevara, *Guerrilla Warfare*, 66.

12. Guevara, *Guerrilla Warfare*, 69.

13. James, *Bolivian Diaries*, 116, 121, 124.

14. Ciro Bustos, *Che Wants to See You: The Untold Story of Che in Bolivia*, trans. Ann Wright (London: Verso, 2013), 264.

15. Bustos, *Che*, 269.

16. Guevara, *Guerrilla Warfare*, 52, 99.

17. James, *Bolivian Diaries*, 219.

18. Guevara, *Guerrilla Warfare*, 103.

19. James, *Bolivian Diaries*, 199.

20. James, *Bolivian Diaries*, 219.

21. Gustavo Gorriti, *The Shining Path: A History of the Millenarian War in Peru*, trans. Robin Kirk (Chapel Hill: University of North Carolina Press, 1999), 88.

22. Carlos Iván Degregori, "Harvesting Storms: Peasant *Rondas* and the Defeat of Sendero Luminoso in Ayacucho," in Steve J. Stern (ed.), *Shining and Other Paths: War and Society in Peru, 1980–1995* (Durham, NC: Duke University Press, 1998), 136, 135.

CHAPTER SIX

After Che: Urban Guerrilla Warfare

The death of Che Guevara and the defeat of his Bolivian *foco* cut short Fidel Castro's concerted efforts of 1966 and 1967 to revive the momentum of revolution in Latin America. The continental revolution; the two, three, many Vietnams strategy; and even rural-based guerrilla war itself rang hollow after the apostle was added to the long list of martyrs to the cause of replicating the Cuban Revolution. Yet within two years of Che's death, a new wave of insurrection rekindled the hopes of the revolutionaries and the fears of Washington and its Latin American allies.

Urban guerrilla warfare, an adaptation of Che's approach to the conquest of power, was in full swing in Uruguay, Brazil, and Argentina by 1970 and had begun in Chile. Even in Brazil, where the urban guerrillas achieved little success, they were more effective than many of the rural *focos* of the 1960s had been. Urban guerrilla warfare was more threatening to the governments of Uruguay and Argentina than rural guerrillas had been anywhere outside of Cuba. Thus the rise of urban guerrilla warfare and its early promise breathed new life into the faltering Latin American revolution.

Although at variance with Che's prescriptions, urban guerrilla warfare represented a revival and continuation of the influence of the Cuban Revolution. The most prominent of the Brazilian urban guerrillas, Carlos Marighela, led the Brazilian delegation to the OLAS meeting in Havana; having absorbed the *fidelista* message of the conference, he broke with the Brazilian Communist Party upon his return and took up the armed struggle against the military government. The Tupamaros consciously based their movement on Che's *foco* principle and set out to create revolutionary conditions in Uruguay through revolutionary action. In Argentina, several of the urban guerrilla organizations traced their lineage to earlier, failed rural *focos*. One Argentine leader explicitly linked Che's death to the guerrillas' turn to the cities: "Che was killed. Therefore, we had to change our way of thinking."[1]

Although seemingly abrupt, the transition from rural to urban guerrilla warfare had antecedents in the early and mid-1960s. Two movements of that period had made extensive use of urban armed units even while concentrating on the countryside. During the height of the Venezuelan guerrilla movement in 1962 and 1963, a major portion of the insurrection was concentrated in the cities, especially Caracas. Clandestine urban cadres organized combat units to conduct demonstrations, sabotage, assassinations, and other activities, culminating in the unsuccessful effort to disrupt the 1963 elections. The Guatemalan guerrillas for a while also had urban units to complement the activities of their primarily rural forces, and some urban activity often accompanied the predominantly rural struggle in other countries. In the area of theory, at least one writer began a vigorous advocacy of urban-based revolutionary war while rural *focos* were still in vogue: Abraham Guillén, an exiled veteran of the Spanish Civil War living in Argentina and Uruguay, published his *Strategies of the Urban Guerrilla* in 1966, prior to Che's Bolivian venture.[2]

Strategies of Urban Guerrilla Warfare

Unlike the major authors who wrote on rural guerrilla war, none of the writers on the urban guerrilla was the protagonist of a successful movement. In contrast to Mao, Giap, and Che Guevara, who wrote up their experiences and presented them as models for emulation, those who wrote on the urban guerrilla drew on historic cases, on critiques of Che's *foco* theory and the attempts to apply it, and on their own unsuccessful or unfinished experiences. As a result, no theorist of urban guerrilla war wrote with the authority of a Mao, a Giap, or a Guevara, and consequently no source comparable to the corpus of Che's works existed to guide the revolutionaries in Latin America's cities.

Abraham Guillén was the most prolific and probably the most widely read author on the urban guerrilla. He based his message partially on urban insurrections in Europe, particularly on the Paris Commune of 1871 and the Russian Revolution of 1917, and on the 1936 defense of Madrid against Franco in which he had participated. Guillén was also a close observer of the Latin American scene who carefully analyzed the failures of the rural *foco* strategy in the countries where it had been applied. After moving from Buenos Aires to Montevideo, he became acquainted with the Tupamaros during their formative phase. Therefore, his thoughts on the urban guerrilla reflect a synthesis of study, experience, and observation.

Although Guillén's revision of Che is quite thorough, the two agreed on the continental strategy of revolutionary linkage. Guillén wrote, "To the 'holy alliance' of the indigenous oligarchy and *yanqui* imperialism we must answer with an offensive of Latin American liberation on all fronts, in all countries, in the cities and the countryside, through a revolutionary war on a continental scale."[3] He went further, proposing the creation of mechanisms to hasten pan–Latin American cooperation in pursuit of revolution. Borrowing from APRA founder Víctor Raúl Haya de la Torre, he posited the creation of continent-wide mass organizations, including labor unions, political parties, youth organizations, and a Latin American liberation front.

Guillén's differences with Che were fully aired in writings that preceded as well as followed Guevara's death. The Spaniard felt that Che's faith in the ability of the *foco* to create conditions for revolutions was misguided: "Foquismo . . . is petty bourgeois in origin as well as outlook—evident in the token number of workers and peasants in the guerrillas' ranks. Actually, it is an insurrectional movement for piling up cadavers, for giving easy victories to the repressive generals trained by the Pentagon."[4] A strong mass line was necessary for victory, specifically "an anti-oligarchical and anti-imperialist popular front based on a program of liberation that brings together workers, peasants, the proletarianized middle class and even a section of the native bourgeoisie fearful of being pushed to the wall by imperialism; [otherwise] the guerrilla will lose the war . . . from failure to obtain the support of the great mass of the population of an underdeveloped country."[5] Guillén inserted a caveat similar to the one that Che had placed in *Guerrilla Warfare*: revolution could only succeed in a country where the ruling class had lost its prestige and legitimacy as the result of some profound crisis or serious economic decline.

Guillén categorically rejected the primacy of the rural struggle. Referring to the failure of the 1965 Peruvian *focos*, he wrote: "To organize a small revolutionary army and to isolate it from the popular masses in a mountainous terrain, without a territorial organization to support it, is to expose it to implacable destruction."[6] In another piece, he argued, "It would be absurd in our epoch of highly developed urban populations to launch the principal front of a revolution in small villages or mountains under conditions in which peasants are no longer a majority and there are few logistical resources for modern warfare."[7] For Guillén, in any country with an urban majority—9 of the 20 Latin American countries by 1970—the main revolutionary movement had to be in the cities; rural guerrillas should operate where feasible, but always in a supporting role—exactly the opposite of Che's position. Despite pretensions to broader application, Guillén seems to have considered Argentina and Uruguay as the prime areas for urban guerrilla warfare. Those countries were preponderantly urban, had large capital cities that dominated national life, and lacked the combined mountain and jungle terrain favored by rural guerrillas, although Argentina's northern Andean region offered enough potential to have attracted a few short-lived rural *focos* in the 1960s.

Despite the availability of writings on theories and strategies of urban guerrilla warfare, urban fighters seemed to be guided above all by pragmatic considerations. After Che's death, they could see more clearly that with their huge urban populations and flat, open terrain, the Cuban model had never been relevant to their situation. The urban guerrillas took guidance from Guillén, Marighela, and others, but unlike the practitioners of the rural *foco*, they had no single anointed theoretician whose words rang with the authority of victory. Strategies and tactics were usually flexible, based on trial and error. One Argentine urban guerrilla stated straightforwardly: "We put things into practice before we made up theories about them"; a Uruguayan counterpart confirmed this approach, arguing that "There is no better revolutionary theory than that derived from revolutionary actions themselves."[8] Freedom from the constraints of dogma may have given the urban guerrillas an advantage over their rural counterparts who read and sought to emulate Che.

The Tupamaros of Uruguay

In a widely circulated interview conducted in 1967, a leader of Uruguay's Tupamaros paraphrased Fidel Castro: "Each revolutionary, each revolutionary group has only one duty: *to prepare* [italics added] to make the revolution."[9] As much as anything, the emphasis on preparation for revolutionary action distinguished the Tupamaros from most other Latin American guerrilla movements, both rural and urban. From its first minor action in July 1963, fully four years of intense preparatory work ensued before the guerrillas launched full-scale war on the government.

The Tupamaros are best known for having pioneered urban guerrilla warfare in Latin America. Despite earlier instances of urban components of guerrilla movements, the Tupamaros were the first to reject Che's tenet of the primacy of the rural struggle. Although acknowledging the desirability of rural warfare as a complementary action, to the Uruguayan guerrillas, the urban theater was the decisive one—the site where the revolution would be won or lost.

The Tupamaros did not generate a theory or grand strategy of urban guerrilla warfare. Writings and interviews reveal that the Tupamaros embraced urban guerrilla warfare as a matter of expediency. A 1967 Tupamaro document made their argument: "The unfavorable characteristics of [rural] geography . . . permit the enemy to use his heavy weapons and aviation . . . It would be a strategic error to isolate ourselves in the countryside, abandoning the unemployed and hungry masses of Montevideo."[10]

Uruguay, a small country of 68,000 square miles and a 1970 population of some 3 million, is mostly flat and largely devoted to pasture. It has the least hospitable terrain in all of Latin America for rural *focos*, so poor that it falls short of the conditions Che described as "unfavorable terrain." Despite having an economy based on meat and wool exports, Uruguay in 1970 was Latin America's second most urbanized country, after Argentina. Eighty percent of its population lived in cities and towns, and half resided in Montevideo, a city of 1.5 million. As one Tupamaro put it, "We have a big city with more than 300 square kilometers of buildings, which allows for the development of an urban struggle."[11]

Despite reversing the fields of action, the Tupamaros shared two fundamental concepts with Che. They identified with the *foco* principle, "the principle that revolutionary action in itself . . . generates revolutionary consciousness, organization, and conditions."[12] They also adhered to the notion of continental revolution and maintained a Committee on International Affairs that developed contacts with revolutionary movements and friendly governments in Latin America and throughout the world. And in common with other Cuba-inspired groups, they viewed the established left as having "more confidence in manifestos, in issuing theoretical statements referring to the Revolution . . . without understanding that it is basically revolutionary actions that precipitate revolutionary situations."[13]

The challenge facing the guerrillas was formidable, in large part because Uruguay, along with Chile, was the bastion of democratic, constitutional government in South America. Often called the "Switzerland of South America" because of its prosperity, political stability, and experimentation with a Swiss-type plural executive system, Uruguay boasted a tradition of democratic government based on regular elections, broad participation, a two-party system, and well-developed individual liberties. Uruguay was Latin America's most advanced welfare state, having nearly three-quarters of its labor force covered by the social security system.

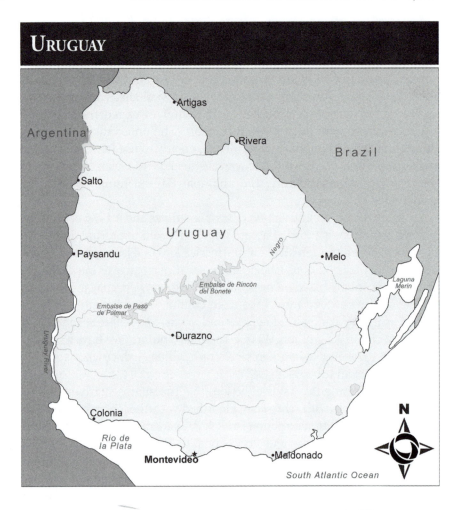

What the Tupamaros saw and hoped to exploit was what they called the Uruguayan crisis. The economy by the 1950s was becoming stagnant; heavily dependent on its raw material export base, Uruguay had exhausted the growth potential of import-substitution industrialization without having modernized its rural sector, whose productivity was far lower than that of the similar Argentine rural economy. A long decline in wool prices exacerbated these conditions. The result of this economic conjuncture in the 1960s was rising unemployment, inflation, a pronounced deterioration in the standard of living of the middle and working classes, and the growth of a marginal sector of slum-dwelling unemployed. The economic decline led to a dramatic growth in labor unrest and strikes, to which the government responded with states of siege several times in the 1960s.

The Tupamaros' analysis also detected a growing hollowness of Uruguayan democracy. An unusual form of proportional representation kept third parties from making gains against the historically dominant Colorados and second-place Blancos. Although there had been no interruption of constitutional continuity, there was mounting evidence of corruption and of citizen cynicism in the 1960s. The Uruguayan situation probably served Guillén as the model of a ruling class that had lost its prestige and legitimacy in a setting of economic decline.

All in all, the Tupamaros concluded that whereas a prosperous and democratic Uruguay had been the exception, "The process of the deterioration of its economy . . . gradually included Uruguay in the rest of the Latin American scene. Therefore, objective conditions in Uruguay are no longer different from those in the rest of Latin America."[14] The Tupamaros' challenge was to create the subjective conditions through revolutionary action and build strong mass support in a polity where the legal struggle was far from exhausted, as reflected in the continuing electoral process and heightened strike activity.

Preparations for the revolutionary struggle began in 1963 with an assault on the Swiss Rifle Club in Nueva Helvecia, led by union organizer and Socialist Party member Raúl Sendic. Formally named the National Liberation Movement (Movimiento de Liberación Nacional, MLN), the guerrillas became better known as the Tupamaros, a name derived from the Inca noble Túpac Amaru who led the greatest indigenous rebellion in the history of Spain's American empire in the Peruvian Andes in 1780, and also from Uruguay's own history.[15] Like guerrillas in other countries, the Tupamaros attracted dissidents from Marxist and left groups who embraced the activist *fidelista* approach to revolution. They made a virtue of the diversity of its members' ideological and party backgrounds. In contrast to most insurrectionary movements, which were tied to a particular party or faction, the Tupamaros recruited broadly under the slogan "nonsectarian armed struggle."

During their four years of underground preparation, the Tupamaros escalated their actions gradually, from break-ins to bank robberies to bombings, while avoiding run-ins with police and troops and refraining from killings. The Tupamaros were initially seen as romantic, benign revolutionaries based on their restraint and on their Robin Hood–style actions to benefit the poor, such as a Christmas Eve "Hunger Commando" hijacking of a food truck and distribution of its contents in the slums. Concurrently, they recruited a large cadre of middle-class students and professionals as well as workers and even members of the armed forces, all of whom lived apparently normal lives but for their clandestine activities. They also established an infrastructure to sustain the armed struggle: supply networks, safe houses, even underground clinics equipped for emergency surgery, as well as long-term recuperative care.

As their numbers and facilities grew, the Tupamaros developed an elaborate organization designed to maximize their fighting potential while insulating the movement against detection and destruction. Based on the concept of compartmentalization, the structure consisted of a central executive committee and columns of 30 to 50 people, each containing cells of between 5 and 10 members. Although coordinated from above, each column was designed to be self-sustaining in the case of trouble at the top; thus the columns were equipped to gather intelligence, maintain supplies, and undertake armed or propaganda action independently, making it theoretically possible for one surviving column to regenerate the movement. So effective was the compartmentalization that, according to a historian of the MLN, "At one point, two members of separate cells . . . recognized each other. It was a quintessential MLN experience: they knew one another from 'legal' life but had no idea the other was a Tupamaro—until that night."[16] Outside the underground itself were support committees that helped in recruiting, securing supplies, and providing needed skills.

The emerging guerrilla movement suffered a serious setback in December 1966, when an unintended encounter with police led to arrests and the discovery of safe houses and supplies. The organization proved resilient, however, and by 1968 the Tupamaros escalated their pressure, moving from the "Robin Hood" stage of self-publicity and exposing the regime to a more aggressive phase of direct challenges to government authority. The first kidnapping came in August 1968, when the Tupamaros seized Ulysses Pereira Reverbel, head of the state electric energy company, and held him for four days. In July 1969 they drew their first blood, attacking and killing some police. By September 1969 they had established a clandestine radio.

"Operation Pando," an event commemorating the second anniversary of Che Guevara's death, was the Tupamaros' real coming-out party. On October 8, 1969, some 50 Tupamaros occupied Pando, a town of 15,000 inhabitants near Montevideo, for several hours. Having arrived individually or in small groups by private and public transportation, in a carefully coordinated action the guerrillas captured the main public buildings, robbed the banks, and harangued the populace. A policeman and three guerrillas were killed and 16 Tupamaros were captured, but the demonstration of guerrilla power was a sobering challenge to governmental authority.

While continuing their bank robberies, bombings, kidnappings, and food distribution in slums, the Tupamaros assumed the state function of dispensing justice by late 1969. This included assassinations of police accused of torturing captured guerrillas and the arrest and, on several occasions, the trial of government and foreign officials for complicity in counterinsurgency activities. Dan Mitrione, an instructor in the USAID police counterinsurgency training program in Uruguay, was seized in July 1970 and held in the guerrillas' "People's Prison" for the release of 150 political prisoners. The maneuver backfired, however, as President Jorge Pacheco Areco refused to negotiate, declared a state of siege, and launched an intense search for People's Prison. The government operation netted nine leading Tupamaros, including Raúl Sendic. The guerrillas retaliated on August 9 by executing Mitrione, whom they accused of teaching sophisticated torture techniques to the police. Full-scale war was on.

For the next two years, the Tupamaros' fortunes fluctuated between spectacular successes and severe setbacks. In November 1970 the guerrillas carried out the largest bank robbery in Uruguayan history. They seized British Ambassador Geoffrey Jackson the following January and held him in People's Prison. In July 1971, 38 Tupamaros escaped from Women's Prison, followed in September by the escape of 106 Tupamaros, including Sendic, from Punta Carretas Prison. Maintaining a sense of humor despite the earnestness of the war, escaping guerrillas painted on the tunnel they had dug: "MLN Transit Authority: Please keep to your left."[17] Three days after the Punta Carretas escape, the guerrillas released Geoffrey Jackson.

As the conflict escalated, the authorities developed progressively tougher responses. Government-sponsored or -tolerated death squads targeted guerrillas and leftists in general. The abduction of Ambassador Jackson brought the most energetic and repressive measures to date. Under a state of siege, 10,000 troops and police cordoned off areas of the capital and conducted building-by-building searches for People's Prison. The Pacheco government placed the military in charge of all antiguerrilla activity in September 1971.

Facing increased government pressure, and influenced by Salvador Allende's recent electoral victory in Chile, the Tupamaros abruptly changed course. In September 1971 they declared a unilateral truce and endorsed the leftist Broad Front coalition in the national elections scheduled for November. The results were disappointing: the Broad Front received only 18 percent of the vote, and conservative Colorado Juan María Bordaberry won the presidency. The Tupamaros resumed the armed insurrection the following month, occupying the town of Paysandú and conducting actions in nearby towns. It appeared that the guerrillas were on the verge of opening a rural front in preparation for a final assault on the government.

On April 15, 1972, the day after the Tupamaros executed four men for involvement in the death squads, the Bordaberry government declared a "state of internal war" and began a census of householders and the registration of all Montevideo residents in an effort to force guerrillas out of safe houses and discourage all collaboration with them. All news of the guerrillas and the counterinsurgency drive was censored. This all-out campaign, combined with valuable information extracted from a captured ranking Tupamaro leader, soon bore fruit. After locating People's Prison in May 1972, the government announced on July 15 that it had captured over 600 Tupamaros, killed 100, and discovered 70 of their safe houses in the past three months. On September 1, counterinsurgency forces wounded and captured Raúl Sendic: to a fellow Tupamaro, "The downfall of Sendic meant it was all over."[18]

Following their successes in counterinsurgency, the military and the Bordaberry administration met increased levels of political opposition from civilians demanding relaxation of security measures and opposing a restrictive new education law designed to control student activism. The military reacted harshly to criticism of its involvement in death squads and alleged brutal treatment of prisoners. Facing a wave of labor unrest and political protest, Bordaberry acceded to the gradual militarization of his government until the culminating coup of June 1973, when he closed Congress and municipal governments and began to rule by decree with a military–civilian cabinet. With its now unfettered power turned on the guerrillas, the government quickly ended the era of significant Tupamaro action.

A postmortem on the Tupamaros suggests that several factors contributed to their defeat. The Uruguayan case did not appear to bear out Che's concept that the *foco* would create conditions for revolution by forcing governments to become repressive. Rather, after the struggle became intense and bloody, the guerrillas appear to have lost much of the support that they had enjoyed during their earlier Robin Hood phase. The effectiveness of the government response helped to deny the guerrillas the wide backing they needed. U.S. aid to the counterinsurgency strengthened the government's response and helped to turn the tide against the guerrillas. Finally, the government displayed a determination to win the war, whatever the cost in political and individual rights. The ultimate defeat of the Tupamaros, however, should not obscure the fact that theirs was the most promising, or threatening, insurrection since Castro's. In contrast to the many rural *focos* of the 1960s, the Tupamaros seriously threatened to topple their country's government and seize power. The Tupamaros' relative success helped sustain the hopes for revolution in Latin America and inspired emulation in Brazil, Chile, and Argentina.

Urban Guerrillas in Chile and Brazil

The urban orientation of guerrilla warfare in Chile was essentially a practical matter. Apart from its isolated southern rainforests, whose potential was limited, Chile offered no good prospects for rural guerrilla warfare. By contrast Santiago, a city of 2.2 million in 1965 and the country's economic and administrative center, appeared to provide an attractive setting for armed insurrection. Urban guerrilla warfare in Chile was primarily the work of the Movement of the Revolutionary Left (Movimiento de Izquierda Revolucionaria, MIR), a group founded in 1965 by students at the University of Concepción. Like the Tupamaros, MIR cultivated support in slum areas through organizational work and donations of expropriated money. Beginning in March 1968, MIR went into action against the reformist government of Eduardo Frei with a campaign of nonlethal bombings directed at the U.S. consulate in Santiago, the Chile-American Institute in Rancagua, the Christian Democrats' primary office, the right-wing newspaper *El Mercurio*, and the residence of conservative Senator Francisco Bulnes. MIR later escalated its attacks to include bank robberies and other armed assaults.

In its first three years of activity, MIR appeared to follow the Tupamaro pattern of a measured escalation of actions designed to demonstrate its power while avoiding premature confrontations with superior government forces. The possibilities of success for the urban guerrilla approach in Chile, however, were not fully tested due to the suspension of MIR's anti-government actions during the 1970 presidential campaign. Despite its conviction that the revolution could not be won at the ballot box, MIR agreed to the suspension in order to avoid creating a major law-and-order issue that might work against the candidacy of leftist Salvador Allende.

After Allende's election, MIR switched roles, becoming an ally of the government, but not always a welcome one. It operated on the fringe of power and beyond the limits of legality to foster mobilization by promoting seizures of land and factories and generally pushing to radicalize the government's policies. MIR simultaneously prepared for the civil war or military coup that it was certain would come. Its organization was badly damaged in the 1973 coup that overthrew Allende, severely limiting its ability to mount effective action against the military dictatorship of General Augusto Pinochet.

Like Chile, Brazil experienced a relatively brief period of warfare in the cities. Yet between 1969 and 1971 the Brazilian urban guerrillas made headlines as a result of their bold moves, which included bank robberies, kidnappings, assaults, prison breaks, and airplane hijackings. Of the various forms of resistance to the military government installed in 1964 and its successors, the urban guerrilla movement was the most dramatic and, while it lasted, the most threatening to the regime.

The context within which the Brazilian urban guerrillas developed was diametrically opposed to that in which the Tupamaros and Chile's MIR evolved. The 1964 government that replaced Goulart was reasonably moderate in comparison with later Brazilian regimes. It did not abolish civilian institutions but rather sought to dominate by reserving the presidency for a military man, strengthening presidential powers at the expense of Congress and the states, and taming the politicians. However, periodic confrontations proved that even the purged politicians were insufficiently pliable, requiring the military to assume more direct control. This progressive tightening of the dictatorship evoked an armed response.

Beginning with a *foco* launched in the Serra do Caparaó in early 1967, a variety of *fidelista* groups attempted to pursue rural guerrilla warfare. All of these *focos* succumbed quickly to the swift reaction of the Brazilian army. By 1968 the underground resistance had begun preparations for armed action in Brazil's cities. In early 1969, following a harsh crackdown that ended all pretense of civilian participation in government, the urban guerrillas swung into action.

Carlos Marighela was the leading Brazilian theoretician of the urban guerrilla. In assessing the possibilities of insurrection against Brazil's firmly entrenched military regime, Marighela concluded that the cities offered the best hope for success. In addition to São Paulo and Rio de Janeiro, with 8.4 and 7.2 million inhabitants, respectively, Brazil in the late 1960s had four other cities of over a million people and five more of over half a million. Overall, Brazil was 55 percent urban. Although it possessed seemingly unlimited jungle terrain, most of that was remote from major population centers, making communications and supply extremely difficult. The quick defeats of rural *focos* convinced Marighela that the cities were the appropriate starting point, but he believed that guerrilla activity would later shift to the countryside and finally produce a field army capable of defeating the government's forces. Thus in contrast to Guillén, Carlos Marighela reaffirmed Che's belief in the primacy of rural struggle in Brazil: "(a) The city is the area of complementary struggle, and the whole urban struggle whether on the guerrilla or mass-movement front, must always be seen as [a] tactical struggle; (b) The decisive struggle will be in the rural area."[19]

Marighela's *Handbook of Urban Guerrilla Warfare*, a training guide for city fighters similar to Che's handbook for rural guerrillas, describes the purposes, organization, and activities of the urban guerrillas. It offers detailed instructions on the use of arms, ambushes, sabotage, escapes, and other practical advice. Ultimately, however, it argues that the success of the urban fighters rests on the same two assumptions that underpin Che's analysis of the rural guerrilla: the support of the populace and the superior qualities of the revolutionary. "The urban guerrilla is characterized by courage and a spirit of initiative. He must be a good tactician and a good shot, and make up for his inferiority in weapons, ammunition, and equipment by his skill and cunning." But above all, "His moral superiority is incontestable."[20] As for popular support, "When they see that the revolutionaries' fire power is being directed against their enemies, the masses—hitherto helpless against the dictatorship—will recognize the guerrillas as their ally and come to their support."[21]

The truncated history of the Brazilian urban guerrillas demonstrates little of either the guerrillas' superiority or the growth of popular support. In contrast to the Tupamaros, the Brazilian guerrillas were divided into various independent groups; despite efforts to unite, fragmentation reduced their effectiveness. During the period of greatest activity, 1969 through 1971, the guerrillas' successes, however spectacular, were outstripped by their failures. Major bank robberies; raids on military and police barracks; kidnappings of the U.S., West German, and Swiss ambassadors; and the exchange of these officials for political prisoners were among the high points of the guerrillas' successes. These accomplishments were overshadowed by the deaths of Marighela and other guerrilla leaders, mass arrests of guerrillas and sympathizers, and the decimation of entire organizations. Like so many of the rural *focos*, the Brazilian urban guerrillas took actions that were too bold, actions certain to elicit strong retaliation before they had the numbers, training, and organization to survive the government's counteroffensive. The Brazilian case also demonstrated the difficulties of challenging a dictatorship that recognized no limits on its use of force.

Argentina's Urban Guerrillas

Despite the predominance of flat, open terrain in much of Argentina, the Andean foothills in the country's northwest offered some prospects for rural guerrilla warfare. Thus, in common with much of Latin America, Argentina was the scene of rural guerrilla outbreaks following Castro's victory in Cuba. In September 1959 a small group, the Uturuncos ("tiger men" in the Quechua language), set up two camps in the mountainous area of Tucumán province. Following its first operation, the seizure of a police station on Christmas Day 1959, the group quickly met its demise. The second rural insurgency surfaced in 1963, when Argentine journalist Jorge Ricardo Masseti, accompanied by three veterans of Castro's Sierra Maestra campaign, crossed into Argentina from Bolivia and began recruiting for their People's Guerrilla Army (Ejército Guerrillero del Pueblo, EGP). This attempt ended after ten months when police captured the majority of its militants. The third insurgency came the year after Che's death in Bolivia. Like its predecessors, it was very short-lived.

Thereafter, influenced by the death of Che and by the Tupamaros in neighboring Uruguay, the Argentina revolutionaries turned to the cities as the site of the armed struggle. Argentina appeared to be particularly well suited to urban insurgency. Greater Buenos Aires, whose 10 million people constituted some 40 percent of the national population, was an attractive venue for urban guerrillas. Three other cities, Córdoba, Rosario, and Mendoza, each had approximately three-quarters of a million inhabitants by 1970.

The Argentine urban guerrillas developed out of the "Cordobazo," a May 1969 workers' uprising in the industrial city of Córdoba against the dictatorship of General Juan Carlos Onganía. In contrast to the Tupamaros in neighboring Argentina, who spent years in patient preparation for action, several guerrilla groups burst upon the scene before the end of 1970. Most of those groups soon coalesced into two: the Trotskyist/Guevarist People's Revolutionary Army (Ejército Revolucionario del Pueblo, ERP) and the Marxist/Peronist Montoneros.

Inspired by the tactics of the Tupamaros, the Argentine urban guerrillas cultivated popular support by carrying out Robin Hood–style actions. Among those were giveaways of stolen milk, meat, blankets, and toys in slums and the donation of 154 ambulances purchased with money extorted from Ford Motor Company. The kidnapping of Stanley Sylvester, British consul and manager of Swift and Company in Rosario, who had recently laid off 4,000 workers, was a major coup; in exchange for his release, the company rehired the workers with compensation, improved working conditions, and distributed food in the city's slums.

Concurrently, the guerrillas mounted a campaign of escalating violence between 1970 and 1973. There were constant bank robberies, attacks on elite establishments such as country clubs and racetracks, assaults on police stations and military bases, and even an attack on the presidenti: The guerrillas administered "revolutionary justice" in the as: of many, including ex-President Pedro Aramburu (1955–195o), wiio nau attempted to de-Peronize the political system and labor unions; General Juan Carlos Sánchez, whose energetic strikebreaking and repression in Rosario had made him a hated figure; and Admiral Emilio R. Berisso, in reprisal for a government massacre of captured guerrillas. Executives of foreign-owned companies, including Fiat, Coca-Cola, and Kodak as well as Swift and Ford, were kidnapped and ransomed or persuaded to pay huge sums as insurance against abduction. Following the example of Operation Pando, the guerrillas occupied at least two small cities. Although the urban fighters suffered some reverses, their successes far outweighed their losses during the early 1970s.

The political context in which the Argentine urban guerrilla war developed was unique. Argentine political life revolved around Peronismo versus anti-Peronismo. Army Colonel Juan Domingo Perón, elected president in 1946, was a populist and authoritarian ruler until the military overthrew and exiled him in 1955. One of the legacies of Perón's presidency was a sharply divided country: On one side was a huge bloc of loyal Perón supporters anchored in the working class and youth and organized into labor unions, a youth organization, and Perón's heterogeneous political party, the *Partido Justicialista*. The Peronists' goal was to secure their leader's return from his exile in Spain and restoration as president. Opposing the Peronists was a bloc consisting of the elites, much of the middle class, and the military, whose primary objectives were to keep Perón's loyalists marginalized from power and to prevent the former president's return from Spain. This deep fissure made the country virtually ungovernable, leading to a succession of short-lived military and weak civilian governments after 1955. Onganía's hard-line dictatorship (1966–1970), which spawned the urban guerrillas, was designed to restore order to Argentina's tumultuous politics.

For the larger of the two main urban guerrilla organizations, the Montoneros, the return of Perón was a strategy for achieving what they hoped would be revolution from above—a hope based on Perón's repeated declarations of his intention to establish a "socialist fatherland." Being Peronist, the Montoneros were programmatically in the mainstream of Argentine politics even while, in terms of strategy, they occupied a fringe position within the heterogeneous Peronist movement. In the words of Montonero leader Mario Firmenich, "guerrilla warfare . . . is the highest level of political struggle."[22] In contrast to their Brazilian, Uruguayan, and Chilean counterparts, many of the Argentine guerrillas shared considerable common ground with mainstream politicians and unionists, and their actions were designed to strengthen those bonds while moving the working class to greater militance. Their armed actions were also designed to make the country even more ungovernable than it had been since 1955, leaving the return of Perón as the only option for restoring political peace. In pursuing a broadly popular and concrete objective—Perón's return—and by virtue of being an element of the political mainstream, the Montoneros, working in tandem with the ERP, were better positioned to succeed than were most other guerrilla movements, both rural and urban. Indeed, the work of the urban guerrillas in destabilizing Argentina was a major factor in the Peronists' success in restoring their leader to power in 1973.

Notes

1. Héctor Víctor Suárez. "The Revolutionary Armed Forces: With Che's Weapons," *Granma Weekly* (Havana), January 17, 1971, in James Kohl and John Litt (eds.), *Urban Guerrilla Warfare in Latin America* (Cambridge, MA: MIT Press, 1974), 379.

2. Abraham Guillén, *Estrategias de la guerrilla urbana* (Montevideo: Ed. Manuales del Pueblo, 1966).

3. Guillén, *Estrategias*, in Donald C. Hodges, ed. and trans., *Philosophy of the Urban Guerrilla: The Revolutionary Writings of Abraham Guillén* (New York: William Morrow, 1973), 230.

4. Guillén, *Estrategias*, in Hodges, *Philosophy*, 269.

5. Guillén, *Estrategias*, in Hodges, *Philosophy*, 253.

6. Guillén, *Estrategias*, in Hodges, *Philosophy*, 233.

7. Guillén, *Estrategias*, in Hodges, *Philosophy*, 254.

8. Suárez, "Revolutionary Armed Forces," in Kohl and Litt, *Urban Guerrilla Warfare*; MLN Tupamaros, *Actas Tupamaras* (Buenos Aires: Schapire Editor, 1971), 7 (author's translation).

9. "30 preguntas a un Tupamaro," *Punto Final* (Santiago, Chile), 2 (58), July 2, 1968, in Antonio Mercader and Jorge de Vera, *Tupamaros: estrategia y acción* (Montevideo: Editorial Alfa, 1969), 55 (author's translation).

10. Mercader and de Vera, *Tupamaros* (Mexico City: Editorial Omega, 1971), 12 (Note the two different editions of Mercader's and de Vera's work).

11. "30 preguntas a un Tupamaro," 57.

12. "30 preguntas a un Tupamaro," 49.

13. Lindsey Blake Churchill, *Becoming the Tupamaros: Solidarity and Transnational Revolutionaries in Uruguay and the United States* (Nashville: Vanderbilt University Press, 2014), 17.

14. Madruga, "Interview with Urbano," 283.

15. The term "Tupamaro" has a specifically Uruguayan context. The term was used to describe the gaucho fighters for independence in the 1810s and 1820s, especially the followers of José Gervasio Artigas.

16. Pablo Brum, *The Robin Hood Guerrillas: The Epic Journey of Uruguay's Tupamaros*, 2nd ed. (No place of publication: CreateSpace, 2014), 221.

17. Kohl and Litt, *Urban Guerrilla Warfare*, 173.

18. Brum, *Robin Hood Guerrillas*, 308.

19. Carlos Marighela, *For the Liberation of Brazil*, trans. John Butt and Rosemary Sheed (Harmondsworth, UK: Penguin Books, 1971), 47.

20. Marighela, *For the Liberation*, 64.

21. Marighela, *For the Liberation*, 48.

22. María José Moyano, *Argentina's Lost Patrol: Armed Struggle, 1969–1979* (New Haven, CT: Yale University Press, 1995), 145.

PART 4

Three Truncated Revolutions

CHAPTER SEVEN

The Peruvian Military Revolution, 1968–1975

When the Peruvian armed forces seized power on October 3, 1968, for the second time in six years, few domestic or foreign observers guessed that the new regime would differ significantly from previous periods of military rule. The radical language of the coup manifesto, denouncing "powerful economic forces . . . motivated by overwhelming greed, [which] retain political and economic power, and frustrate the popular desire for basic structural reforms" was generally considered window dressing.[1] Yet within a year, the government headed by General Juan Velasco Alvarado had attracted attention by its bold beginnings in reform, and by 1970 it was clear that the Peruvian military was committed to a thorough structural transformation of the country.

The anomaly of the Peruvian armed forces' bucking the prevailing hemispheric trend to lead what they called a "revolution" made the Velasco government the subject of intense international scrutiny. As a result of its sweeping reforms in domestic and foreign policy, the Peruvian regime was taken as a model by military men in several Latin American countries who formed "*peruanista*" factions within their institutions. By the time of Velasco's removal from office in 1975, Peru had undergone more significant change than any other Latin American country since the Cuban Revolution, with the possible exception of Chile under Allende. Although many of Velasco's reforms were reversed by subsequent governments, others, including land reform, endured to mark the seven years of Velasco's presidency as an important watershed in Peru's modern history.

Coming after a decade of frustration for Latin America's revolutionaries whose attempts to replicate the Cuban Revolution had met abject defeat, the Peruvian military regime offered new hope for change. Disillusioned by their own failures at insurrection and attracted by the government's reforms, some of Peru's *fidelistas* supported the Velasco regime and a few, including former *foco* leader Héctor Béjar, became important collaborators. Fidel Castro praised the Velasco government for its reforms and its anti-imperialist stance. Thus the Peruvian government, especially in conjunction with the Allende government in Chile, elected in 1970, opened a new perspective on revolution in Latin America: the prospect of revolution, or at least structural reform, from above. Whereas the purists might reject halfway measures, Fidel's implicit blessing of the Peruvian military regime and the frustration of a decade of failed insurrection made the notion of revolution from above an appealing one for much of the Latin American left. The return of Perón in 1973, the populist administration of Luis Echeverría in Mexico (1970–1976), the nationalist government of Omar Torrijos in Panama (1970–1981), the leftist military government of Juan José Torres in Bolivia (1970–1971), and the *"peruanista"* military regime of Guillermo Rodríguez Lara in Ecuador (1972–1976) suggested that the Peruvian armed forces had initiated a new, if transitory, phase in the politics of change in Latin America.

One of the salient traits of the Peruvian military government was its *sui generis* nature. The regime that called itself the "Revolutionary Government of the Armed Forces" has been identified by scholars as revolutionary, reformist, corporatist, nationalist, state capitalist, populist, fascist, modernizing, and experimental. Of its various characteristics, the most visible thread linking the main pronouncements and policies of the Velasco government was unrelenting nationalism. As one would expect, an institution whose ostensible duty is defense of the homeland will be inherently nationalistic. In the broadest sense, the military adopted the mission of nation-building, of creating a true country out of the hollow shell of a republic. Its social reforms were designed to bring the excluded majority of Peruvians—those marginalized by race, language, geography, and poverty—into the national mainstream. Its economic and diplomatic policies attempted to achieve true independence for a country long subject to an exaggerated dependency. Its moves to strengthen the state were likewise motivated by nationalism, by the impulse to transform a state subservient to national and foreign capital into a state sufficiently powerful to represent the broader interest of the nation under construction over the narrow special interests that had held sway.

Background to the Military Revolution

Peru in the 1960s was a textbook case of a country ripe for revolution or reform. Whether viewed through the lenses of *fidelismo* or those of the Alliance for Progress, Peru exhibited most of the problems and hallmarks of underdevelopment and social atavism. Although Peru ranked eighth in Latin American per capita income at $338 per year in 1960, distribution of this modest income was extremely skewed. Forty percent of Peru's 10 million people in 1960 spoke Quechua, Aymara, or another native tongue as their first language. Adult illiteracy was over 50 percent nationally and much higher in the Indian strongholds of the Andes. Peru's land distribution was characterized by extremes: 1.2 percent of the country's largest landowners owned 75 percent of usable surface, whereas 84 percent held 6 percent of the land in plots averaging under two hectares. In addition, millions of rural Peruvians were landless, many of whom lived and worked in subhuman conditions on semi-feudal haciendas in the Andes. The country's formal economy was based on agricultural and mineral exports, much of those controlled by foreign, mainly U.S., interests. On the positive side, Peru's exports were more diversified than those of most hemispheric countries, a fact that insulated the country somewhat against world market price swings. The dynamic new fish meal industry had become the largest export sector by the 1960s.

Peruvian thinkers had been highly critical of the country's condition, especially of the land tenure system and the plight of the Indian since Manuel González Prada wrote at the turn of the 20th century. José Carlos Mariátegui, founder of Peru's Communist Party, wrote *Seven Essays on Peruvian Reality* in 1928.[2] A critical examination focusing on land, Indians, and dependency, Mariátegui's analysis remained essentially accurate in the 1960s. The struggle to rectify those conditions gave rise to the APRA, the prototype of Latin America's democratic left, in the 1920s. However, a blood feud between the army and APRA, stemming from a 1932 uprising involving excesses on both sides, combined with skillful political manipulation by Peru's elites, kept the APRA from power and thus postponed substantive reform until it was long overdue. By the 1950s APRA itself, having endured years of repression, had opted for restoration of its legal status in exchange for moderating its position on reform.

Signs of peasant, labor, and student unrest appeared in the 1950s and proliferated in the early 1960s as the Cuban Revolution and the Alliance for Progress accelerated the incipient mass awakening. In common with most of Latin America, Peru experienced the formation of *fidelista* parties and factions, new demands for radical change, the growth of peasant

PERU

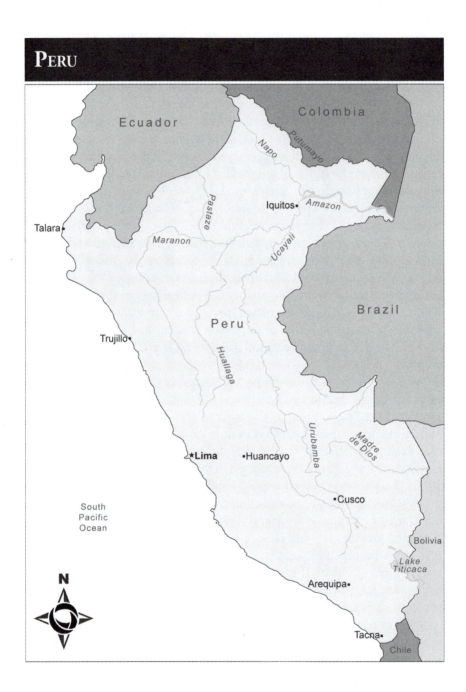

Ecuador

Colombia

Napo

Putumayo

Talara•

Pastaze

Iquitos•

Amazon

Maranon

Ucayali

Peru

Brazil

Trujillo•

Huallaga

★Lima

•Huancayo

Urubamba

Madre de Dios

•Cusco

South
Pacific
Ocean

Bolivia

Lake
Titicaca

Arequipa•

N

Tacna•

Chile

organization and militancy, and a general intensification of political activism. Responding to Hugo Blanco's peasant movement in the Valley of La Convención, all major candidates in the 1962 national elections called for agrarian reform; after the military annulled those elections to forestall a possible APRA victory, the 1963 campaigns reiterated the major parties' commitment to land redistribution. With the victory of moderate reformer Fernando Belaúnde Terry, some 300,000 individuals from approximately 400 Indian communities carried out their own agrarian reform by occupying dozens of haciendas; many were never removed. Meanwhile, guerrilla *focos* were launched, and quickly defeated, in 1963 and 1965.

Against this backdrop of heightened demands for change and a broad consensus on the need for at least moderate reform, a stalemate in national politics led to the continuing postponement of meaningful reform. Sacrificing principle for political expediency, APRA representatives in Congress allied themselves with their erstwhile enemies, the party of ex-dictator Manuel Odría, to block or water down Belaúnde's moderate reform proposals. In addition to this paralysis of the political system, economic problems, labor unrest, and continuing rural agitation plagued the Belaúnde administration. The outcome of negotiations with Esso subsidiary International Petroleum Company (IPC), Peru's primary oil producer and a major symbol of U.S. imperialism to many Peruvians, severely weakened the government. In August 1968 Belaúnde announced, but did not divulge, the terms of the Pact of Talara, the proposed resolution of a long-standing dispute over the company's legal status and exploitation rights. When the content of the agreement leaked, revealing major concessions to the company and a scandal involving a missing page of the document, Belaúnde's government was damaged beyond repair. The more nationalist and reformist factions of the officer corps seized the opportunity to remove an inept civilian government and install an administration committed to their views. This action also foreclosed the possibility of an APRA victory in the upcoming national elections.

The military's intervention under those circumstances did not portend the changes in store. The new government's first action, the outright expropriation of IPC, was interpreted as merely the culmination of a process botched by Belaúnde rather than the opening salvo in a vigorous campaign of economic nationalism. Although Latin America had experienced a few reformist governments led by military men—among them Marmaduke Grove, who established the Chilean Socialist Republic of 1932; the Toro and Busch governments in Bolivia in the 1930s; Juan Perón in Argentina in the 1940s and 1950s; and the Árbenz regime in Guatemala in the early 1950s—military-dominated governments usually upheld the status quo.

Following a spate of uprisings by leftist officers in the early 1960s, of which only the October 1960 coup in El Salvador succeeded, the climate of military politics in the era of the Cuban Revolution was decidedly reactionary. Although the 1962–1963 military junta had shown flexibility in establishing Peru's first agrarian reform in the agitated Valley of La Convención, that had been an emergency response to a grave situation and did not appear to presage the radical reforms carried out by the government installed in 1968.

No single factor explains the Peruvian military's radical departure from precedent and from the general pattern of military politics in the 1960s and 1970s. Strong representation of men of provincial middle-class origin in the officer corps is cited as evidence that the military was essentially a middle-class institution with no binding ties to the Peruvian oligarchy. The advanced training offered in the Center for Advanced Military Studies (Centro de Altos Estudios Militares, CAEM) included a large dose of social sciences focused on Peru, taught by civilians from a progressive perspective. This instruction contributed to the military's belief that its job of providing national security went beyond military questions to encompass the development and modernization of a backward country. The equation of national security with modernization and development flowed naturally from the study of Peruvian history: Peru's loss to Chile in the War of the Pacific (1879–1884) was generally attributed to the country's backwardness, above all to the marginal condition of its Indian majority. Field experience in civic action and counterinsurgency provided the officer corps with first-hand knowledge of social conditions in the poorest areas of the country and made it aware of the threat posed by rural mobilization fostered by those conditions. Frustration with civilian politicians for failing to resolve the country's pressing problems was another factor encouraging the armed forces to abandon their traditional role of guardian of established interests.

Although these considerations offer insights into the Peruvian military's course of action after 1968, they also describe to some degree the characteristics and experience of the militaries of several other countries— militaries that did not embrace reform as their response to the impact of the Cuban Revolution. Two other significant factors help to set Peru's military apart from other cases and explain its unique behavior. One was the composition of the group that organized the coup and subsequently ran the government. The coup instigators were progressives who sought substantive change in Peru's economy and society; after installing themselves in power, they were able to keep the influence of conservative officers to a minimum. Whereas the president and cabinet-level officials were generals, a large cadre of colonels who were committed to quite radical change had been prime movers in the coup; they assumed a direct role in government through the Advisory Committee to the Presidency (Comité de Asesores a la Presidencia, COAP) which exercised strong influence over policy formulation. Within a year or two, most of those colonels were promoted and placed in positions of greater authority.

With the conservatives neutralized, General Velasco mediated constantly between the radicals and the more moderate nationalists, balancing the radicals' demands for a fundamental redistribution of wealth and power in Peru with the moderates' desire to strengthen national capitalism through policies designed to increase productivity. While the government's policies normally reflected some compromise, Velasco's personal inclinations cemented the ascendancy of the more radical faction throughout most of his presidency. As reported by a military colleague, Velasco revealed those personal inclinations in a private conversation: "Power spreads its tentacles from above. Everywhere the rich pull the strings. The big companies call the shots: who will be the next president or the new prime minister. Tell me, where is the people's autonomy?" The colleague continued, "[A]t a given moment he decided that the armed forces simply had to intervene."[3]

A comparison with the other South American militaries that established long-term dictatorships in the 1960s and 1970s further illuminates the Peruvian armed forces' different orientation and policies. The military governments in Brazil (1964–1985), Uruguay (1973–1985), Chile (1973–1990), and Argentina (1976–1983) abolished civilian political institutions and governed as dictatorships, as did the Peruvian military. But the other four adopted right-wing policies favoring the elites and used extreme repression, reaching the level of state terrorism, to accomplish their mission of eradicating the left in their countries. Those military regimes were established amid serious, immediate threats of revolution. In Brazil and Chile, soldiers removed presidents they saw as moving dangerously far to the left; in Uruguay and Argentina, the militaries acted to counter urban guerrilla insurgencies that threatened to topple civilian governments and seize power. In each case the immediate threat to national security was translated as Communism or *fidelismo*, and the military's task in restoring peace was to destroy Marxist influence in all its forms. In Peru, by contrast, despite rising levels of turmoil and mobilization, the military faced no immediate threat of revolution; rather, it faced an inept civilian government and supporting institutions that failed to enact the reforms deemed necessary to prevent revolution. The Peruvian officers, then, had the luxury of reflection and deliberation in formulating policies after seizing power, rather than having to strike swiftly and decisively at revolutionary forces that appeared as immediate threats to vested interests.

The Reshaping of Peruvian Society

When the military took power, it had no blueprint for achieving its broad nationalist objectives, but only a vague "Plan Inca." Thus it took several years and a series of reform measures before the Velasco government's vision of a new Peru came into focus. Because of the relatively closed nature of discussion and planning within the military institution and the time lags separating the several phases of reform, observers at various points believed that the "revolution" had run its course. But despite hiatuses between the announcement and implementation of the successive reform measures, the Velasco government displayed a constantly deepening commitment to radical change.

The military launched its program of transformation with the Agrarian Reform Law of June 24, 1969. Announcing it on the newly proclaimed "day of the peasant," Velasco proclaimed that the law "will end forever the unjust social order that impoverished and oppressed the millions of landless peasants who have always been forced to work the land for others."[4] He added dramatically: "The landlord is no longer going to eat from your poverty."[5] Action of some sort on agrarian reform was not unexpected. The military's 1962 program in La Convención and Belaúnde's moderate 1964 agrarian reform law had legitimized the issue, while widespread frustration over the slow pace of land distribution had plagued the latter years of Belaúnde's administration. Critics of Peru's land tenure system had focused for nearly a century on the inefficiency and social injustice of the highland haciendas, and the 1962 and 1964 laws had been aimed at eliminating or modernizing some of those holdings.

To the shock of virtually all observers, Velasco first applied agrarian reform to the modern export-producing plantations on the coast. When the government moved within days after issuing the law to expropriate the capital-intensive holdings of the Grace Company and several of Peru's most powerful families, Velasco's commitment to radical change became clear. Expropriation of coastal plantations, some of which included industrial components such as cane-based paper mills and distilleries, was not a blow for economic modernization; in fact, previous plans had specifically exempted the coastal plantations because of the danger of disrupting export earnings as well as the political power of the owners. This was a blow directed at Peru's oligarchy and an important segment of foreign capital, and also at the APRA, the military's historic enemy, much of whose strength lay in the agricultural workers' unions of the north coast sugar zone.

When agrarian reform reached the Andes some months after the law's enactment, the primary emphasis was on ending a backward system of land tenure and social domination. The typical Andean hacienda was undercapitalized and underproductive; it was worked by a resident labor force paid primarily in land use rights and by seasonal labor drawn from nearby Indian communities and pockets of landless peasants. In the Andean regions, the challenge to agrarian reformers was not simply redistribution of land; in contrast to the highly productive coastal agriculture, land in the Andes would require major investment in order to afford even a modest living for its inhabitants.

In both regions, reformed agricultural property was placed under cooperative ownership rather than being distributed in individual holdings. On the coast, conflict ensued along several axes over which groups were to be included in the cooperatives and with what rights: field versus industrial workers; unskilled versus skilled workers; workers versus professionals, such as accountants, agronomists, and chemists; and resident versus nonresident workers. In the Andes, resident workers of expropriated haciendas were challenged by neighboring Indian communities, many of which were overpopulated and had historic claims against haciendas for stealing their land; landless seasonal workers also pressed claims to land.

These competing claims for land unleashed a wave of mobilization in the countryside that the authorities only gradually brought under control. One effect of the competition for land was a progressive deepening of the reform process as expropriations were extended beyond the limits of the law to satisfy the manifest land hunger. Most reformed holdings on the coast were organized into individual Agricultural Production Cooperatives (Cooperativas Agrícolas de Producción) run by elected worker committees but with final authority residing in a manager appointed by the government. In the Andes, the competing claims were commonly resolved by the creation of Agricultural Societies of Social Interest (Sociedades Agrícolas de Interés Social) which integrated hacienda and community lands in a single extensive production unit. In order to address income disparities among land recipients in a broader area, some region-wide units were created to transfer resources and income from the wealthier to the poorer holdings.

By the end of the Velasco presidency, both the traditional Andean hacienda and the large private coastal hacienda had virtually disappeared. By the end of the 1970s, between 25 and 40 percent of Peru's agricultural population had received land, most of them in cooperative ownership.

Approximately 10 million hectares—nearly half of the country's agricultural land—had been expropriated; much of the remainder belonged to Indian communities. By contrast, Belaúnde's moderate agrarian reform had expropriated around 1 million hectares.

Inevitably, such an ambitious agrarian reform did not serve all those in need of land. Nonresident landless peasants were the most often neglected, and many of them simply switched bosses from hacienda owners to cooperative members. In some areas, including the south-central Andean department of Ayacucho where Sendero Luminoso had its stronghold, population pressures were such that land-short Indian communities could not be given additional land. In general, technical support for improved crop and livestock yields lagged far behind goals. But after all the shortcomings are noted, it remains that in less than a decade the military accomplished much of what critics had called for since the 19th century, and more. They not only eliminated the backward Andean hacienda, but they also redistributed the modern sector of the agricultural economy, using agrarian reform to attack the Peruvian power structure.[6]

Another redistributive reform, the General Law of Industries of July 1970, applied the principle of worker self-management that undergirded agrarian reform to the industrial sector. Manufacturing firms with six or more workers or a gross annual income of over a million soles (approximately $25,000) were required to establish a *comunidad industrial* (industrial community) consisting of all permanent employees. The industrial community received 15 percent of the company's pre-tax net income each year with which to purchase shares in the firm until the workers achieved 50 percent ownership of total shares. In addition, workers received 10 percent of annual pre-tax profits as profit sharing. As of September 1974, there were 3,446 industrial communities with approximately 200,000 members. Another 100,000 workers participated in similar communities in the fish meal, mining, and telecommunications sectors.

The industrial community was designed to increase productivity by tying worker income to company profits and to dampen class conflict and wean workers away from unions by extending the benefits of ownership. The preamble of the law stated: "In one person shall be united the double quality of employer and employee. Capitalist exploitation will cease . . . Class struggle will be a thing of the past."[7] Inevitably, as with agrarian reform, this radical departure from the status quo generated conflict between labor and management and among workers of differing skills, pay levels, and longevity. Effective worker self-management required education of the labor force in all aspects of the company's operations. Many owners found ways to underreport profits through transfers, inflation of costs, and other devices so as to contribute less to the workers than was owed. Partly for this reason, industrial communities owned only some 15 percent of their companies by the end of the Velasco regime.

The most sweeping formulation of worker ownership and self-management was that contained in the military government's Social Property Law of May 1974, the result of over four years of preparation and extensive intramural and public debate. Reflecting the influence of Christian Democratic notions of communitarianism and of the Yugoslav practice of worker self-management—two Yugoslav consultants helped prepare the draft—the social property law laid the basis for what the regime hoped would become the dominant sector within a pluralistic economy. The social property sector would consist of firms in almost any line of production or business composed solely of workers who would run each firm through a democratic process. Ownership of the firm, however, would reside in the entire social property sector, and part of the income of each firm would be applied to a fund for creating new worker-managed companies. Overseeing the sector was a government-appointed council with power over wages, establishment of new companies, and general administration.

With the social property law, the government's concept of the pluralistic Peruvian economy was finally defined. The four elements would be the state sector, consisting primarily of mining, petroleum, and basic industries; the reformed private sector featuring industrial communities; the private sector of small firms and companies of any size not required to have industrial communities; and social property, which would encompass existing and future cooperatives in agriculture as well as the new firms to be created throughout the economy. Given the government's control over credit resources, the bulk of new investment would be channeled into the social property area, which would be the primary engine of growth and become the largest sector within 15 years.

The social property law represented the most radical expression of the Peruvian military experiment. It was to be the centerpiece of the new Peru, which would be "neither capitalist nor Communist" and would afford full participation to all citizens. Although the government made a start in creating social property firms, even under the most favorable circumstances its projection of the sector's growth to dominance was unrealistic. Although by this time some innovative region-wide cooperative ownership arrangements had been established under agrarian reform, the push for social property throughout the economy ended after Velasco's removal from office in 1975.

Secondary means of redistributing resources toward the poor majority of Peruvians included the expansion and transformation of the educational system and new policies for the urban squatter communities. The Velasco government emphasized basic literacy, bilingual education for the speakers of Indian languages, and vocational and technical education to counter the traditional orientation of Peruvian education toward the liberal arts and law, which reformers blamed for perpetuating the values of Peru's exploitive class system. Velasco also believed that educational reform would "forge a new kind of man with a new morality that emphasizes solidarity, labor, authentic liberty, social justice, and the responsibilities and rights of every Peruvian man and woman."[8] Because of its democratic and practical orientation, the educational reform encountered stiff resistance from two bastions of privilege: universities and private schools.

The military government saw the mushrooming population of the squatter settlements, or *barriadas*, surrounding Lima and provincial cities as both a problem and an opportunity. To alleviate harsh conditions as well as cultivate support, especially among the million *barriada* dwellers who constituted a fourth of Lima's population, the government gave priority to setting up self-help programs, extending utilities to the zones, and granting titles to plots that normally had been occupied in illegal land invasions. Symbolizing the new approach was a new name for the *barriadas*: "*pueblos jóvenes*," or young towns.

The Quest for National Sovereignty

To complement its restructuring of Peruvian society, the Velasco government implemented a series of measures designed to achieve Peruvian sovereignty, both economic and political. These measures included the transformation of the Peruvian state from a pliant tool of vested national and foreign interests into a powerful entity capable of defining and implementing national goals and policies. Second, the regime established new guidelines for foreign investment that would result in national control of key sectors of the economy. Third, Velasco's government worked to end Peru's notable subservience to the United States by charting an aggressively independent course in foreign relations.

By Latin American standards, the pre-1968 Peruvian state was very weak economically. Private capital dominated every sector of the economy, with foreign investment playing a major or decisive role in most areas, including mining, agriculture, petroleum, communications, utilities, and even retailing. The telephone company, most other utilities, and Peru's national and international airlines were privately held; Peru was one of very few countries, along with the United States and Canada, in which all major railroads were not state owned. If it was to achieve the economic power to transform Peruvian society, the government would have to enhance the state's role in the economy.

Strengthening of the state's economic role flowed from three policies. Agrarian reform and creation of the industrial communities weakened the economic power of both national and foreign private capital. Nationalization of private investments outside of agriculture put direct ownership of major economic sectors in state hands. And new restrictions on foreign investment would prevent international capital from regaining the enormous influence that it had enjoyed before 1968.

In nationalizing petroleum and expropriating the coastal haciendas, the Velasco government made impressive progress in its first year toward breaking the economic power of the national oligarchy and major foreign investors. In 1970 the regime turned its attention to the remaining sectors of the economy. The key provision for promoting state economic power was the General Law of Industries, which also established the industrial community. This law reserved natural resources and "basic industries" for state ownership. Enactment of the law launched a phase of negotiations with owners, both foreign and national, over the terms of expropriation and compensation. Within five years, the government took ownership of the fish meal industry, most mining and metal refining, railroads and the international airline, some pharmaceutical firms, most electric utilities, cement plants, banking and insurance companies, and the telephone company. It also established a state import-export monopoly over key commodities and invested as a partner with private capital in numerous enterprises, including television and radio stations. While the state sector grew quickly and impressively, the government retained flexibility by working out operating agreements with private firms in some activities, including oil exploration. By 1975 the state's share of total national investment had risen from 13 percent a decade earlier to nearly 50 percent, moving Peru toward the levels of state economic involvement found in Mexico, Chile, and Argentina.

Even while expropriating the "commanding heights" of the economy, the military government pursued new foreign capital to meet Peru's development needs, but under radically different terms of investment that came to be known as the "Velasco Doctrine." President Velasco first announced a new attitude toward foreign investment in a July 1970 speech: "We are not a weak group of nations at the mercy of foreign capital. They need our raw materials and our markets. And if we need capital goods and advanced technology, the evident bilaterality of these needs must lead to new arrangements that protect the present and future interests of Latin America."[9] The Velasco Doctrine essentially sought to foster economic growth without the dependency normally resulting from foreign investment in developing countries. Translated into policy, the Velasco Doctrine was one of the military government's most innovative and widely admired initiatives; it became Decision 24 of the Andean Pact, the six-member regional common market headquartered in Lima.

Under the new rules, foreign capital was invited to invest in needed areas on a temporary, phase-out basis, preferably in partnership with national capital; when the total investment had been recovered and a reasonable, agreed-upon profit had been made, the majority share of the foreign investment would become state property. The final regulation of the Andean Pact allowed a maximum annual profit repatriation of 14 percent of total investment and required divestiture to reduce the foreign share of joint ventures to less than 50 percent within 15 years. Thus rather than rejecting foreign investment, the Peruvian government sought to shape it into a positive force for the country's development. Despite the new restrictions and U.S. pressure against the international lending agencies, foreign capital continued to flow into the country until near the end of the Velasco presidency.

The political aspect of state development involved a similar approach: weakening autonomous political and economic organizations capable of challenging the state and replacing them with government-controlled entities designed to incorporate and represent the populace along economic and functional lines. Such corporatism has deep roots in Latin America, both in Iberian colonial institutions and in 20th-century responses to the emergence of class conflict and radical politics. The Velasco government went beyond the normal corporatist objective of subordinating independent organizations, such as political parties, labor unions, and economic interest groups, to the state. It attempted to use the corporate structure as a tool for integrating the previously marginalized majority—especially *campesinos* and *barriada* dwellers—into the national polity and, in the process, turning them into active supporters of the government.

Consistent with its rejection of unnecessary repression, the government normally tolerated institutions that were too strong to take on or too weak to cause problems. It did not challenge the church as an institution. The political parties and national labor confederations retained considerable freedom of action so long as their opposition to the government was restrained, while the regime worked to weaken them by wooing away their constituencies through reform and playing rivals off against one another. On the other hand, the government did not tolerate open challenges or covert attempts to sabotage its policies. It abolished the national teachers' union, for example, for striking in defiance of the regime and replaced it with a government-sponsored union. The National Agrarian Society (Sociedad Nacional Agraria), the interest group of large-scale agricultural producers, was abolished in 1972 for opposing agrarian reform; its members were merged with the peasant syndicates into the government-controlled National Agrarian Confederation (Confederación Agraria Nacional), which officially represented the entire agricultural population. Although not abolished, the Sociedad Industrial Nacional was reorganized so as to be more pliant to government wishes.

The capstone of the government's corporatist endeavors was the National System to Support Social Mobilization (Sistema Nacional de Apoyo a la Movilización Social, SINAMOS), founded in 1971. SINAMOS was to be a vast organization, running from local units to the national level, to support the military government in the aftermath of the dismantling or marginalization of the major parties and unions. It was intended to decentralize decision making and provide access to government for the marginal populations that the military was attempting to integrate into national life as well as for those groups, such as labor and professionals, whose existing associations were being suppressed. The challenge was to grant the organizations enough freedom of action so that they could attract members while assuring that they did not become independent groups capable of acting against government interests.

Predictably, the creation of such a vast program designed to achieve a delicate balance between co-optation and the fostering of grassroots democracy caused considerable reaction and chaos. Because of the great expectations raised for their betterment, peasants, squatters, and workers proved more inclined to press for additional benefits than to express their gratitude to the government for gains already made. APRA, with its hundreds of thousands of loyal members and its control over major labor and professional groups, also proved impervious to governmental pressure and stood as an important obstacle to the success of SINAMOS-backed organizations. Overall, SINAMOS failed to develop the degree of support the government desired, resulting in the debilitating irony that Peru's first government to carry out redistributive measures favoring the poor was one without a broad base of organized popular support.

The final nationalist goal of the armed forces in office was to establish an independent foreign policy, distancing Peru from its traditional close and subservient relationship with the United States. One step in asserting its independence was the establishment of diplomatic relations with the Soviet Union, China, Cuba, and other socialist countries. Peru also signed a trade pact with Moscow and acquired significant amounts of Soviet arms, giving the Soviet Union its first military presence in the hemisphere outside of Cuba. Widely admired within the Third World for its reforms and its innovative reformulation of the rules of foreign investment, Peru quickly assumed a leadership role in the Nonaligned Movement.

The Velasco government displayed its independence of the United States in other ways as well. In the early months of the regime, Velasco denied compensation for IPC's expropriated properties, alleging that the company owed Peru $690 million in excess profits and unpaid taxes, and defied Washington to implement economic sanctions. Enforcement of Peru's claim to 200 miles of territorial waters against U.S. fishing boats also strained relations, as did Washington's suspension of military aid and Lima's subsequent expulsion of the U.S. military mission in Peru. These provocations were somewhat offset by moderation on other fronts. Apart from the IPC case, reasonable offers of compensation followed most expropriations of U.S. properties. For its part, Washington failed to apply the Hickenlooper Amendment, which required the cutting of aid to countries failing to pay for nationalized U.S. investments, preferring a quiet financial pressure that eventually took a toll on Peru's economy. U.S. restraint was largely explained by a situation that was unique in the era of the Cuban Revolution: a military regime was carrying out reforms which, if conducted by a civilian government, would likely have led Washington to promote a military coup to save the country from Communism. The fact that the radicals were in uniform thus had a moderating effect on the U.S. response to a genuine revolution.

Assessing the outcomes of his nationalist policies, Velasco said in a 1977 interview: "Peru was no longer a subjugated country [*un país vendido*], a nation that had to kneel down. I kicked them [the Americans] away! We didn't need them, we had grown up enough and we did not need to ask them about everything."[10]

Fall of the Velasco Government

By 1974 a number of general trends and specific circumstances had converged to weaken the Velasco regime. One long-term trend that affected the government was a rising level of conflict expressed in strikes, antiregime demonstrations, and riots. Much of the conflict was generated by the reform process itself, which unleashed demands for change but rarely satisfied any important group. Agrarian reform, for example, might have been expected to produce a fairly contented group of new landowners who would form a solid core of support for Velasco. Rather, as discussed earlier, agrarian reform produced several axes of conflict, leaving much of the countryside in a state of mobilization. Workers belonging to industrial communities might also have been expected to support the government, but rather than demonstrating gratitude, they tended to vent their dissatisfaction with the slow pace of accumulation of worker shares in their firms; in 1972, as an example, the Confederation of Industrial Communities demanded the immediate granting of 50 percent worker ownership, rather than following the gradual process defined by law, and forced the resignation of the relevant government official. Adding to the problem of unmet expectations was the fact that the government had created organizations at every level that were designed to generate support, but which served instead as vehicles for expressing discontent and mobilizing people against the government. APRA, which had a pervasive presence in most important economic sectors, also worked to undermine the government while building its own clientele.

Economic problems had become serious by 1974. Peru's balance of trade suffered in 1972 when the fish meal industry, the leading export sector, nearly collapsed as a result of climatic changes (*el niño*) affecting the Humboldt Current. The government had borrowed heavily to finance state-led development, with good results to 1974; then, along with many Latin American countries, Peru found itself deeply in debt but, with the prices of its exports down, unable to pay its obligations. This led to the imposition of austerity measures in 1975 that exacerbated the endemic conflict affecting the country.

The year 1974 was the high-water mark of reform and the beginning of a reaction against the regime's more radical policies and their proponents. Even some of the regime's supporters regarded the social property law of May as too radical and unworkable. Whereas the effect of that law was to be gradual, the impact of a July decree expropriating the Lima press was immediate. Expropriation of the press met two government objectives. On one hand, the participatory system would be strengthened by the granting of newspapers to labor, agricultural cooperatives, professionals, and the other main sectoral organizations that the regime had created. At a practical level, the move would silence the increasingly strident criticism that the press was aiming at Velasco. This measure was widely viewed as a step toward totalitarianism on the part of a regime that heretofore had been surprisingly tolerant of dissent. An unexpectedly violent reaction to the press expropriation forced the government into a more repressive posture and hastened its demise.

As the popular unrest, economic problems, and reactions to reform took their toll on the regime, the declining health of General Velasco provided the opportunity for open discussion of the succession and a considerable amount of jockeying for position within the armed forces. Velasco's health problems had forced him to relinquish power in February 1973 for three months, during which a leg was amputated. Further economic deterioration in 1975, combined with the mounting problems besetting the government, opened the way for a peaceful coup led by heir-apparent General Francisco Morales Bermúdez, a member of the moderate faction of Velasco's supporters. The new government reflected a shift in power within the officer corps away from the radicals, who were associated with turmoil and economic difficulties, toward those espousing the more moderate developmentalist line.

After initially proclaiming itself the continuation of Velasco's revolution, the Morales Bermúdez government quickly moved to end the more radical policies of its predecessor. While the distribution of expropriated agricultural land continued, the social property sector was allowed to go bankrupt, and a modification of the 1970 industry law exempted all but the largest firms from worker co-management. Recognizing the failure of SINAMOS and the urgent need for civilian support, Morales Bermúdez turned to the military's historic enemy, APRA, which in exchange for major concessions exercised its discipline to curtail the level of antigovernment agitation. Facing a crisis of debt payments, the new regime was forced to deal on unfavorable terms with foreign banks, which in exchange for emergency loans regained a degree of control over the Peruvian economy, thwarting the quest for more equitable relations with the capital-exporting countries which had briefly made Peru a leader of the Third World.

When they took power, the leaders of the Velasco government estimated that the thorough transformation of Peru that they envisioned would require until at least 1990, or 22 years. The experiment in revolution from above ended after only seven, long before all the country's pressing problems could be addressed and before the main reform programs that the military implemented could have a chance to bear fruit. It is impossible to determine whether the vision of a new Peru that General Velasco and his more radical collaborators had—a vision of a country neither capitalist nor Communist, based on full citizen participation and anchored in economic independence—could have been achieved under even the most favorable circumstances. Nonetheless, the Peruvian military government of 1968–1975 had the distinction of leading one of Latin America's most ambitious attempts to cope with underdevelopment and social injustice. In the aftermath of Che Guevara's death, the Velasco experiment also demonstrated that revolution was possible, even by unorthodox and unanticipated means.

Notes

1. George D. E. Philip, *The Rise and Fall of the Peruvian Military Radicals, 1968–1976* (London: The Athlone Press, 1978), 13.

2. José Carlos Mariátegui, *Seven Interpretive Essays on Peruvian Reality*, trans Marjory Urquidi (Austin: University of Texas Press, 1971).

3. Dirk Kruijt, *Revolution by Decree: Peru 1968–1975* (Amsterdam: Thela Publishers, 1994), 73.

4. Juan Velasco, "The Master Will No Longer Feed Off Your Poverty," in Orin Starn, Carlos Iván Degregori, and Robin Kirk (eds.), *The Peru Reader: History, Culture, Politics* (Durham, NC: Duke University Press, 1995), 279–280.

5. Enrique Mayer, *Ugly Stories of the Peruvian Agrarian Reform* (Durham, NC: Duke University Press, 2009), 20.

6. According to Enrique Mayer, an authority on the Peruvian agrarian reform, "Although the 'feudal' hacienda in the highlands was already in decline, Velasco's reform liquidated it for good." Mayer, *Ugly Stories*, 232.

7. Kruijt, *Revolution*, 127.

8. Dulce Manzano, *Bringing Down the Educational Wall: Political Regimes, Ideology, and the Expansion of Education* (New York: Cambridge University Press, 2017), 195.

9. Shane Hunt, "Direct Foreign Investment in Peru: New Rules for an Old Game," in Abraham F. Lowenthal (ed.), *The Peruvian Experiment: Continuity and Change under Military Rule* (Princeton, NJ: Princeton University Press, 1975), 312.

10. Lourdes Hurtado, "Velasco, Nationalist Rhetoric, and Military Culture in Cold War Peru," in Carlos Aguirre and Paulo Drinot (eds.), *The Peculiar Revolution: Rethinking the Peruvian Experiment under Military Rule* (Austin: University of Texas Press, 2017), 181.

CHAPTER EIGHT

Chile Under Allende, 1970–1973: A Peaceful Road to Socialism?

The election of Salvador Allende as president of Chile in September 1970 attracted immediate, worldwide attention. For the next three years, events in Chile were observed, recorded, and analyzed by legions of journalists, social scientists, and political operatives from around the globe. Allende, a member of Chile's Socialist Party and leader of a Marxist-dominated coalition of six parties, had campaigned on the promise to move Chile as quickly as possible to socialism. His election presented a situation unique not only to Latin America, but to the world. In contrast to the member parties of the Socialist International, such as the British Labour Party, the German Social Democratic Party, the Venezuelan AD, or the Peruvian APRA, and to the proponents of Arab socialism, Allende was a traditional Marxist who believed that socialism meant state ownership of the means of production and distribution—not merely a welfare state. In contrast to the countries where socialism had been established—the Soviet Union, Eastern Europe, China, and Cuba—Allende took power without insurrection or military conquest. Besides being a freely elected president, Allende professed allegiance to Chile's well-established pluralist political system—a further contrast with the one-party dictatorial socialist states. Thus Chile provided the laboratory test for the question that heretofore had remained hypothetical: Is there a peaceful road to socialism?

The election of Allende revived the hopes of Latin America's revolutionaries as well as the worries of the conservatives and the U.S. government.
Together with the Peruvian experiment next door, Allende's election gave
credence to the notion that revolution, after all, might be achieved by means
other than armed insurrection, which had proved elusive after 1959. Even
Fidel Castro had to reassess. Without discarding the established Cuban
line, he gave his implicit blessing to the Chilean path by visiting the country for nearly a month in 1971. Combined with his praise for the Peruvian
military, Fidel's endorsement of Allende and his apparent retreat from rigid
adherence to the Cuban model seemed to offer an opening for a reconciliation of the Latin American left, which the Cuban Revolution had splin-
tered. Even though it was widely acknowledged that the Chilean political
system was unique within Latin America and that a Marxist electoral triumph was highly unlikely in any other country, the United States feared
that a second socialist country in the hemisphere, in combination with a
radical regime in Peru, might create an effective anti-U.S. axis in Latin
America. Among the implications of Allende's election, according to the
CIA, were a threat to "hemispheric cohesion" and "a definite psychological advance for the Marxist idea."[1]

Chile and the Cuban Revolution

Along with Uruguay and Costa Rica, Chile was the most stable of Latin
America's constitutional democracies. The Chilean pattern of elected civilian governments developed in the 19th century, at a time when government in most of Spanish America alternated between instability and
authoritarian rule. The urban middle and working classes were incorporated into the political system during the 1920s and 1930s, occasioning a
period of instability and the last direct military intervention before 1973.
By 1938, when Chile became the only Latin American country to elect a
Popular Front government, the party system had evolved into three well-
defined blocs: a Marxist left, composed of the Communist and Socialist
parties; the middle-class Radical Party in the center; and the historic Liberal and Conservative parties on the right. Presidents were elected from
the center or right, while Congress reflected a fairly stable balance among
the three blocs, with the Radicals normally holding the balance of power.

Featuring a tradition of civilian rule, respect for civil liberties, and
competitive elections, the Chilean political system in the late 1950s still
excluded large segments of the adult population. The rural labor force and
smallholders continued to be under the control of large landowners, who
either barred them from the electoral process or manipulated their votes

CHILE

Peru

Arica

Iquique

Bolivia

Brazil

Paraguay

Antofagasta

Chile

La Serena

Argentina

Uruguay

South
Pacific
Ocean

Valparaiso ★Santiago

Talca

Concepcion

Andes Mountains

Puerto Montt

South
Atlantic
Ocean

N

Punta Arenas

Tierra del
Fuego

0   150   300km
0   150   300mi

in favor of Conservative or Liberal candidates. Literacy requirements, difficult voter registration procedures, and the absence of effective organization also marginalized residents of the burgeoning shantytowns of Santiago and Valparaíso. The exclusion of these broad sectors made the Chilean political edifice less solid than it appeared—a weakness readily exposed by the influence of the Cuban Revolution.

In common with the rest of Latin America, Chile experienced the impact of the Cuban Revolution in several ways, including a rise in demands for change, the radicalization of existing political groups, and a leftward shift of the political agenda. The influence of greatest consequence for Chile was the development of political consciousness and organization, leading to a broad mobilization among the marginal groups—especially rural labor. Attempts to organize rural labor were not new in the 1960s: the left had tried to unionize agricultural workers since 1919, with little success. After the Cuban Revolution and the rise of agrarian reform as a pan–Latin American issue, the Marxist parties set out more aggressively to organize rural unions and proselytize landless workers and smallholders. Their efforts were matched by the Christian Democratic Party (Partido Demócrata Cristiano, PDC), a dynamic new political force founded in 1957 that espoused a program of structural reform and sought to develop support among the same marginalized groups.

Despite legal obstacles and the determined resistance of landowners, Marxists and Christian Democrats made rapid headway in breaking landowners' control of the peasantry, to the point that by 1961 the Conservative and Liberal parties joined the Radicals in calling on the right-wing government of Jorge Alessandri, elected in 1958, to undertake a moderate, preemptive agrarian reform. The resulting 1962 agrarian reform law, which made inefficiently worked large properties subject to expropriation and subdivision, had predictably little effect on the structure of rural property; but it was an accurate reflection of the rapid leftward shift of the terms of political debate in Chile.

Eduardo Frei and the "Revolution in Liberty," 1964–1970

Against the backdrop of a groundswell of demand for change and strong sympathy for the Cuban Revolution, the half-hearted preemptive strategies of the Alessandri government proved ineffectual. This was demonstrated conclusively in the results of a March 1964 congressional by-election in heavily rural Curicó province, a traditionally safe stronghold of the right, where the dramatic rise of the Marxist and PDC vote among agricultural workers and smallholders buried the right's candidate. Sensing the collapse of landowners' control of the rural vote, and with it the eclipse of the right's electoral strength at the national level, the Conservatives and Liberals took a drastic step to avoid a potential Marxist victory in the September 1964 presidential election. Aware that a three-candidate field could open the way for Socialist candidate Salvador Allende, they broke an electoral alliance with the Radical Party and freed their supporters' votes. For most, this meant voting for Christian Democrat Eduardo Frei, a reformer, but a lesser evil than Allende. Frei welcomed the right's support but rejected its efforts to moderate his reformist campaign platform.

In the absence of a rightist candidate, the 1964 presidential election offered voters only two viable options: change or more change. Salvador Allende, running for the third time as the candidate of the predominantly Marxist Popular Action Front (Frente de Acción Popular, FRAP), promised to move the country toward socialism by nationalizing key sectors of the economy, including the U.S.-owned copper mines, increasing state investment, raising taxes on the wealthy, creating a mixed agricultural economy, and promoting unionization. Frei's program was similar and equally ambitious but, reflecting the Christian Democratic ideology, less statist; hence its slogan, "Revolution in Liberty." Frei promised an agrarian reform that would create 100,000 new landowners in six years; huge investments in education and housing; Chileanization or government co-ownership of copper; profit sharing in industry; and a plan called "people's development" (*promoción popular*) to provide organization and political input for slum dwellers, peasants, women, and other underrepresented groups.

The choice facing the Chilean electorate—two candidates promising revolution—reflected the radicalization of Chilean politics since the previous presidential election in 1958. Although neither candidate's program mentioned it, the 1964 election was also a referendum on the Cuban Revolution. With Castro now firmly in the Soviet camp, Frei supporters were quick to suggest that an Allende victory would lead Chile inexorably to domination by Moscow. Allende supporters pointed to Frei's ties to the United States and the similarity between his program and the Alliance for Progress, which they deemed a Yankee plot to thwart social reform and national liberation. More clearly than any other Latin American election of the 1960s, the 1964 Chilean race was in effect a contest between the Cuban- and the U.S.-promoted models of reform and development. The CIA funneled over $2.6 million into Frei's campaign—over half the total cost—apparently without the candidate's knowledge or approval, and Frei supporters brought in Fidel Castro's estranged sister Juana to testify to the horrors of Communism. Frei won, as expected, receiving 55.6 percent of the vote to Allende's 38.6, with 4.9 percent going to the Radical Party's candidate.[2]

Frei's greatest challenge as president was to satisfy the urgent demand for social reform and economic improvement that had been heightened by the Cuban Revolution and by campaign promises to rural workers and urban shantytown dwellers. It was an implicit assumption that if the Christian Democratic–Alliance for Progress approach did not satisfy the demands unleashed, Allende and his Marxist alternative would become all the more attractive by the next presidential election in 1970. Thus the United States contributed generously to the Frei government through Alliance for Progress funds and an array of other grants and loans.

Eduardo Frei left office with a solid record of accomplishment. He achieved the Chileanization of the copper companies, gaining 51 percent government control with options to purchase the remaining 49 percent. The government also acquired all or part of the U.S.-owned telephone and telegraph companies. It established thousands of organizations, such as the ubiquitous Mothers' Centers (*Centros de Madres*), to foster self-help projects and articulate the interests of the poor. For a large part of the rural population, Frei's unionization and minimum wage laws brought about material improvement and social and political liberation from landowner control.

The Christian Democrats could not reach their ambitious goals, however, in every area. Inflation remained a problem, and due to a severe drought and some disinvestment in agriculture, economic growth failed to reach the government's projections. Although falling short of his goals in education and housing, Frei made impressive progress in both areas. In agrarian reform, he made a substantial beginning in dismantling the hacienda system, but established less than a third of the promised 100,000 new small farms.

Despite a record of reform that would have qualified as radical prior to 1959, the Frei government failed to satisfy the aspirations of Chile's mobilized lower classes for change and improvement. This was especially true in the rural sector, where the very success of Frei's union law had given workers the means of pressing their growing demands for land, with which the agrarian reform did not keep pace. Frustrated by what it considered the slow pace of reform, the PDC left wing broke off in 1969 to form the Popular Unitary Action Movement (Movimiento de Acción Popular Unitario, MAPU).

At the same time, the government that was too moderate for the left alarmed the right. Perhaps most worrisome to the upper classes were their perceptions that the Christian Democrats lacked a firm commitment to capitalist private property and that the government's expropriations of rural properties were politically motivated. They also experienced under Frei, for the first time, a government that did not consistently interpret and apply the law in their favor and defend their interests against redistributive threats. Thus increasing pressure from the left began to be matched by a resurgence of the right as vested interests, and some of the middle classes decided to stiffen the fight against reform so as to keep Chile, as they saw it, from falling into the abyss.

After a disastrous 1965 congressional election which saw the combined Liberal and Conservative share of the vote fall to 12 percent, leaving them with 7 of 45 Senate seats and only 9 of 147 seats in the Chamber of Deputies, the historic right-wing parties dissolved themselves in 1967 to reappear as the National Party. After a strong showing in the 1969 congressional election, the right adopted a more aggressive posture and decided to take a stand in 1970 by running its own presidential candidate, despite the increased risk of a Marxist victory. It was this reversion to the normal three-bloc presidential election that opened the way for Salvador Allende.

The Election of Allende

Salvador Allende was the 1970 presidential candidate of a coalition considerably broader than the one he had headed in 1964. Besides the Socialists and Communists, the People's Unity (Unidad Popular, UP) included four non-Marxist parties whose presence in the coalition was designed, in part, to allay fears of a rigidly Marxist regime: the Radical Party, now stripped of its former power but still commanding some middle-class votes; MAPU, the former Christian Democratic left; and two smaller groups, Independent Popular Action (Acción Popular Independiente) and the Social Democratic Party (Partido Social Democrático). Allende promised an acceleration of the reforms already underway and extensive nationalizations to move Chile toward socialism. As before, the United States spent millions of dollars to stop Allende.

The right backed former President Jorge Alessandri, a respected and pragmatic conservative. Alessandri's candidacy was labeled "independent" so as to avoid too close an identification with the historic right and to appeal to middle-class voters disillusioned with the leftward shift of both the PDC and the Radicals. While not rejecting the continuation of all reform, Alessandri made clear his intention of curbing the more radical changes instituted under Frei.

The Christian Democrats selected Radomiro Tomic of the party's left bloc as their candidate. Tomic saw Allende as his chief rival, and accordingly designed a campaign to compete for the left vote. He called for a significant deepening of reform, including the full nationalization of copper, completion of agrarian reform, and expropriation of substantial parts of the economy. In adopting his left strategy, Tomic distanced himself from Frei, who, despite the wear of nearly six years as president, remained Chile's most popular politician. Some analyses suggest that Tomic's strategy cost him middle-class votes with no compensating increase in working-class support, strengthening Alessandri without significantly hurting Allende.

With Alessandri enjoying a slight lead in the polls, Allende's victory was a mild surprise. Allende received 36.5 percent of the valid vote to Alessandri's 35.2, with Tomic getting 28.0 percent. Two reactions to Allende's victory captured the ambivalent attitudes of the right. The Santiago stock market fell overnight by half, indicating deep-seated fear of Allende; and two impeccably tailored elderly gentlemen who had voted for Alessandri, interviewed at random for international television, responded stoically, "One must know how to lose."[3] This combination of fear and resignation guided the behavior of the Chilean right for the first year of the Allende administration.

The election results showed that after six years of substantive reform, a large majority of Chileans supported an acceleration of change: by nearly 2 to 1 they voted for programs that went well beyond Frei's 1964 platform. Although Allende's percentage of the vote would make him a minority president, such was the norm given Chile's multiparty system and the absence of a runoff provision; Frei, who had obtained a majority in 1964 due to the absence of a rightist candidate, had been the only candidate to top 50 percent of the popular vote since 1942.

Although being a minority president was not usually a serious handicap, implementation of Allende's ambitious program of reform would require a congressional majority, which he lacked. Thus Allende would have to translate the Chilean electorate's mandate for change into votes in the next congressional elections, which were not scheduled until 1973 (in Chile, presidential and congressional elections did not coincide). His challenge was to woo the large segment of Tomic supporters, mostly middle and working class, to the UP, and in doing so he faced three obstacles. The 30-month hiatus between presidential and congressional elections would diminish almost any president's ability to translate his early popularity into congressional votes. The high degree of party loyalty characteristic of the Chilean electorate, moreover, would complicate Allende's task. Finally, the most fundamental problem would be to preserve the commitment of

Tomic's middle-class constituency to reform in the context of the promised transition to socialism.

Allende's first challenge came from the U.S. government, supported by elements of the Chilean right. Having spent millions of dollars and employed all sorts of dirty tricks over the years to prevent Allende's election, the United States now turned to blocking his installation as president. There was no grace period of watching and waiting to see what Allende would do or trying to moderate him after he took office. President Richard Nixon and National Security Advisor Henry Kissinger, both reportedly infuriated at Allende's victory, set out immediately to prevent his inauguration, scheduled for November 3. Nixon vowed to make the Chilean economy "scream," and Kissinger reported that the president wanted "no stone unturned" in the effort to thwart Allende."[4] International Telephone and Telegraph (ITT), which feared the loss of its large Chilean investments, encouraged these efforts; ITT president Harold Geneen constantly badgered the White House for action and spent over a million dollars of corporate funds to keep Allende from office.

One of Washington's approaches to blocking Allende, known as "Track I," invoked a legal means of denying him the presidency. By the 1925 constitution, Congress actually elected the president when no candidate received an absolute majority of the popular vote—the normal case in Chile—by choosing between the top two vote recipients. In the past, Congress had always elected the candidate receiving the greatest number of votes, but given the situation in 1970 this congressional power offered an attractive option to the Chilean right and the Nixon administration. Rightist politicians approached the popular President Frei, asking his aid in persuading the PDC congressmen to vote for Alessandri; in exchange, Alessandri would resign after his inauguration, and Frei, who was legally barred from succeeding himself, could then be a candidate in new elections. The United States pressured the Christian Democrats in every way possible and authorized the payment of bribe money to supplement its efforts at persuasion. The Track I option disappeared, however, when Frei refused to participate in the scheme and Allende accepted a set of constitutional amendments known as the "Statute of Democratic Guarantees." The PDC-sponsored guarantees were designed to strengthen the legal status of private education, the press, political parties, unions, and the military against any possible totalitarian tendencies that Allende or his government might harbor. Satisfied that the constitutional amendments protected liberal democracy, the Christian Democrat members of Congress voted for Allende.

Concurrently with the political maneuvering, Washington pursued "Track II," a plan for a military coup to prevent Allende's assumption of power. Despite the long odds, in view of the Chilean military's record and its repeated statements of adherence to the constitution, the CIA made contacts within the armed forces while planning economic sabotage and propaganda to prepare the climate for a transitional military government. With constitutionalist General René Schneider as army commander in chief, the problem was to find an officer of sufficiently high rank to mobilize the number of troops needed for a successful coup. After much fumbling, and even after the CIA had given up, a group of military personnel and anti-Allende civilians took action, accidentally killing General Schneider in an attempt to kidnap him. Rather than serving its intended purpose, the coup attempt backfired, generating support instead for the constitutional process and Allende's confirmation by Congress.

The period between Allende's popular election on September 4 and his inauguration on November 3, normally a time of festivities and of high hopes for the incoming president, was instead a continuous crisis. It was also a harbinger of what Allende could expect from the Nixon administration. Two days after the inauguration, Kissinger warned the U.S. National Security Council that Chile would "become part of the Soviet/Socialist world . . . and it might constitute a support base and entry point for expansion of Soviet and Cuban presence and activity in the region."[5] The following day, Kissinger wrote Nixon that "The election of Allende as President of Chile poses for us one of the most serious challenges ever faced in this hemisphere . . . ."[6]

The Revolution of Red Wine and *Empanadas,* November 1970–October 1971

In a press conference early in his administration, Allende promised "a revolution *a la chilena* with red wine and *empanadas* (meat and onion pies)."[7] His reference to the festive diet of the Chilean *pueblo* was an apt metaphor for his first year in office, which was characterized by an atmosphere of enthusiasm and optimism within the government and a broad segment of the population. Among the president's early initiatives were redistributive measures and populist gestures designed to cement the loyalty of the working class: free milk for school children and nursing mothers, rent reductions, and rescheduling construction of the Santiago subway so as to serve working-class neighborhoods first. Workers also benefited from some old-fashioned pump priming based on an expanded public works program, increased social security and pension payments, and a modification of the wage and salary adjustment mechanism adopted in the 1940s to cope with

Chile's permanent inflation. With money in their pockets from a 25 percent increase in real income, workers went on a year-long consumption spree that touched off a minor boom in industry and services and raised the level of employment.

"We must make haste—slowly," is an aphorism attributed to Salvador Allende at the outset of his presidency.[8] Despite opposition control of Congress, movement toward fulfilling UP's campaign program of structural reform was anything but slow during Allende's first year. The only major policy for which Allende obtained congressional support was the nationalization of all remaining U.S. interests in copper, which passed by unanimous vote. For the rest of his programs Allende had to rely on the extensive powers of the presidency and on clever use of laws and regulatory powers. In nationalizing the economy, he found that many foreign and domestic companies were willing to accept very low buyout offers in the climate of economic and political uncertainty that followed his inauguration. In addition, Allende discovered and used an obscure 1932 emergency decree-law, enacted during the Great Depression, that empowered the government to expropriate any enterprise not meeting rigid production criteria. The UP government also manipulated the long-established system of wage and price controls in ways designed to force targeted companies toward bankruptcy and used to its advantage existing law allowing the government to assume the management of firms undergoing labor conflicts.

Extensive nationalizations in banking, insurance, communications, transportation, textiles, cement, and manufacturing, combined with the copper nationalization, gave the state control of the "commanding heights" of the economy within Allende's first year. With legislation and machinery already in place for agrarian reform, the UP government accelerated the pace of expropriations and found a loophole that allowed it to create embryonic state farms in place of the small private holdings that the Christian Democrats had fostered. Meanwhile, Allende reestablished diplomatic relations with Cuba during his second week in office, making Chile the first Latin American country to resume ties severed as a result of the 1964 OAS action.

The April 1971 municipal elections reflected the success of Allende's first five months as president. Because of the extreme centralization of Chilean government, municipal elections, as in France, were considered a referendum on the national government rather than a contest over local issues. The UP improved its electoral performance by 13.2 points, from the 36.5 percent that Allende received in September, to 49.7 percent, including 1 percent for an independent pro-government party, in April. The combined opposition received 48 percent, giving the UP a majority of valid votes.

In terms of voter support, April 1971 was the high point for the UP. Allende was unfortunate that congressional elections, held every four years, were not scheduled until March 1973; in contrast, Frei had had the advantage of congressional elections within five months of his inauguration, allowing him to translate his personal popularity into a majority in the Chamber of Deputies and to ensure enactment of his legislative program. Although Allende did not enjoy a similar opportunity, critics point out that his campaign promise to revamp Chilean government institutions by strengthening presidential powers, creating a unicameral legislature, and reforming the judiciary might have been enacted if he had taken the risk of submitting those proposals to a plebiscite following the UP victory in April 1971.

By the end of Allende's first year there were signs of trouble for his government. On the economic front, Allende's expensive programs of nationalizations and pump priming had used up a large portion of Chile's foreign currency reserves. Delay in compensating the copper companies— ultimately, the refusal of all compensation—provided a ready excuse for a U.S. credit boycott that forced the government to find alternative sources of foreign loans. Insecurity of rural property led to serious disinvestment in crops and herds in the private sector.

There were also signs of increased political trouble for the regime. Spurred by Allende's victory and by elements of the left, illegal property seizures increased in the cities as well as in the countryside. A PDC victory in a Valparaíso congressional by-election in July 1971 was the government's first electoral reversal. Although both parties denied collusion, the National Party had declined to nominate a candidate for the seat, launching an undeclared right–center alliance that soon became explicit. Just as the opposition alliance was forming, Senator Carlos Altamirano of the Socialist Party's extreme left wing—a bloc that flirted with insurrection even while participating in the political system—became secretary-general of Allende's own party. The ingredients of confrontation and polarization were in place, and a PDC proposal for a constitutional amendment to limit Allende's powers of expropriation, introduced in October 1971, set the climate for the ensuing period of escalating conflict between government and opposition.

Confrontation and Polarization, October 1971–September 1972

Allende's fight to succeed as president was an uphill battle from the beginning, and by his second year in office the problems that would

bring about his overthrow were out in the open. Perhaps his most fundamental difficulty was that the UP controlled only one branch of government. Having a cooperative Congress would have made a great difference,
but the passage of time diminished the prospects of achieving a congressional majority in 1973. The judiciary, dominated by conservatives,
presented many problems for Allende. Its antipathy toward UP objectives
was especially significant given the refusal of Congress to pass the government's bills; being forced to enact its program by stretching existing
laws and powers and constrained by the primacy of capitalist definitions
of property in a transition to socialism, the UP was constantly frustrated
at the judiciary's ability to slow or halt its progress. The UP electoral program included judicial reform, and Allende formally proposed it to Congress, but to no avail.

Finally, there was the ultimate arbiter of politics: the armed forces.
Despite Chile's long history of rarely interrupted civilian government,
everyone knew that the armed forces, by action or inaction, would decide
whether Allende would finish his six-year term. Allende's challenge in rela-
tion to the military was to keep it loyal to its tradition of nonintervention;
to accomplish that, the president would have to avoid a major crisis of the
kind that would make the military's intolerance of disorder override its
commitment to nonintervention.

As its second year in office began, the UP faced mounting economic
problems as well as the increasing intransigence of the opposition and the
United States. The primary economic problem was inflation, a chronic condition in Chile but one that by 1972 was moving well beyond the 1960s
range of 8 to 46 percent and would reach over 300 percent by September 1973. The inflationary spiral resulted largely from the government's
massive spending on property acquisitions, subsidies to nationalized firms,
and wages, but was greatly compounded by congressional refusal to approve
budgets. In order to maintain the momentum of his first year, Allende
turned increasingly to the government printing presses that churned
out enough currency to pay the bills but also to stimulate inflation and
devaluation.

Besides the stiffening of domestic opposition, Allende had to deal with
a Nixon administration firmly committed to his overthrow. In addition to
the credit boycott, Washington funneled money through the CIA to opposition parties and to *El Mercurio*, the conservative dean of the Santiago
press and a staunch opponent of the UP agenda. Between September 1971
and April 1972, the Nixon administration authorized the expenditure of
over $2.5 million on these anti-UP forces—part of the $8 million total
spent to destabilize the Chilean government—while instructing the CIA

to explore every possible avenue to a coup. The U.S. press, although not consistently supportive of the Nixon position, did its part to shape U.S. public opinion against Allende by focusing on matters such as meat rationing without noting that Chilean governments had controlled supplies and prices of basic foods since the 1930s.

The UP's political fortunes also took a turn for the worse in the months following Allende's first anniversary in office. Fidel Castro came for an announced 10-day visit in November 1971 but stayed three and a half weeks. The visit had some improbable and light moments, such as Fidel's visit to the annual livestock show of the very conservative and elite National Society of Agriculture (Sociedad Nacional de Agricultura), but his very presence in Chile conjured up visions of Marxist dictatorship. Fidel's customary bombastic discourse did not help, either: after he labeled the opposition "fascist," the right and center press and parties accused Castro of interference in Chile's internal affairs.

The power struggle between president and Congress reached a new level in January 1972 with the first of several congressional impeachments of cabinet ministers. In the same month the opposition retained two congressional seats in by-elections; more troubling for the government than the failure to gain those seats was the decline of 5.5 percent in the UP vote since the previous April. In March 1972, 13 cases of arms from Cuba labeled as works of art were discovered to have been imported without customs inspection upon the approval of the minister of the interior. Because the arms were not for the military, this caused a furor about the government's suspected implication in arming popular militias and led to an opposition-sponsored arms control law that Allende signed over the objections of some of his coalition partners.

Underlying the increasing confrontation and polarization were a growing mass mobilization and the government's ambivalent attitude toward controlling it. Throughout rural Chile, unauthorized worker occupations of estates led to frequent violence as landowners armed themselves and banded together to defend their properties. Although this phenomenon had begun under the Frei government, its exacerbation after the 1970 election created chaos in the countryside and disrupted production. The promoters of these seizures were generally UP members or sympathizers, sometimes agrarian reform officials themselves, who sought to radicalize the revolution with all possible speed. In Santiago and other cities, similar extralegal expropriations were proceeding apace, especially in the industrial belt of the capital, where workers and left activists seized dozens of factories.

This "hypermobilization" of the rural and urban working class posed a difficult dilemma for the Allende administration. On one hand, Allende had constitutional responsibility as president to enforce the law, which, of course, guaranteed private ownership rights unless a valid expropriation order was given, and he repeatedly stated his commitment to the rule of law. On the other hand, the workers were Allende's constituency, and for ideological as well as practical reasons he was understandably loathe to use the force of a "people's" government against the people. The government's responses to the wave of unauthorized seizures of factories and haciendas reflected Allende's vacillation over property rights and the rule of law. Some properties were returned to their owners, usually after promises to the occupiers of expeditious legal expropriation; many were not returned at all; and in some cases the government expelled the workers by force.

The government's inconsistency reflected more than sentimental considerations about the use of force on the people. More basically, it was the product of the deep division within the UP coalition and within Allende's own Socialist Party over strategy and tactics for making the revolution. On the left, a strong minority of the UP and its allies advocated pushing ahead with all speed to break the back of capitalism and install a true people's government before the opposition could regroup and react. The left believed that stimulating rather than restraining the popular mobilization would help accomplish this goal and that the government itself should encourage extralegal acts rather than enforce bourgeois law.

The left wing of the Socialists, led by party Secretary-General Carlos Altamirano, had long expressed disdain for Chile's political institutions and had argued the need for insurrection at the appropriate time. MAPU generally supported the Altamirano position. Outside the government but tacitly allied with it was the MIR, the revolutionary group that had moderated its approach in support of Allende's presidential candidacy. The MIR operated openly on the fringe of government, fostering takeovers, developing shantytown organizations, proselytizing the populace, and generally pushing Allende as hard as it could toward ever bolder steps.

The more conservative majority of the UP consisted of the Communists, the Allende Socialists, the Radicals, and the smaller groups other than MAPU. Their position was to push vigorously toward socialism primarily through legal means by extending state control and redistributing income. They were not willing to take the risk, which the UP left and the MIR implicitly accepted, of provoking an armed reaction against the government; they preferred consolidation of gains at a certain point, if necessary, over continual confrontation. These deep divisions within the UP were aired and debated, but not resolved, at a conference in February 1972, and the schisms persisted to the end of Allende's presidency.

The government's vacillation on the rule of law was a major factor in the UP's political failure. To win a congressional majority in 1973, the UP would have to retain or expand the bare majority it had received in the 1971 municipal elections. The PDC's hold on significant portions of the working class—a majority of the rural unions, several skilled workers' unions, and women—meant that Allende's chances of converting the lower-class majority of Chileans into a UP electoral majority were slim. Therefore he had to rely on a significant portion of Chile's large middle classes for electoral support.

The middle sectors tended to view rising levels of confrontation and the government's vacillation on law enforcement with apprehension, and the opposition press constantly fed their fears with reports and photo spreads of land seizures, worker marches, MIR activities, and discoveries of arms caches. Accelerating inflation and shortages of food and consumer goods further eroded support for or tolerance of Allende among the middle classes. Moreover, the leveling tendency, reflected in the integration of the historically separate white- and blue-collar workers' social security systems, undoubtedly fueled their growing disenchantment with the government. Substantial parts of the middle class revealed their antigovernment sentiments in October 1972, when a truck owners' strike, called to protest a government plan to nationalize the trucking sector, precipitated action by Chile's economic and professional associations, or *gremios*.

Counterattack and Overthrow, October 1972–September 1973

The *gremio* movement had begun during the Frei administration, when the virtual eclipse of rightist electoral power and congressional representation impelled Chile's economic elites to seek alternative means of defending their interests. Although long-established organizations such as the National Society of Agriculture, the Society for Industrial Development (Sociedad de Fomento Fabril), and the Central Chamber of Commerce (Cámara Central de Comercio) had acted as pressure groups for many years, heightened threats to their interests in the 1960s stimulated the expansion of membership and coordination of efforts across sectoral lines. To counter the threat of reform, the large capitalists modified their traditional elitist approach by stressing the commonality of interests among all merchants, from the major import-export houses to the humble shopkeeper, all farmers, manufacturers, and professionals. Thus by the time of Allende's election, tens of thousands of small farmers, artisans, taxi owners, and market stall operators were organizationally affiliated with Chile's traditional elites in the multiclass *gremio* movement, a loose confederation of interest groups dominated by the elites and coordinated by a central command.

The October 1972 truckers' strike launched a mass movement of opposition to Allende based on strategies and tactics borrowed from labor unions and left parties. Described as "the mass line of the bourgeoisie," the movement featured a "bosses' strike" or lockout by business owners and a shutdown of transportation, professional services, shops of all kinds, and even strikes by some 100,000 PDC-controlled agricultural workers.[9] Accompanying these actions were housewives' "marches of the empty pots," student demonstrations, and general street agitation normally associated with the left. Government supporters responded by occupying some of the factories and businesses from which they were locked out. The elite organizations of large-scale entrepreneurs cleverly remained in the background during the strike, leaving the spotlight on leaders of the middle-class associations who could more effectively portray the action as a broad-based, popular rejection of Marxism.

This innovative approach to upper- and middle-class self-defense was very effective. The shutdown of provisioning to the cities necessitated establishment of emergency supply networks involving additional regulations and revealed the government's vulnerability to coordinated private-sector action. The strike was resolved after four weeks, but only by the appointment of three military officers to Allende's cabinet.

The president invited the military into his cabinet to restore order and to build confidence in his government. While the military's objective was to contribute to stability and thus to reinforce its ability to remain out of "politics," the generals and admirals inevitably became involved in controversial, politically charged policies. Many officers disliked the resulting identification of the armed forces with UP policies, and as the government's problems continued to mount, they came increasingly to reject participation, preferring to let the government sink on its own until public opinion would welcome a coup. After the initial three military ministers resigned in March 1973, the council of generals rejected Allende's requests for renewed military participation in his government. Although military participation gave Allende a short respite after the *gremios'* 1972 strike, it resolved no major problem and ultimately helped to discredit the noninterventionist position within the officer corps.

The March 1973 congressional elections followed an acrimonious campaign. Recognizing the slim chance of victory, Allende had stopped talking about a congressional majority and claimed that 40 percent of the vote would be an endorsement of UP rule. The National Party, aiming by now at Allende's removal, called for the opposition to achieve the two-thirds of Congress needed to impeach the president. The outcome allowed both sides to claim victory: 44.0 percent of the valid vote for UP candidates to 55.7 percent for the opposition. The UP's total was 7.5 percentage points above Allende's 1970 figure but nearly 6 below the 1971 municipal election results. The few seats that the UP gained did not change the majority and because virtually every vote now was party line, the 1973 election cemented the deadlock between president and Congress, reinforcing the polarization of Chilean politics.

The president's annual address to Congress on May 21 gave Allende a final opportunity to recount his government's accomplishments. Judged against the UP campaign platform, the achievements of two and a half years were impressive. Expropriation of 3,570 rural properties, amounting to 35 percent of Chile's total agricultural surface, had left only a small number of holdings exceeding the legal maximum. The government had nationalized over 200 of the country's largest enterprises, which accounted for 30 percent of Chilean production, exceeding Allende's goal of 91 companies listed after his election. A third of wholesale distribution and 90 percent of bank credit were under state control, and income redistribution had proceeded effectively. In sum, Allende had moved Chile well along the road toward socialism.

While emphasizing the UP's successes, Allende's speech also acknowledged that Chile had entered a stage of crisis. By May 1973 the Chilean economy was near collapse, beset by runaway inflation, rapidly declining production, shortages of essential goods, lack of new investment, and mounting deficits. Rising street violence, numerous incidents of assassination and sabotage, rumors of workers' militias, the arming of the right-wing Fatherland and Liberty (Patria y Libertad), and the establishment of neighborhood vigilance patrols reflected the growing instability that was rapidly undermining Chile's institutional foundations. The sense of crisis was so great that by the next month elements within the military were working out plans for a coup and the UP was moving to counter it. The small, easily suppressed rising of Santiago's Second Armored Regiment on June 29 served notice that the brink had almost been reached.

On July 25 the *gremios* launched another national strike, this one clearly designed to shut down the economy as long as necessary to secure Allende's removal. Several additional groups, including large contingents of PDC-controlled labor, joined forces with the *gremios* that had conducted the October 1972 movement. Rejecting all attempts at conciliation, the *gremios* continued their action until, caught between the antigovernment mobilization and the counter-actions of its own supporters, the Allende government's authority virtually evaporated.

In the midst of escalating violence, economic paralysis, and political deadlock, the armed forces in August received a provocation that hastened their preparations for removing Allende. Naval intelligence reported a plot by sailors in Valparaíso and Talcahuano to rise against their commanders and accused the MIR, Socialist Senator Carlos Altamirano, and MAPU Deputy Oscar Garretón of promoting the planned revolt. Coinciding with that revelation was Allende's first use of his commander in chief's powers over military retirements and promotions to place officers of his confidence in strategic positions in the military hierarchy. Although unrelated to the naval plot, this reversal of Allende's hands-off policy, motivated by his growing sense of danger, could be interpreted by the officer corps as coordinated subversion from above and below. As with their Brazilian counterparts in 1964, the perception of tampering with military discipline was the final straw for the Chilean officers. The last serious obstacle to the coup disappeared when constitutionalist General Carlos Prats, rebuffed by his colleagues, resigned as army commander on August 22. President Allende named General Augusto C. Pinochet his successor; at his swearing-in ceremony, Pinochet pledged to uphold the constitution.

Any lingering hesitation on the part of military leaders vanished on September 9, when Socialist Party leader Altamirano made a radio-broadcast speech defying the military to prosecute him for subversion and rejecting all compromise with the opposition. When it came on September 11, a week before Chile's national holiday, the coup was efficient and brutal. As the presidential palace burned around him, Allende made his last radio address:

> Workers of my fatherland: I have faith in Chile and its destiny. Other men will transcend this gray and bitter moment in which treason seeks to impose its will. Carry on in the knowledge that, sooner rather than later, the great avenues along which free men will pass to build a better society will open wide again. Long live Chile! Long live the people! Long live the workers! These are my last words and I am certain that my sacrifice will not be in vain.[10]

Although the train of events of Allende's final weeks appeared to make the coup unavoidable, different decisions at critical junctures throughout the UP administration might have postponed or prevented the denouement of September 11, 1973. If Allende had held the plebiscite on his proposed institutional reforms soon after the April 1971 municipal elections and won, he would have been able to accomplish much of his program without recourse to maneuvers of dubious legality; had his plebiscite lost, he might have charted a less ambitious course and avoided the polarization that gripped the country by 1972. Restraining the UP left and the MIR might have enabled Allende to restore order and finish his term, although this would have slowed the momentum of his movement toward socialism.

Throughout Allende's presidency, the UP and PDC periodically conducted negotiations designed to surmount specific crises and generally to arrest the erosion of political stability. Each time, narrow partisan interests and inflexibility on the UP left and PDC right prevented agreements that might have saved Chile's political institutions from destruction. A different outcome of the last PDC–UP dialogue, held at the end of July 1973, might well have dissuaded the military from acting. Allende's resignation would certainly have prevented the coup, but that was a step that he was unwilling to take. However, the growing turmoil convinced Allende to stake his continuance in office on a plebiscite, which he planned to announce in the late morning of September 11. Unfortunately, the beleaguered president arrived too late at the decision that most likely would have prevented the coup and years of harsh military dictatorship.

The overthrow of Allende was a severe blow to the hopes of Latin America's left. Many were quick to proclaim that the *vía electoral* had been an illusion all along, that there is no peaceful road to socialism. Those who had believed that its unique tradition and the strength of its political institutions made Chile an exception were forced to recognize that, beneath its trappings of constitutional stability and military nonintervention, Chile was, after all, part of Latin America. For a substantial portion of the many Chileans who welcomed the coup as their salvation, joy quickly turned to misery as the military showed its true face. For the millions of poor Chileans who lost their *"compañero Presidente,"* military rule would confirm their worst nightmares.

Notes

1. U.S. Congress, Senate Select Committee on Intelligence Activities, *Alleged Assassination Plots Involving Foreign, Leaders: Interim Report* (1975), 229, in Paul E. Sigmund, *The Overthrow of Allende and the Politics of Chile, 1964–1976* (Pittsburgh: University of Pittsburgh Press, 1977), 113.

2. These figures are percentages of the total vote and do not account for blank or invalid votes (in this election, 0.9 percent). The term "valid vote" as

used in this chapter refers to a percentage of the total vote with blank and invalid votes subtracted.

3. The author viewed the telecast, September 5, 1970.

4. Tanya Harmer, *Allende's Chile and the Inter-American Cold War* (Chapel Hill: University of North Carolina Press, 2011), 60.

5. Jonathan Haslam, *The Nixon Administration and the Death of Allende's Chile: A Case of Assisted Suicide* (London: Verso, 2005), 56.

6. Kristian Gustafson, *Hostile Intent: U.S. Covert Operations in Chile, 1964–1974* (Washington, D.C.: Potomac Books, 2007), 139.

7. Sigmund, *Overthrow of Allende*, 131.

8. David J. Morris, *We Must Make Haste—Slowly: The Process of Revolution in Chile* (New York: Vintage Books, 1973), 119.

9. Armand Mattelart, "La bourgeoisie à l'école de Lénine: Le 'gremialisme' et la ligne de masse de la bourgeoisie chilienne," *Politique Aujourd'hui* (Paris), 1–2 (January-February 1974), 23–46.

10. Elizabeth Quay Hutchison, Thomas Miller Klubock, Nara B. Milanich, and Peter Winn, eds., *The Chile Reader: History, Culture, Politics* (Durham, NC: Duke University Press, 2014), 431.

The Sandinista Revolution in Nicaragua, 1979–1990

Twenty years after Fidel Castro seized power in Cuba, his dream of a Latin American revolution appeared dead. Efforts to replicate the Cuban Revolution through rural guerrilla warfare had failed, most of them dismally. Despite initial success in Uruguay and Argentina, the urban variant of guerrilla warfare ultimately succumbed to counterinsurgency measures and to its own limitations. Revolution by decree under the Peruvian military and by the ballot box in Chile appeared promising until both experiments came to abrupt ends. By 1979 the most tangible results of two decades of attempted revolution were legions of dead revolutionaries and state terrorist regimes that governed half of Latin America's people.

The victory of the Sandinista National Liberation Front (Frente Sandinista de Liberación Nacional, FSLN) and its allies over the Nicaraguan government of Anastasio Somoza Debayle revived the dynamic of revolution in Latin America. The FSLN had launched a rural *foco* in 1961, which met the standard fate of the guerrilla movements of the early 1960s. Despite military reversals and the loss of key personnel over the years, the FSLN persisted and gradually built effective rural and urban support networks. Taking advantage of changing conditions in Nicaragua, the FSLN by the mid-1970s emerged as a potent force and clearly the leading armed opposition to Somoza. Aided by the regime's increasingly repressive character, the guerrillas were able to achieve a broad political-military front that toppled the dictatorship on July 19, 1979.

Although the Sandinista revolution had important repercussions within the hemisphere, it did not have an impact comparable to that of the Cuban

Revolution 20 years earlier. This was due in part to the prevailing climate of reaction in the late 1970s and early 1980s, which limited the possibility of popular response in many countries. It also reflected the nature of the Nicaraguan revolution itself. The Sandinista leadership was collective, and hence no charismatic Fidel Castro appeared to ignite the passions of the Latin American masses. Nor was there a Che Guevara to propagate a heroic version of victory capable of inciting widespread emulation. Finally, the policies of the revolutionary government were relatively moderate in both the domestic and foreign spheres, in contrast to the radical measures and rapid pace of the Cuban Revolution.

Nonetheless, the Sandinista revolution clearly set the agenda for the politics of Central America for over a decade and had some impact beyond the region. As the Cuban Revolution had done two decades earlier throughout Latin America, the Sandinistas' success encouraged insurrection in Central America by demonstrating that victory was possible. The Sandinista revolution and the subsequent destabilization of Central America elicited a reaction similar to Washington's response to the Cuban Revolution: the United States attempted simultaneously to snuff out revolution at the source—through blatant military intervention and strong economic and diplomatic pressures against the Sandinista government—while investing heavily in military aid in the region to prevent the spread of revolution. Thus although more limited geographically in its impact, the Sandinista revolution became nearly as much of a preoccupation for Washington in the 1980s as the Cuban Revolution had been in the 1960s.

Background to Revolution

Nicaragua's *ancien régime*, the Somoza dynasty, came to power in 1936 after more than two decades during which Nicaragua had been an unofficial U.S. protectorate. From its first occupation in 1912 to final withdrawal in 1933, the United States maintained troops in Nicaragua for all but one year. Most of the time a small detachment of Marines sufficed to guarantee political stability and U.S. interests, but from 1927 to 1933 up to 5,500 Marines were in the field against the guerrilla forces of General Augusto C. Sandino, an ardent nationalist and reformer who broke with the elite–military consensus that tolerated U.S. control. The Marines left the country after establishing the National Guard to replace the Nicaraguan army, which because of its politicization was seen as the main source of the country's endemic instability; having equal numbers of members of the rival Conservative and Liberal parties on its general staff, the National Guard was designed to be politically neutral. U.S. personnel chose Anastasio

Somoza García, an affable, English-speaking young officer, to head the National Guard. Within four years of the U.S. withdrawal, Somoza had assassinated Sandino, purged the Guard's officer corps of Conservatives, packed it with fellow Liberals, and assumed the presidency. With the Guard as his base, Somoza quickly subverted U.S. intentions and used the "apolitical" new force as the springboard for establishing Latin America's most durable 20th-century family dynasty.

Three Somozas served as president during the family's 43-year reign: Anastasio Somoza García between 1937 and 1956, son Luis Somoza Debayle from 1956 to 1963, and son Anastasio "Tachito" Somoza Debayle between 1967 and 1979. Trusted lieutenants wore the presidential sash during brief interludes, but no one other than a Somoza ever served as commander of the National Guard. The Guard had an official monopoly on armed force, serving as army, air force, police, and customs agency and

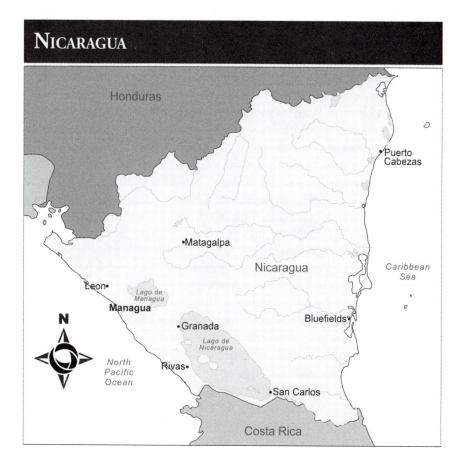

fulfilling numerous other government functions. The original Somoza molded the Guard into an instrument of family power by personally selecting officers, giving them ample opportunity for enrichment, treating the troops generously and paternalistically, and segregating them from the general populace so as to create an elite institution never lacking in volunteers.

Unwavering U.S. support was a second pillar of the Somoza dynasty. With the advent of the Cold War, the Somozas' value to Washington increased: they were aggressively anticommunist at home and reliably pro-United States in the United Nations and the OAS. Nicaragua provided the embarkation point for the U.S.-sponsored invasion of Cuba in 1961 and was one of six Latin American countries to send troops to the Dominican Republic in 1965. In return, Washington gave generous military and economic aid, a succession of friendly and unquestioning ambassadors, and the stamp of approval that dissuaded most Somoza adversaries from action. The dynasty rested also on a branch of the historic Liberal Party that Somoza renamed the Nationalist Liberal Party, the support or tolerance of the country's elites, the marginalization of the masses, and the economic power of the Somoza clan.

When the impact of the Cuban Revolution swept over the hemisphere, Central America was relatively unaffected, with the exception of Guatemala, where the recent Árbenz reforms had weakened the foundations of traditional elite rule. With its backward, predominantly agrarian economy and its entrenched dictatorial rule, Nicaragua lacked the social and political institutions to respond effectively to the stimuli from Cuba. The middle class and urban proletariat were small and weak and, in contrast to most hemispheric countries with democratic governments, unions, student organizations, left parties, and opposition press were proscribed or tightly controlled, leaving few organized means of mobilizing support for reform or revolution. When such movements did materialize, the National Guard proved effective in repressing them. An increase in exile invasions, formation of a few *fidelista* groups, and the appearance of several small guerrilla *focos* marked the early 1960s, but the powerful Somoza dynasty felt merely a ripple from the tidal wave sweeping Latin America.

In its quest to immunize Latin America against revolution, the Alliance for Progress inadvertently helped to create conditions that would make Nicaragua vulnerable to radical change by the late 1970s. As elsewhere, new institutions and bureaucracies sprang up to administer agrarian reform, health, education, and low-cost housing programs, raising expectations of change. More significant was the Central American Common Market, founded in 1960 and implemented with Alliance funding, which broke down tariff barriers among its five member states and for the first time created markets of sufficient size to support some industrialization. The economic impact on Nicaragua was immediate and substantial: expansion of manufacturing, processing, and intraregional trade brought a period of economic boom in the 1960s, but by the early 1970s progress gave way to economic cycles that eroded the gains of the previous decade.

A 1972 earthquake that killed some 10,000 people and leveled much of Managua is generally credited with beginning the unraveling of the Somoza regime. Developments during and after the disaster brought the corruption and venality of the National Guard and Tachito Somoza himself into the national and international spotlights. Charged with security during the emergency and direction of the subsequent relief effort, the Guard openly looted stores and sold donated relief supplies. Internationally circulated photographs of National Guard jeeps bulging with looted appliances captured the essence of the breakdown of discipline in the pillar of the regime. Somoza himself profited from the disaster, granting his companies lucrative demolition and construction contracts and decreeing the rebuilding of Managua on nearby land that he and close associates owned. One of his maneuvers, illustrative of the unseemly greed of a man already worth tens, if not hundreds, of millions, was to buy a plot of land after the earthquake at $30,000 and sell it three weeks later to his National Housing Institute for $3 million in U.S. relief funds; the land remained barren of housing.

Somoza's avarice, his near-monopolization of the lucrative post-earthquake land and construction business, and diminishing economic growth in the 1970s created a split within the bourgeoisie between the Somocistas and the increasingly marginalized groups who were not part of the inner circle. The economic wedge that Somoza had driven between himself and his fellow elites soon manifested itself in a political realignment and a growing upper- and middle-class opposition movement. Some of this opposition involved an intensification of historic party rivalries between Conservatives and Liberals, with some smaller parties also involved. The most significant new twist, however, was the creation in 1974 of the nonpartisan Democratic Liberation Union (Unión Democrática de Liberación, UDEL) led by the Conservative publisher of *La Prensa*, Pedro Joaquín Chamorro.

The FSLN

When it made international headlines in December 1974 by taking a group of regime dignitaries and diplomats hostage at a soiree honoring U.S. Ambassador Turner Shelton, the FSLN had been in the field for

13 years. After visiting Cuba, Carlos Fonseca Amador, a student leader and Communist from the northern town of Matagalpa, became disillusioned with the Communists' reluctance to pursue the armed struggle. He broke away and, with his friends Tomás Borge and Silvio Mayorga, formed a small revolutionary group inspired by Marxism, *fidelismo*, and intense nationalism. Operating from a base in Honduras, the group attempted unsuccessfully in 1961 and again in 1963 to establish itself in Nicaragua. The second defeat at the hands of Somoza's National Guard led the guerrillas to reassess the validity of a purely *foco* approach, and for the next four years they concentrated on building peasant support and establishing an urban network for recruitment and fundraising. Yet the FSLN's return to military action in 1967 was no more successful than its earlier armed forays. In an encounter near Pancasán in the north, the Guard killed several guerrillas, including founder Silvio Mayorga, and destroyed their peasant network.

Despite this setback, the Sandinistas patiently rebuilt their rural structure—an endeavor that they referred to in borrowed Maoist terms as "gathering forces in silence." The key to developing rural support, they learned, was to break down peasant distrust of city people by living and working with the rural folk and using their strong family ties and godparenthood relationships to establish support networks across wide areas. This work was so successful that when they returned to the offensive in 1970, the guerrillas survived and expanded. National Guard repression of peasants in the north now backfired, creating additional support for the Sandinistas. Omar Cabezas' colorful memoir of the struggle, *Fire from the Mountain*, clearly reveals the guerrillas' success at winning peasant support—a crucial ingredient lacking in most Latin American guerrilla actions of the 1960s: "We took hold of the *campesinos*' hands, broad, powerful, roughened hands. 'These callouses,' we asked, 'how did you get them?' And they would tell us how they came from machetes, from working the land. If they got those callouses from working the land, we asked, why did that land belong to the boss and not to them? We were trying to awaken the *campesino* to his own dream."[1]

Despite the growth of guerrilla strength and the development of a substantial urban resistance, the 1974 raid on the Somocista Christmas party was a bold and risky move. But given the elite credentials of those captured—Ambassador Shelton not included, for he had left just prior to the attack—Somoza acceded to most of the FSLN demands in exchange for the freeing of the hostages. He released 18 Sandinistas from jail and flew them to Cuba, paid a $5 million ransom, and ordered Nicaraguan newspapers and radio stations to disseminate two FSLN communiqués.

By revealing the guerrillas' strength and the regime's vulnerability, the hostage taking thrust the heretofore obscure FSLN into the limelight.

The following three years brought mixed fortunes to the FSLN while moving Nicaragua closer to revolution. Under a state of siege declared during the hostage crisis, Somoza formed Special Antiterrorist Activity Brigades within the Guard to spearhead the fight against the guerrillas. During the next 32 months, with civil liberties suspended, curfews imposed, and censorship tightened, the government severely repressed peasants, workers, and slum dwellers—all potential collaborators—as well as FSLN fighters and supporters. The intensification of state repression in a country long accustomed to institutionalized but inconsistent brutality had the effect of broadening and stiffening the opposition to Somoza.

The FSLN suffered numerous casualties and arrests during the 1975–1977 period, but was still able to augment its ranks as disaffection spread. Yet by early 1978 the Sandinistas had less than 500 armed fighters against the Guard's 7,000 troops. Moreover, the repression contributed to a split in FSLN ranks over strategy and, to a lesser extent, over ideology. Although the break among the three "tendencies" was never formalized, each group tended to go its own way militarily and organizationally until late 1978. The Proletarians (Proletarios), influenced by Jaime Wheelock, focused on the cities, organizing in factories and slums to broaden the movement's base and carrying out some urban guerrilla actions. The Prolonged People's War (Guerra Popular Prolongada) faction, led by Tomás Borge and Henry Ruíz, opted to continue and strengthen the Maoist strategy of gradual accumulation of forces in the countryside for an eventual peasant army capable of defeating the Guard. The Third Way (Terceristas), led by Daniel and Humberto Ortega and Víctor Tirado López, believed in pressing the insurrection wherever and by whatever means possible, even at the risk of being overly bold. This group was the most flexible ideologically as well. Taking advantage of the growing opposition to Somoza, it recruited non-Marxists of various stripes, diluting the FSLN's original Marxist identity.

The election of Jimmy Carter to the U.S. presidency had serious repercussions for Somoza's fight to preserve the dynasty. State Department pressure to improve the human rights climate in Nicaragua led to a lifting of the state of siege in September 1977, reducing the repression and allowing a freer manifestation of the growing antiregime sentiment. The FSLN factions pressed their advantage with stepped-up military activity, but, reinforced with new equipment and recruits, the Guard turned back the guerrilla offensive without major difficulty.

The Overthrow of Somoza, January 1978–July 1979

Although the three years since the FSLN hostage taking had weakened the Somoza regime, the government's demise was far from certain as 1978 dawned. A critical turning point came on January 10, 1978, when assassins gunned down Pedro Joaquín Chamorro, founder of UDEL, publisher of *La Prensa*, and a long-time and widely respected critic of the regime. Owners of a blood plasma company, who included relatives and close collaborators of the dictator, ordered Chamorro's killing in retribution for a *La Prensa* article exposing the company's exportation of plasma, with which Nicaragua was chronically undersupplied. Within hours of the event, over 50,000 people gathered at Chamorro's house to mourn and protest his death. Disturbances followed in cities throughout the country.

The Chamorro assassination unleashed the forces that, building upon the events of the past five years, brought Somoza down within a year and a half. UDEL, the elites' opposition group, called a general business strike that shut down some 80 percent of national economic activity. Resembling the Chilean *gremio* movement that had played a major role in the overthrow of Allende, this nationwide movement gained the support of trade and production associations, political parties, labor unions, and new opposition groups that sprang up. The business strike combined with tax boycotts and other economic actions began to weaken the regime's economic foundation.

As the active opposition grew, a new umbrella organization, the Broad Opposition Front (Frente Amplio Opositor, FAO), was established to coordinate the actions of bourgeois and middle-class organizations, parties, and some labor unions. Aggregating moderate to conservative anti-regime opinion, the FAO pushed for reform, not revolution: it called for Somoza's resignation, political democracy, an end to corruption, a vague agrarian reform, and improved social services. Leaders of the FAO and component groups suffered arrest and persecution as Somoza took an increasingly hard line toward the political opposition.

Encouraged by the United States and the OAS, the FAO conducted negotiations with Somoza for some four months beginning in September 1978. Determined to serve out his current presidential term through 1981 and to leave the National Guard and his Nationalist Liberal Party intact thereafter, Somoza proved recalcitrant, leading the FAO to offer more concessions than many of its constituents condoned. As the negotiations proceeded toward impasse, important groups left the FAO, weakening the moderate political opposition and strengthening the groups, especially the FSLN, that advocated armed struggle in order to prevent the dictator's replacement with a "Somocismo sin Somoza" (Somozaism without Somoza).

In addition to igniting a strident political opposition, the Chamorro assassination catalyzed a series of spontaneous uprisings that revealed the depth of popular opposition to the regime and the Guard. The first of these occurred in February 1978 in Monimbó, the Indian neighborhood of the colonial town of Masaya. The Guard attacked residents celebrating the renaming of a small plaza for the late Chamorro; in an unprecedented response, the residents defended themselves with rocks and makeshift weapons and drove out the troops. Then in an action that presaged the Guard's counteroffensive against the mounting wave of popular insurrection throughout the country, troops cordoned off Monimbó, shelled it, bombed it, and finally attacked house to house with armor, killing 200 people in the process. Two more insurrections took place in February and March in other towns, and the method of retaking the areas was the same. By early 1978, Somoza was literally at war with his people.

The unexpected ferocity of popular insurrection took both the FSLN and the moderate political opposition by surprise. For the Terceristas, the uprisings provided an opportunity to test their thesis that revolution could be provoked in the short run by heightened activity. Accordingly, in August 1978 they staged an operation reminiscent of but far bolder than the 1974 hostage taking. A command of 25 Sandinistas disguised as a National Guard patrol occupied the National Palace while the Chamber of Deputies was meeting and captured over 2,000 hostages, including most of the deputies, administration officials, journalists, bureaucrats, and citizens doing business in the building. After two days, the guerrillas won the release of important Sandinistas from prison, a large ransom, and safe passage out of the country. Thousands of sympathizers turned out to cheer the convoy of guerrillas and released Sandinistas on its way to the airport.

This spectacular operation soon had the desired effect of stimulating mobilization against the regime. September 1978 was marked by uprisings in at least eight cities, including Managua, León, Matagalpa, and Estelí. Under a new state of siege, the Guard retook the cities one by one, using the same tactics unveiled in Monimbó, destroying extensive business and residential areas, and killing between 1,500 and 2,000 people, mostly civilians. During follow-up operations in October, the Guard took its revenge by brutalizing the cities' inhabitants, especially the youth who had participated massively in the insurrections. But rather than intimidating the populace, the terror unleashed to defend the dynasty only strengthened the will to resist. Despite internal censorship, the international media disseminated news of Somoza's draconian response to rebellion, bringing growing international pressure on the dictator to negotiate a settlement. By early 1979 the United States and the OAS were urging his resignation, several Latin American countries had broken diplomatic relations, and a few were aiding the rebels. The regime's loss of the customary unequivocal U.S. support was a demoralizing financial, political, and diplomatic blow.

The dramatic events of 1978 had a galvanizing effect on the FSLN. The awesome demonstration of popular will to fight and willingness to die, from Monimbó through the September insurrections, convinced the Sandinistas that the regime's end was near. Concurrently, the determination and strength of the bourgeois-led political opposition, combined with international pressures for negotiations, raised the specter of a political settlement that would bring the UDEL and its allies to power and exclude the FSLN. Facing these challenges and opportunities, the FSLN factions in early 1979 set aside their differences, reunited under a single directorate, and stepped up recruitment in the cities and countryside. Aided by their clandestine Radio Sandino, which allowed them to circumvent government censorship, the FSLN had some 1,200 fighters in the field by the beginning of May 1979. On the political front, they supported the formation of two broad-based organizations to compete with UDEL and FAO: the People United Movement (Movimiento Pueblo Unido) led by Moisés Hassan and their own National Patriotic Front (Frente Patriótico Nacional).

On May 30, 1979, the FSLN announced its "final offensive" to topple the government. Their ranks swollen by additional fighters and thousands of collaborators, the Sandinistas launched simultaneous urban insurrections and military operations north, east, and south of Managua. The north, where the FSLN had concentrated its efforts over the years, fell quickly. The Guard made its best stand in the south, where fierce fighting lasted several weeks between the Costa Rican border and the city of Rivas. After the fall of Rivas and Masaya, the only important regime-held territory was part of the capital. Fighting now for its institutional survival and the lives of its members, the Guard rallied to drive the FSLN out of Managua's popular barrios and back to Masaya on June 24.

Washington's response to the looming Sandinista victory was to revive its earlier attempt to fashion a settlement that would exclude the FSLN. The Carter administration proposed a multinational peacekeeping force to stop the fighting so that a political solution could be found; the OAS firmly rejected the proposal on June 21. The FSLN leadership then agreed to talk with U.S. representatives, but with victory in sight, they were unmoved by Washington's plea for a new bourgeois-led government. Finally recognizing the hopelessness of his situation, on July 6 Somoza agreed to resign upon receiving the signal from Washington. When the FSLN mounted its final drive on the capital, Somoza abandoned the country for exile in

Paraguay, at the invitation of long-term dictator General Alfredo Stroess-ner.[2] Nicaragua's Congress then named a provisional government that collapsed within 48 hours as the Sandinista army entered Managua on July 19. It and the last remnants of the dynasty fled Nicaragua in Guate-malan air force planes as the new provisional government flew in from San José, Costa Rica, in the Mexican presidential jet. Sergio Ramírez, an FSLN ally and member of the provisional government (the Governing Junta of National Reconstruction), described the scene on July 20 when the new government was introduced in the capital:

> The five of us who were members of the Government Junta taking the place of Somoza entered from a side of the plaza on top of a fire truck with its siren blaring . . . The guerrilla troops that had become our provisional bodyguards were firing shots in the air from the truck's running boards and platforms . . . There were shouts of joy, cascading applause, choruses of slogans, tears that washed faces and laughter lighting up the faces bathed in tears, marimba music coming from speakers on a truck . . . There were also bunches of people up in the trees in the neighboring Central Park, in the cathedral towers' cornices, and on the National Palace's roof.[3]

The cost in human life and injury and in material damage was stagger-ing: some 15,000 were killed during the final offensive, and between 40,000 and 50,000 of Nicaragua's 2.9 million people had been killed between 1977 and the final victory. Yet Nicaragua's war was just beginning.

Institutionalizing the Revolution, 1979–1987

The seven and a half years between the fall of Somoza and the adoption of a new constitution were marked by intense political competition. Yet the entire process of institutionalizing the revolution was characterized by a high degree of consistency in the balance of forces and in the composi-tion and functioning of the government. By virtue of its military victory and subsequent control of the armed forces, the moral authority derived from its 18-year struggle against the dynasty, and the support it had devel-oped among the rural and urban masses, the FSLN was clearly the domi-nant political entity from the outset. At the same time, the Sandinistas' own heterogeneity and commitment to two political principles—pluralism and participatory democracy—moderated the power that the FSLN was capable of wielding and resulted in considerable flexibility.

The FSLN consisted of a number of mass organizations, the party itself, and a nine-member National Directorate that set party policy. Most of the mass organizations dated from the later years of the war against Somoza as the FSLN turned increasingly to building broad support. The most powerful mass organization was the armed forces, which was built on the foundation of the FSLN's guerrilla force and replaced the hated National Guard. The close connection between the FSLN and the armed forces was clear: the military's official title was the Sandinista People's Army (Ejército Popular Sandinista), and the minister of defense from the beginning was Humberto Ortega, brother of Daniel and a member of the FSLN National Directorate.

The FSLN's voluntary mass organizations included the Luisa Amanda Espinosa Nicaraguan Women's Association, the July 19th Sandinista Youth, and an extensive network of rural and urban unions grouped under the Sandinista Workers' Central. The largest union was the Association of Agricultural Workers; in 1981, smallholders split off into a separate National Union of Farmers and Cattlemen (Unión Nacional de Agricultores y Ganaderos, UNAG). Although non-Sandinista unions of both left and right orientation remained a significant minority within the labor movement, there was no important competition to the Sandinistas' control of youth, women, and rural workers and smallholders.

The Sandinista Defense Committees (Comités de Defensa Sandinista, CDSs) were the FSLN's primary mass organization among the urban poor. Set up along neighborhood lines, these groups, reminiscent of Cuba's CDRs, were formed during the insurrection against Somoza to support FSLN fighters; at their height in the two years after the victory, the CDSs enrolled an estimated 500,000 people, or a third of Nicaragua's adult population. The CDSs carried out public functions, including the maintenance of order and distribution of basic commodities and rationing cards. Their security functions diminished as the revolutionary state apparatus and an urban police force took shape, but the CDSs continued to exercise a sort of revolutionary vigilance, mobilize neighborhood residents for political rallies, and organize clean-up campaigns and other collective projects. By the late 1980s the CDSs had declined greatly in membership and vigor, reflecting the cooling of the post-victory enthusiasm and the rigors of a shattered economy that cut into individuals' time for voluntary action.

The National Directorate, the FSLN's governing body, consisted of nine long-term FSLN members and combat veterans, all of whom held the highest military rank of *comandante*. The Directorate balanced the differing views from within the heterogeneous movement, assessed input from the mass organizations, and articulated policy positions on a day-to-day basis. Most Directorate members also held key government positions: Daniel Ortega as chairman of the original junta and after 1984 as president; Humberto Ortega as minister of defense; Directorate Chairman

Tomás Borge as minister of interior charged with internal security; Bayardo Arce as president of the Council of State to 1984; Carlos Núñez as president of the national assembly after 1984; Jaime Wheelock as minister of agriculture; and so on. This overlap between the National Directorate and the government ensured the FSLN's preeminence in policy making and implementation and provided consistency in the general direction of the revolution.

The FSLN exercised its power within a setting of political pluralism in which numerous parties and economic interest groups exercised broad rights of political organization and expression. The composition of the first post-Somoza government, the Governing Junta of National Reconstruction, reflected the breadth of the struggle against the dynasty: two representatives of the bourgeois opposition, including Violeta Barrios de Chamorro, widow of the slain *La Prensa* editor; two representatives of the pro-Sandinista political opposition; and Daniel Ortega of the FSLN's National Directorate. The appointed, corporately structured 51-member Council of State was an advisory body that proposed policy to the Governing Junta. Its composition reflected both the breadth of the apparatus and the FSLN's ultimate power over it. The main anti-Somoza factions had agreed on the Council's composition prior to the victory; however, in April 1980 the FSLN demanded additional seats to accommodate the new or enlarged mass organizations that it had created. The FSLN claimed that the new seats were necessary to foster participatory democracy, while the opposition charged the FSLN with packing the Council with its own people. The FSLN prevailed, and the two bourgeois Junta members resigned but were replaced by members with generally similar views.

Political opposition to Sandinista dominance continued to be vigorous and relatively free. By the end of the 1980s there were 21 political parties registered in Nicaragua; a range of economic interest associations headed by the Superior Council of Private Enterprise (Consejo Superior de la Empresa Privada, COSEP); and several opposition newspapers, magazines, and radio stations. Although it would be incorrect to suggest that the FSLN had a perfect record in safeguarding all rights of the opposition, the pluralist political system was clearly at odds with President Ronald Reagan's repeated characterization of Nicaragua as a "totalitarian" state. A comparison with Mexico, another pluralist system with one-party dominance, would suggest that pluralism in Nicaragua was quite effective. The constant pressure from opposition groups, combined with the FSLN's insistence on hearing and incorporating input from the mass organizations, resulted in policies that were more pragmatic than dogmatic.

The November 1984 general election and the 1987 constitution final-
ized the shape of the post-Somoza political system. The election took place
under intense U.S. pressure and international scrutiny. The Reagan administration declared in advance that the election would be fraudulent and
pressured the right opposition to boycott as a means of denying legitimacy
to the winners. The FSLN undoubtedly used the advantages of incumbency
during the campaign and instituted some security measures that the opposition claimed restricted its ability to campaign. Despite the boycott by
several right parties and interest groups, 75 percent of registered voters
participated in what international observers certified as a fair election. Daniel
Ortega was elected president with 63 percent of the vote, and the FSLN
obtained 61 of 96 National Assembly seats. Three parties to the right of
the FSLN won a total of 29 seats, and three Marxist parties on the FSLN's
left, including the Communists, received a total of 6 seats.

The final step in institutionalizing the revolution was the adoption of
a new constitution, which took effect in January 1987. Before writing a
draft, the government held open community meetings (*cabildos abiertos*)
throughout the country to obtain a maximum of citizen participation in
the process. The document that emerged from nearly two years of deliberation and debate defined Nicaragua as a social democracy based on an
elected government; inviolable individual liberties; and enumerated social,
economic, and cultural rights. The document guaranteed political pluralism, a mixed economy, and nonalignment in foreign affairs. Insofar as the
1987 constitution embodied the goals of the Nicaraguan Revolution, it
is apparent that Nicaragua had chosen a new path to the future, but a much
more moderate one than the path Fidel Castro selected for Cuba.

At War with the United States

As it moved to institutionalize and implement its revolution, Nicaragua
faced the daunting challenge of war with the United States. From the
moment of victory, the FSLN's Marxist orientation, the glorification of "revolution," and the government's early moves to establish an independent
foreign policy—which included relations with Cuba and the Soviet
Union—elicited reactions in Washington that ranged from skepticism to
hostility. Underlying Nicaragua's nationalistic foreign policy was a deep-
seated awareness of the United States' historic dominance of the country.
In the words of Sergio Ramírez, "Anti-imperialism was always the most
profound expression of the Sandinista movement. No other country in
Latin America had been the victim of as many abuses and military inter-
ventions by the United States as Nicaragua."[4]

The U.S. Congress expressed its concern by attaching numerous conditions to President Carter's bill for aid to Nicaragua, such as the holding of elections and prohibition of U.S. funding for any projects with Cuban involvement. Carter himself covertly authorized $1 million for anti-Sandinista activities and denied the new government's requests for military assistance. But with Ronald Reagan in the White House beginning in January 1981, suspicion of the Sandinistas gave way to the firm Cold War conviction that the Sandinistas were tools of Moscow and Havana. Citing alleged Nicaraguan aid to the rebels in El Salvador, Reagan immediately halted all economic aid, pressured international agencies to cut off loans, and began financing the counterrevolutionaries, or "Contras"—a loose grouping of Somoza adherents, National Guardsmen, and former Somoza opponents who had lost out in the power struggle with the FSLN. Reagan authorized $19 million in aid to the Contras in 1981 alone, and Congress appropriated $43 million in Contra aid for the 1983 and 1984 fiscal years. Reagan also pressured the Honduran government to grant the use of its territory and bases for U.S. military exercises, some 40 of which had taken place by 1985. These exercises served the dual purposes of intimidating the Nicaraguan government and bringing into Honduras massive amounts of weapons and supplies, which departing U.S. troops left behind for the Contras.

By early 1982, the Contras began attacking from their refuge in Honduras, penetrating deeply into Nicaragua by the end of 1983. In 1984 the United States stepped up its military pressure by mining Nicaragua's three major harbors, blowing up oil storage tanks, and increasing the scope of its Honduran-based exercises. Reacting to the administration's blatant violations of international law, which the World Court condemned, Congress placed restrictions on aid to the Contras and, in 1985, banned military assistance altogether while authorizing $27 million in "humanitarian" aid. Reagan nonetheless managed to continue financing the Contras by various extralegal means, including the bizarre "Iran-Contra" affair. Meanwhile in 1985, citing "policies and actions of the Government of Nicaragua [which] constitute an unusual and extraordinary threat to the national security and foreign policy of the United States," Reagan banned all trade with Nicaragua.[5] The president also kept pressure on Congress, publicly referring to the Nicaraguan government as "a Communist totalitarian state" and eulogizing the Contras as "freedom fighters" and "the moral equivalent of our Founding Fathers," until it authorized $100 million for the war in June 1986.[6]

In 1987, the high-water mark of the war, the Contras had approximately 15,000 troops in the field against the government—a government with which the United States maintained correct, if chilly, diplomatic relations. In addition to holding some territory, the Contras targeted the newly built rural schools and clinics that were central to the government's program of social improvement. To meet the growing threat, the government built its regular army to some 60,000 troops and set up a reserve system of 200,000, including 40,000 active, and a militia approaching 100,000. It was forced to institute conscription in 1983, and by 1986 the military effort was consuming over half the national budget. The government's development of an effective counterinsurgency program drove the Contras out of most parts of the country by 1988. Reacting to the Contras' ineffectiveness and scandals in the handling of U.S. funds, Congress refused to fund the contras after 1987.

Naked U.S. aggression against Nicaragua was not well received in Latin America, especially after the state terrorist regimes began to fall in the early 1980s. Beginning in 1983, the "Contadora Group" of Venezuela, Colombia, Panama, and Mexico sought in vain to bring Washington and Managua together to negotiate a settlement. With the escalation of war in Nicaragua and El Salvador, a resurgence of violence and repression in Guatemala, and the beginnings of political unrest in Honduras, Central American leaders themselves took the initiative in seeking a region-wide settlement. Under the leadership of Costa Rican President Oscar Arias, who received the Nobel Peace Prize for his efforts, the Central American Peace Accord signed on August 7, 1987, at Esquipulas, Guatemala, laid the basis for the eventual end of the U.S. war on Nicaragua.

Implementing the Revolution

Despite the immense burden of fighting the U.S. war, the reshaping of Nicaragua's economy and society progressed well. As it did in constructing the new political system, the FSLN used moderation in implementing economic and social change. The revolutionary government's moderation surprised many observers who expected a predominantly Marxist regime to follow Cuba's example and move quickly toward socialism. Several factors explain the relatively slow pace of change. First, the FSLN had compromised its ideological purity during the final years of the anti-Somoza struggle when its membership broadened beyond its original Marxist core. Second, the Nicaraguan revolution coincided with a growing skepticism among Marxists about Soviet-style economics, the beginning of *perestroika* in the Soviet Union and similar reforms in China, and strong trends toward privatization in the Third World. Fidel Castro himself reportedly advised the Sandinistas to preserve a substantial private sector. Finally, unrelenting

U.S. pressure may have influenced the government toward moderation in order to avoid provoking a return of the Marines who had occupied the country for over 20 years earlier in the century. Observers pondered whether the FSLN's commitment to political and economic pluralism was transitory or permanent; considering the embodiment of those principles in the 1987 constitution and the world trends away from state ownership and single-party states, it appears that the Sandinistas were simply up-to-date in their economic and political ideas.

From the outset, the new government offered assurances that it would not socialize all the economy, Cuban style. In broad terms, the state sector of the national economy increased from an extremely low 15 percent under Somoza to approximately 45 percent in 1984 and remained at that general level—a normal one for Latin America—through 1989. Growth of the state sector began with the nationalization of Somoza- and Somocista-owned properties, which included extensive agricultural holdings, the national airline, processing and manufacturing plants, construction firms, real estate, and other investments. Overall, the state inherited some 20 to 25 percent of the national economy, which accounted for approximately half of the expanded state sector, from Somoza and pro-Somoza exiles. Nationalization of banking, insurance, foreign trade, mining, forestry, transportation, and some manufacturing furthered the growth of the state sector. The overall tendency in nationalization was to take over the largest holdings in land, manufacturing, finance, and commerce and to fortify small and medium private property.

A closer look at changes in agriculture, which employed approximately half of Nicaragua's economically active population in 1980, illustrates the evolution of property under the Sandinistas. The only action in the first two years was the expropriation of Somoza-owned holdings, which included about 20 percent of the country's productive land. The 1981 agrarian reform law was quite conservative: it targeted large, inefficient, and abandoned holdings and those whose land was leased or sharecropped and guaranteed the integrity of efficient holdings of any size. With these limitations, the 1981 law failed to provide sufficient land to satisfy peasant demands.

The escalating Contra war underscored to the Sandinistas the importance of peasant support. Therefore, agrarian reform accelerated in 1985 with an easing of the restrictions on expropriation and a de-emphasis on state farms and production cooperatives. By 1988, the state sector had shrunk from 20 to 13 percent of total agricultural surface. Large private owners held 12 percent, cooperatives 15 percent, and small- and medium-sized producers controlled 60 percent. The size and power of UNAG, the small and medium owners' organization with 125,000 members in 1986, combined with the shrinkage of the state farm sector, reflected the dominant position of peasants and small entrepreneurs in a capitalist agricultural economy.

Although property relations changed significantly in agriculture and throughout the economy, preservation of the mixed economy meant that a majority of the population continued to be employees and wage laborers in the private sector, self-employed farmers, petty merchants or artisans, and the unemployed and underemployed. The government's commitment to revolution involved improving the standard of living of the poor by redistributing income, goods, and services by two basic methods. One deeply rooted approach was to empower these citizens to improve their conditions through membership in the mass organizations—labor unions, CDSs, youth organizations, and women's organizations. Effective unions would fight for members' bread-and-butter issues, while in the Sandinista concept of participatory democracy, all the mass organizations would provide input into policy formulation in their members' interests. In addition, CDSs often functioned as neighborhood improvement committees which could enhance members' living conditions.

The more direct approach to spreading the benefits of revolution was through government spending on social services and subsidies for essential goods. In the first five years after the victory, the government made an impressive beginning in redistributing welfare through food subsidies; rent controls; increased expenditure on education, housing, and public health; and reestablishment and reform of the collapsed social security system. A Cuban-style literacy crusade in 1980 took 100,000 volunteers into every corner of the country to teach basic literacy to the illiterate 40 percent of adult Nicaraguans; the result was a reported reduction of illiteracy to around 13 percent. Free public elementary education expanded. University admission policies were standardized and tuition virtually eliminated, allowing the poor to attend the formerly elite private institutions. Establishment of basic rural clinics, vaccination campaigns, and other public health measures produced good results in reducing infant mortality and crippling diseases despite the constant Contra attacks on the rural establishments.

The pronounced initial thrust toward indirect and direct redistribution of income and services slowed markedly under the weight of the drastic economic decline caused by war, the trade and credit embargoes, falling prices for Nicaragua's exports, and disruptions in production accompanying the partial socialization of the economy. Moreover, the government's commitment to preserving the private sector required it periodically to crack down on the working class by prohibiting strikes, controlling wages, and taking other measures that contradicted its program of redistribution.

Although the Contras never threatened to defeat the Nicaraguan government, the expense of fighting the war, in addition to the cost in lives, devastated the Sandinistas' efforts to improve the material conditions of the majority and inevitably wore down the initially high levels of popular enthusiasm for the FSLN. The inability to deliver, combined with the economic policies favoring the private sector, led to the development of a left critique aptly expressed by a representative of the Marxist-Leninist Popular Action Movement (Movimiento de Acción Popular Marxista-Leninista) in Congress, who charged that "The Contra-Sandinista war is nothing but a smoke screen to allow both sides to screw the proletariat."[7]

After a decade, the Nicaraguan Revolution had assumed an identity of its own. Led primarily by Marxists, it was an anti-imperialist but capitalist revolution anchored in the support of the lower and middle classes. At the 10th anniversary of the Sandinista victory, Nicaragua appeared to be evolving toward the model of Mexico after its 1910 revolution rather than toward the Cuban model. In contrast to the Mexican case, however, the FSLN leadership submitted its accomplishments and its continuance in power to the test of fair and open elections.

The End of the Sandinista Revolution

The 1990 election was a referendum on the decade of Sandinista governance. Originally scheduled for November 1990, it took place instead in February. The 1987 Central American Peace Accord had bound all signatories to seek national reconciliation by ceasing hostilities, ending aid to guerrillas fighting other governments, and holding free elections. Constantly pressured by the Reagan administration, which continued by all possible means to sabotage any peace that would leave the Sandinistas in power, the Ortega government moved much faster than any other to meet the conditions of the accord so as to end the long, debilitating war and begin rebuilding. Thus it agreed to hold elections, in which repatriated Contras would participate, nine months ahead of the date stipulated in the new constitution.

The election took place under the cloud of massive U.S. intervention. Unconcerned about the glaring electoral fraud and irregularities common to many Latin American countries recently demonstrated in the 1988 Mexican election, the United States held Nicaragua to a higher standard of electoral purity—guaranteed by thousands of international observers—than some U.S. entities could claim. In addition, Washington openly financed the opposition's campaign with at least $7.7 million from the congressionally funded National Endowment for Democracy and covertly spent at least $5 million more, for a total investment of a minimum of $8.50 per voter.[8] Following the pattern set during the Reagan administration, President George H. W. Bush announced shortly before the election that a Sandinista victory, even though certified as fair, would not be enough to relax U.S. sanctions: nothing short of a change of government would satisfy Washington.

The election results proved the polls wrong, and by a large margin. Violeta Barrios de Chamorro, widow of slain publisher Pedro Joaquín Chamorro and a member of the first post-Somoza government, was the presidential candidate of the National Opposition Union (Unión Nacional Opositora, UNO)—a broad coalition of 14 parties ranging from conservative to Communist. She received 54.7 percent of the vote to 40.8 for the FSLN candidate, President Daniel Ortega. UNO won 51 seats in Congress, the FSLN 39, and independents 2.

The election results revealed the success of Reagan's policy of wearing Nicaragua down through war and economic blockade. The impoverishment of an already poor country, the death toll of some 50,000 in the Contra war—a ratio of dead to total population approximately 75 times greater than U.S. losses in Vietnam—and the unpopularity of the military draft necessitated by the war eventually proved more compelling to the population than did their loyalty to the group that had played the leading role in ridding them of Somoza. Just as surely as if the U.S. Marines had invaded or the CIA had orchestrated a coup, the Reagan policy brought down the FSLN government. As Fidel Castro observed, Daniel Ortega had allowed himself to be maneuvered into playing by Washington's rules—a fatal error born of desperation. Ortega explained the FSLN defeat by saying that "The Nicaraguan people went to vote with a pistol pointed at their heads."[9]

Notes

1. Omar Cabezas, *Fire from the Mountain: The Making of a Sandinista*, trans. Kathleen Weaver (New York: Crown, 1985), 210.

2. Argentine urban guerrillas assassinated Somoza in Asunción in September 1980 by blowing up his automobile with a bazooka.

3. Sergio Ramírez, *Adiós Muchachos: A Memoir of the Sandinista Revolution*, trans. Stacey Alba D. Skar (Durham, NC: Duke University Press, 2012), 35–36.

4. Ramírez, *Adiós Muchachos*, 93.

5. E. Bradford Burns, *At War in Nicaragua: The Reagan Doctrine and the Politics of Nostalgia* (New York: Harper & Row, 1987), 32.

6. Burns, *At War*, 35.

7. Interview with Deputy Carlos Cuadras by Robert J. Alexander and the author, June 22, 1988.

8. Part of the U.S. funding went to ostensibly independent but clearly UNO-affiliated groups. Note that foreign funding of political campaigns in the United States is prohibited by law.

9. *El País* (Madrid), April 25, 1990, 15.

PART 5

The Reaction

CHAPTER TEN

State Terrorism in South America

The wave of revolutionary activity spreading from Cuba spawned a potent reaction across Latin America. Castro's rejection of electoral democracy and his embrace of Communism, with the resulting elimination of civil and political rights, disappointed many Latin Americans who applauded the changes in Cuban society and the island's liberation from U.S. domination. Latin America's wealthy and privileged were keenly aware of the fate of their Cuban counterparts, who lost their property and status and opted for exile over life under socialism. Latin American military officers observed with grave concern the dissolution of the Cuban national military and its replacement with Castro's own Rebel Armed Forces. Thus the same Cuban Revolution that mobilized many for change engendered in other segments of the population an equally strong determination to fight against the spread of Cuban-style revolution—whether to prevent the eclipse of the civil and political rights suppressed in Cuba; to preserve their wealth, privileges, and way of life; or both.

The rise of revolutionary movements in the wake of the Cuban Revolution had a destabilizing effect on Latin America's predominantly elected, civilian governments and compromised their ability to maintain order and preserve their citizens' security. The result in many countries was military intervention. The armed forces had traditionally played dual roles. Their primary role, according to constitutions and laws, was national defense, which under the influence of National Security Doctrine came to mean defense against the internal threat posed by Marxists and other "subversives." Their other role involved politics. At times, ambitious and self-serving officers—such as Rafael Trujillo in the Dominican Republic,

Anastasio Somoza García in Nicaragua, or Fulgencio Batista in Cuba—seized power in pursuit of their own ends; more frequently, officers took power to guide their countries through times of crisis. For example, the militaries seized power in virtually every country between 1930 and 1932, when the Great Depression caused severe economic dislocations, social tensions, and political instability that existing governments were unable to handle. The crisis created by the Cuban Revolution was far greater: to the elites, it was an existential threat that warranted extreme measures, including repression that in some countries rose to the level of state terrorism.

The New Military Regimes

The armed forces overthrew civilian governments in several countries in the early 1960s in order to contain the mobilizations precipitated by the Cuban Revolution. But the Brazilian military's 1964 coup against the Goulart government marked a change in patterns of military governance: the Brazilian armed forces pioneered the development of a new type of regime tailored to the era of the Cuban Revolution. The primary purpose of the new military government was to make Brazil immune to revolution, and its main instruments were political purification and economic development. In Chile and Uruguay, the countries with Latin America's strongest constitutionalist traditions, the armed forces seized power in 1973 to erect states similar to the Brazilian one. With the 1976 coup in Argentina, over two-thirds of South America's people lived under extremely repressive military regimes just 15 years after President John F. Kennedy predicted the demise of the "strong man" in Latin America.

Underlying the rise of the new South American military regimes, and common among Latin American military institutions in the 1960s, was the National Security Doctrine derived from the Cold War and the Cuban Revolution. With the shift of emphasis in the Inter-American Military System from external to internal threats, Latin American officers began to study social and economic conditions in their own countries as a supplement to the traditional curriculum geared to external defense. Armed with this new knowledge gained in schools such as Brazil's Superior War College (Escola Superior de Guerra) and Peru's Center for Advanced Military Studies (Centro de Altos Estudios Militares, CAEM), the armed forces set out to insulate their countries against the threat of revolution. National security required rapid economic development to eliminate the poverty upon which revolutionaries preyed. More importantly, with the primary exception of Peru's officers, who pursued a different course, the armed forces embraced the notion that national security also required the elimination of Marxists and other "subversives" and the destruction of electoral democracies that allowed these elements to participate, even thrive, in national politics. This would then permit the forced political reeducation of the populace to root out all ideas of Marxism and its credo of class conflict. The patriotic mission of the armed forces would be complete only when the country had been thoroughly immunized against revolution.

The Brazilian, Uruguayan, Chilean, and Argentine military regimes of the 1960s through the 1980s were shaped according to national circumstances, and all had antecedents that linked them to the traditional military regimes common throughout the history of republican Latin America. However, these regimes shared important characteristics that set them apart from the standard military government and defined a discrete regime prototype. All four were established to combat forces unleashed or movements accelerated by the Cuban Revolution: Goulart and the mobilized lower classes in Brazil, urban guerrillas in Uruguay and Argentina, and a Marxist-dominated government propelled into office by surging demands for revolutionary change in Chile. All were governments of the armed forces as institutions rather than military-supported personal or clique dictatorships—although General Augusto Pinochet gained great personal power within the framework of the Chilean military government. The four regimes sought to promote rapid economic growth, with mixed results. All employed civilian technocrats, who supposedly operated independently of political pressures, to direct their economies. They were stridently anticommunist and, of course, anti-Castro. These regimes were committed, like the Peruvian armed forces, to remaining in office as long as it took to make their countries revolution resistant. Finally, these military dictatorships rejected any constraints on their powers of repression, becoming terrorist states.

Terrorism comes in two basic forms: terrorism against the state and terrorism by the state. Based on recent experience, we tend to think of terrorism as actions against states perpetrated by groups such as the Basque separatist Euskadi Ta Askatasuna (ETA), the Irish Republican Army (IRA), Al-Qaeda, and the Islamic State in Iraq and Syria (ISIS). Both forms of terrorism share essential characteristics. One of the broader, more inclusive definitions of terrorism comes from Frederick H. Gareau:

> Terrorism consists of deliberate acts of a physical and/or psychological nature perpetrated on select groups of victims. Its intent is to mold the thinking and behavior not only of these targeted groups, but more

importantly, of larger sectors of society that identify [with] or share the view and aspirations of the targeted groups or who might easily be led to do so. The intent of the terrorists is to intimidate or coerce both groups by causing them intense fear, anxiety, apprehension, panic, dread, and/ or horror.[1]

Terrorism against the state is designed to force the targeted government to change its policies, to overthrow that government, or even to destroy the state. The intent of terrorism carried out by the state is to eliminate people considered actual or potential enemies of the regime and to marginalize those not eliminated through creating intense fear. In Latin America, the enemies of the regime were the Marxists and other "subversives" who challenged the established order, whether by arms or by political means.

The Brazilian Military in Power, 1964–1985

When the Brazilian armed forces overthrew President João Goulart in March 1964, it was not immediately evident that a new model of military governance was in the making. The government of Marshal Humberto Castelo Branco (1964–1967) set out to correct what it considered Goulart's mistaken economic policies and to cleanse the political system of dangerous elements. But within a short time the government was using a new term, "manipulated democracy," to describe and defend its increasingly profound reshaping of the political system and the economy. By 1969, with the accession of the third of Brazil's five military presidents, the government had become an undisguised dictatorship using terrorism against its citizens as a means of retaining power and implementing policy—the model for the new style of military regime.

The first five years of military rule were dominated by the moderate faction of the armed forces, which sought to govern within the framework of civilian institutions, but on the military's terms. The pattern from 1964 through 1968, however, was the progressive stripping away of the substance of popular participation in the face of continuing civilian resistance to the military's policies. Institutional Act no. 1 of April 1964 reaffirmed the validity of the 1946 constitution, then modified the document by calling for congressional election of the president, enhancing presidential powers vis-à-vis Congress and the states, and empowering the president to suspend citizens' political rights for 10 years and remove office holders for subversion or corruption. Under this act the military's candidate, Castelo Branco, was elected, hundreds of leftist and moderate politicians lost political rights and office, and the government took over labor

unions and outlawed the peasant leagues that had threatened to destabilize Brazil before the military coup.

This manipulation of the political system might have secured the desired
compliance were it not for the government's economic policies. These featured austerity measures to fight inflation and the reopening of Brazil to
virtually unrestricted foreign investment, underpinned by a guarantee
against expropriation of U.S. investments. With strikes banned, wages controlled, and government spending on social services sharply reduced, real
wages fell precipitously, unemployment increased, and the subsistence poor
experienced a shrinking margin of survival. These economic policies,
combined with a normal dislike for military rule, fueled a resistance that
drove the military hard-liners to demand firmer measures and eventually
to assume complete control of government.

Institutional Act no. 2 of October 1965, the next step toward military
absolutism, was a response to state elections held earlier in that month.
Having issued a new electoral code, regulated parties, and extended the
purge of politicians, the government expected its candidates to win easily.
Their defeat, a failure of "manipulated democracy," elicited further tightening under the October act, which enabled the president to dissolve Congress
and rule by decree, banned existing political parties, packed the supreme
court, and remanded those charged with subversion to military courts.
Institutional Act no. 3 of February 1966 ended popular election of governors and mayors of state capitals.

Reflecting the struggle between moderates and hard-liners, Castelo
Branco still tried to salvage a semblance of democracy by reviving parties
and creating a two-party system consisting of a pro-government party (the
"yes sir" party) with a majority in Congress and a minority opposition party
(the "yes" party) whose members were inoffensive enough to have survived
the purges. Most changes contained in the institutional acts and presidential decrees were incorporated in the new 1967 constitution, along with
press restrictions and a sweeping internal security law that stripped away
individual liberties. Marshal Artur da Costa e Silva, who succeeded Castelo
Branco in March 1967, thus entered office armed with what appeared to be
sufficient legal authority to rule absolutely behind a facade of constitutionalism and civilian participation. However, 1968 brought Brazilian involvement in the international year of student rebellion and a wave of illegal
strikes protesting the continuing decline in real income. The final victory of
the hard-liners over the advocates of manipulation came in December 1968
when, despite severe government pressure, the normally pliant Congress
refused to waive the immunity of an opposition deputy who had offended
the armed forces. This display of independence and intractability led

to Institutional Act no. 5 of December 1968, which suspended the 1967 constitution, dissolved Congress and the state legislatures, tightened censorship, eliminated habeas corpus, and cancelled the political rights of thousands more Brazilians.

When he took over as president in November 1969, after Costa e Silva had suffered a disabling stroke, General Emílio Garrastazú Médici (1969–1974) inherited a state apparatus with powers unprecedented in republican Brazil, even under Getúlio Vargas' fascist-inspired Estado Nôvo (1937–1945). With the beginning of urban guerrilla warfare in 1969 in response to the incremental elimination of legal means of opposition, Médici found ample opportunity to use the tools of repression at his disposal. In addition to attacking the guerrillas, the government followed the strategy—later developed into a fine and deadly art in other state terrorist regimes—of focusing repression on actual and potential supporters of the guerrillas to dissuade them from active involvement and thereby to isolate the guerrillas. Arbitrary arrest and detention, indeterminate jail sentences, torture, and assassination became standard instruments of government policy in the fight against subversion; in addition to its own police and military agents, government-sanctioned or -condoned private death squads carried out the same work. The government was now able to operate with no limitations on its use of repression, except the persistent but largely ineffectual pressure that the Catholic Church could muster. Because the guerrillas were defeated relatively easily, the Brazilian military government did not employ its repressive powers to the full extent possible. Yet in their quest for national security, the successive governments since 1964 had created the first fully developed antirevolutionary terrorist state.

Accompanying the rise of a naked military dictatorship and, to the outside world, partially masking the repressive nature of the regime was the Brazilian economic "miracle." Beginning in 1967, the technocratic economists charged with promoting rapid development had replaced the initial anti-inflation austerity plan with an aggressive policy of state-stimulated growth. Although based on private foreign and domestic capital and a contraction of state investment, the policy directed by economist Antônio Delfim Neto was managed by state controls over prices, wages, credit, and inputs. The result of the initial dampening of inflation followed by rapid expansion of production was a period of spectacular economic growth, culminating in 1969–1974 with an average annual increase of over 10 percent in the gross domestic product.

The Brazilian miracle, highly touted by the government and widely admired abroad, had its dark side. A disproportionate amount of the growth took place in the industrial and coffee-exporting southeast, already the country's wealthiest area, while the impoverished northeast continued to stagnate. A major share of growth took place among the transnational corporations that flooded post-1964 Brazil. With growth concentrated in capital-intensive industries, unemployment rose significantly, and the wealthy benefited from income redistribution in their favor during the miracle.

The administration of General Ernesto Geisel (1974–1979) was essentially a continuation of the terrorist state with a few modifications. Having promised a *distensão*, or gradual opening toward broader participation, Geisel reined in the use of repression and tolerated some public discussion and criticism, but did not hesitate to use the full range of authoritarian power when necessary. During his presidency the miracle began to fall apart. Oil-importing Brazil was hurt by the Organization of Petroleum Exporting Countries' (OPEC's) pricing policies beginning in 1973; recession in the industrial countries hindered exports; and the easy credit of the early and mid-1970s began to take its toll as Brazil faced a huge foreign debt with dwindling resources. Opponents of the regime found a powerful, if inconsistent, ally in the Carter administration, whose emphasis on human rights put Washington and Brasília on a collision course. Students, workers, and even businesspeople began to show signs of unrest late in the Geisel presidency, and in the climate of greater tolerance Geisel allowed an opposition presidential candidate to run against the man he had chosen to conclude the political opening.

When he took office in March 1979, General João Baptista Figueiredo publicly expressed the armed forces' desire to return to the barracks. One of his first acts was to sign an amnesty covering political crimes committed since 1964 by the government as well as by the opposition. The subsequent gradual dismantling of the terrorist state under Baptista Figueiredo reflected several factors. The military had failed in its goal of lifting the country out of poverty, and prospects for rekindling the brief miracle were dim. Despite some impressive economic growth, Brazil's basic problems of poverty, social injustice, illiteracy, poor health, and regional disparities had grown worse under military rule. The regime had also failed to develop public support beyond some of the privileged groups; hence, it could govern only through the use or threat of repression. Yet at a point 20 years after Castro took power in Cuba and 15 years after the overthrow of Goulart, the armed forces could take comfort in what appeared to be the reduced threat of revolution in Brazil and in Latin America outside of Central America.

Assessing its future, the officer corps opted to rid itself of the increasingly unpopular and unrewarding task of governance. Added to this calculation, some military leaders undoubtedly continued to embrace the older view that the military's political role should be limited to its traditional moderating power—the correction or removal of offending or ineffectual governments, not the right to govern. The return to civilian rule was a phased-in process lasting almost a decade, beginning with the restoration of party rights and elections for state governors in 1982, won by opposition groups. The 1985 presidential election would install the first nonmilitary president in 21 years, but fearing the consequences of a free and direct popular election, the administration prescribed an indirect election procedure to ensure acceptable results. With the election of opposition candidate Tancredo Neves, who was incapacitated before taking office, and the accession of his vice president, José Sarney, Brazil was ready for the final steps: a new constitution, approved in 1988, and the first direct presidential election in three decades. With the inauguration of President Fernando Collor de Mello in March 1990, Brazil returned to civilian constitutional government after 26 years of direct or indirect military rule.

Military rule in Brazil involved extensive, institutionalized human rights violations. A report on torture secretly compiled by the Archdiocese of São Paulo and published in 1985 did not attempt to quantify the extent of torture, but quoted a former military officer: "Torture was an essential part of the military justice system in Brazil."[2] It also identified 242 clandestine torture centers and 444 individual torturers. Finally overcoming resistance from the military, the government established a National Truth Commission in 2012 to investigate human rights under the dictatorship. Its December 2014 report listed 434 persons murdered or disappeared and named 377 regime figures implicated in human rights violations, including extensive torture. One of the tortured was then-President Dilma Rousseff, who delivered the commission's report to the public with tears in her eyes.

The Uruguayan Military Regime, 1973–1985

The Uruguayan military regime that took power in the aftermath of the struggle against the Tupamaros had much in common with its Brazilian counterpart. Its mission was to institute major changes in political life and in the economy in order to make the country resistant to revolution, but in practice it proved unwilling to alter the economy and use the degree of repression necessary to make a clean break with the past. After only seven years in power, the armed forces began searching for the means of extricating themselves from the government, and the transition to civilian rule was complete by 1985.

The militarization of Uruguay was a gradual process, beginning with the decision of President Jorge Pacheco Areco in September 1971 to place the armed forces directly in charge of fighting the Tupamaros. After a year of intense counterinsurgency actions under a state of internal war, the Tupamaros were essentially defeated, but convinced of the need to sanitize Uruguay's liberal political system to prevent a recurrence of destabilization and insurrection, the military increased its demands for power. Thus a national security council, chaired by the country's ranking military officer, was created as a new governmental entity in February 1973. Siding with the armed forces against the politicians, President Juan María Bordaberry dissolved Congress in June and replaced it with an appointed, military-dominated council of state. The appointment of military officers to administer state enterprises, ministries, and other agencies furthered the militarization of the state. In 1976 the military replaced Bordaberry with another civilian figurehead, Aparicio Méndez.

The "institutionalization of the revolutionary process" continued.[3] It drew from the Brazilian model progressively to strip the hybrid military–civilian government of all substance of citizen participation by curtailing parties, taking over trade unions, and establishing strict censorship. "Institutional Acts" gave a legal patina to policies directly contradicting the constitution, whose integrity the military claimed to be preserving through its stewardship. The institutional acts provided the armed forces a strong formal role in government, infringed the autonomy of the courts, and suspended the political rights of some 15,000 mainline as well as left politicians for 15 years. Education came under military control, prompting a university dean to remark, "We must abolish research since it is harmful to education."[4] With this groundwork laid, the military routinized arbitrary arrest and sentencing, torture, and murder of dissidents and suspects.

The Uruguayan military's plan to reverse a two-decade economic decline was to force the economy to become competitive internationally through the standard World Bank and International Monetary Fund (IMF) formula of tariff reductions, privatization of the huge state sector, and a decrease in government spending and direction of the economy. Yet despite possessing the power to do so, the government was unwilling to administer a "shock" to the economy, keeping instead a broad range of price controls until 1979 and lowering tariffs incrementally and selectively to ease the transition to a market economy. Although modest improvements occurred in various economic indicators, Uruguay experienced no "miracle" of the Brazilian or the Chilean type, and a 1982 crisis reversed the positive trend. Meanwhile, social costs were high: real wages fell significantly, unemployment doubled, and social services contracted.

Just as the beginnings of the Uruguayan military regime were gradual and unspectacular, so was its end. Unable to rid itself of all of the country's traditional political values, and perhaps badly miscalculating public sentiment, the military called for a referendum on institutionalizing the political system it had devised. In that November 1980 election, 57 percent of the voters pronounced against the new regime, launching a four-year process of military withdrawal. The traditional political parties were reauthorized in 1982, and elections were scheduled for 1984. General strikes and a broad popular mobilization in 1984 even convinced the military to legalize the left and allow most of its candidates to run for office. After 12 years, the elections returned Uruguay to civilian rule in 1985 under the leadership of President Julio Sanguinetti of the Colorado Party.

A study published in 1989 named 165 persons who were disappeared by the Uruguayan military regime or by the cooperative state terrorist regime in neighboring Argentina, along with 102 individuals killed. It did not attempt to quantify torture, but quoted a military man as saying "One can say that everyone arrested in Uruguay is tortured. There is no one who is not tortured."[5] The government belatedly established a truth commission, the Commission for Peace (Comisión Para la Paz), in 2000, but its 2003 report found concrete evidence on only 38 disappeared persons.

State Terrorism in Chile: The Pinochet Dictatorship, 1973–1990

Despite the Chilean armed forces' history of nonintervention in politics—a tradition that set them apart from most Latin American militaries—few Chileans were surprised by the September 11, 1973, coup given the extreme polarization, the hardship imposed by the *gremios*' strikes, and the rise of violence. However, their expectation that the military would follow the standard Latin American coup script—deposing the government with minimal force, exiling its leading personnel, stabilizing the country, and overseeing elections to restore civilian governance after a year or two—was a serious miscalculation.

The coup was shockingly brutal. When President Allende refused to leave the historic La Moneda presidential palace, the air force strafed and bombed it, burning a major symbol of Chilean democracy. After ordering his staff to leave, Allende shot himself to death. The newly formed military junta decreed a state of siege befitting "a state or time of war," and the air force representative on the junta declared it necessary to extirpate the "Marxist cancer."[6] The junta dissolved the political parties, closed Congress, purged union and university leadership, and imposed strict censorship, thereby eliminating most potential sources of opposition. The military cashiered pro-Allende officers and threatened the careers of those who failed to demonstrate sufficient commitment to the unfolding mission of cleansing Chile of all traces of Marxism and subversion. It soon became clear that the military expected to hold power indefinitely and use all means necessary to eliminate the threat of revolution, permanently and completely.

Allende supporters and collaborators, whose political beliefs and affiliations had been perfectly legal until the moment of the coup, became ex post facto criminals and enemies of the state. The junta ordered hundreds of persons associated with the Allende government to turn themselves in; having done nothing illegal from their perspective, many complied to clear their names and were never seen again. Massive roundups of UP supporters filled military installations, soccer stadiums, and other improvised detention sites where hundreds were tortured and killed. Hastily formed military tribunals sentenced scores of enemies of the new state to death without a semblance of due process. In rural areas, former landowners settled scores with their former workers who had acquired hacienda lands through Frei's and Allende's agrarian reform.

Despite the censorship, reports and photographs depicting bodies lying in streets and floating in rivers, long lines of prisoners chained together, and a grim General Pinochet looking sinister in dark glasses circulated internationally. Whereas the Nixon administration embraced the new regime and quickly extended diplomatic recognition, the United Nations and governments around the world condemned the coup and the extreme violence that accompanied it.

The Nixon administration's support of the coup and the state terrorist regime that emerged from it resonated far beyond Chile's borders. It sent a clear signal to all of Latin America that regimes employing repression, even state terrorism, could count on U.S. support. It was a green light to Latin America's right wing and armed forces to use all means necessary to eradicate the left and, with that, to erase the advances that workers and, in some countries, *campesinos* had made through lengthy struggles. The ramifications of U.S. approval of Chilean state terrorism were soon felt throughout the region, including in Operation Condor, an armed alliance of several repressive South American regimes that hunted and killed leftists across international borders.

The junta's March 1974 "Declaration of Principles" unveiled the outlines of the military's design for a new Chile. It declared that the military regime "does not fear or hesitate to declare itself anti-Marxist." The armed forces would need to hold power indefinitely "because the task of reconstructing the country morally, institutionally, and materially requires profound and prolonged action." To accomplish this multifaceted reconstruction, it would be "absolutely necessary to change the mentality of Chileans" by replacing Marxism and its credo of class struggle with the values of family, class harmony, conservative Catholicism, and Chilean nationalism.[7] On the economic front, the regime aimed to replace state direction of the economy as developed in the 1930s and 1940s and deepened under presidents Frei and Allende with the free market model taught by Milton Friedman at the University of Chicago and to turn economic policy over to Friedman's Chilean students, the "Chicago Boys."

The Directorate of National Intelligence (Dirección de Inteligencia Nacional, DINA), a secret police composed of military, police, and civilians that operated without constraints, was the primary instrument for eradicating the Chilean left. Run by General Manuel Contreras, the DINA originated in an extremist faction of the army that enthusiastically embraced National Security Doctrine and countersubversive warfare. Pinochet used his close relationship with Contreras and the DINA to maneuver in only 15 months from head of the junta to president of the republic; although the junta officially governed throughout the lengthy dictatorship, Pinochet's unrivalled power made him the de facto ruler of Chile.

The DINA established secret detention centers where abducted leftists were tortured, often under the supervision of medical doctors, and sometimes killed. Villa Grimaldi, a confiscated estate on the outskirts of Santiago, was the largest and most notorious of the centers. Gladys Díaz, a survivor, recalled her experience in Villa Grimaldi.

> "Sometimes it's electricity; sometimes drugs . . . the submarine, when they stick your head in sewer water and they leave you there until you almost drown, they take you out, they stick you in again; the 'telephone' that breaks your—I have a broken eardrum. . . . When there wasn't physical torture there was psychological torture. . . . They put on tapes of voices of children to make me think that my son had been captured. The defense mechanisms that a person uses in certain extreme situations are infinite. . . . I sometimes dreamed about beautiful things—that gave me some consolation. I remember having awakened to the sound of the warbling of . . . a little bird that was outside, and how I was able to keep the sound of that bird's singing in my ears for days, enjoying it."[8]

The DINA's priority targets were the underground operatives of the Communist and Socialist parties and the Movement of the Revolutionary Left (MIR). These clandestine units had been formed at the time of the coup to retain their parties' presence in the country in the face of the murder or exile of most of the left's leadership. By 1976, the last remnants of the left underground had been eradicated, and Pinochet's control over the country was absolute.

At the beginning of the dictatorship, Chile had no human rights organizations to defend people against state terrorism. The Catholic Church quickly stepped up, improvising emergency services for victims and their families in conjunction with other religious groups and international humanitarian agencies. In 1976, the Archdiocese of Santiago established its Vicariate of Solidarity (Vicaría de la Solidaridad), which became the largest and most active of a dozen human rights organizations that developed under difficult circumstances. Despite its unstinting efforts, the human rights movement was unable to rein in the repression, but did contribute to easing it in some cases while providing aid and solace to victims of torture and families of the murdered and disappeared. The Vicaría's lawyers filed some 9,000 writs of habeas corpus with the courts in attempts to free arrested persons; all but a handful were denied by judges intimidated by or sympathetic to the regime. Eventually, a decade after the dictatorship's end, the Vicaría's court filings proved invaluable for bringing hundreds of former repressors to justice.

The dictatorship's halcyon years were 1977 through 1981. After severely contracting from the Chicago Boys' radical policies, the economy began to boom and unemployment declined. With the underground opposition eliminated, repression was reduced but not eliminated. Despite the steadfast anti-regime activism of exiles spread throughout the world, international opposition to the regime was largely ineffectual. The 1976 election of U.S. President Jimmy Carter, who embraced human rights as a determinant of foreign policy, ended the strong U.S. support the regime had enjoyed under Nixon and his national security advisor, Henry Kissinger. However, by making superficial changes, including replacing the notorious DINA with a nearly identical secret police under a different name and leader, Pinochet avoided serious confrontation with Carter. In 1980, Pinochet enacted a new constitution that confirmed his dictatorial powers for an eight-year term, with the possibility of extending his rule for another eight years, and configured a "protected democracy" for a distant post-Pinochet Chile.

The superheated Chilean economy began to falter in late 1981 as bankruptcies multiplied and unemployment again mushroomed. Spontaneous protests in the Santiago *poblaciones* (slums) soon gave way to organized demonstrations as leaders of the outlawed political parties forged alliances and pushed to force Pinochet out of office before the end of his eight-year term. The appearance of the first active opposition since 1976 brought heightened repression. Then, in response to a failed 1986 assassination attempt against Pinochet, the regime unleashed more severe repression that forced the opposition to abandon its quest to drive Pinochet from office and to focus instead on defeating him on his own terms: at the ballot box. The 1980 constitution called for a plebiscite before the end of Pinochet's eight years on whether to give him or a designated successor another eight-year term.

As 1988 approached, the neighboring state terrorist regimes in Argentina, Uruguay, and Brazil had ended, and President Ronald Reagan's initial support had waned over concerns that a rigged plebiscite could reignite the opposition movement and bring a new leftist government to power. Moreover, recognizing that most of the formerly Marxist left had embraced European-style social democracy and were no threat to the Chicago Boys' economic model, many of Pinochet's supporters pushed for a clean plebiscite. Facing these pressures, despite harassing the opposition, Pinochet was forced to conduct a relatively fair election. A broad alliance of 16 center and left parties formed the Alliance of Parties for the NO (Concertación de Partidos por el NO), campaigned vigorously, and defeated the overconfident dictator by a margin of 55 to 43 percent. Fellow junta members had to restrain an enraged Pinochet from annulling the outcome. But despite the electoral loss, Pinochet and the military tightly controlled the transition to civilian government.

Given the plebiscite's outcome, the constitution dictated that an election should be held in 1989 and a president and new Congress inaugurated on March 11, 1990, 16.5 years to the day after the coup that derailed Chilean democracy. Supported by the same broad coalition that defeated Pinochet, Christian Democrat Patricio Aylwin won 55 percent of the vote against two right-wing candidates. The Concertación also won control of the Chamber of Deputies; but due to the electoral code that skewed the vote in favor of the right and the presence of nine Pinochet appointees in the 47-member Senate, the Concertación faced certain rejection of any laws unacceptable to the right and to Pinochet himself, who had extended his commandership of the army, and thus his power, for eight more years, to 1998. This was the protected democracy that Pinochet bequeathed Chile.

In his introduction to the English-language edition of the report of the Truth and Reconciliation Commission formed under the Aylwin government, human rights lawyer José Zalaquett wrote that Chile experienced "an intense political repression which resulted in political killings and 'disappearances,' the imprisonment or exile of countless Chileans, and the widespread use of torture. These massive human rights violations shocked the world."[9] The commission found that the dictatorship had killed or disappeared over 3,200 people, a number that has risen with the passage of time. Subsequent investigations established that the regime had tortured at least 38,000 individuals. Another 200,000 people saved their lives by going into exile. Such was the harvest of state terrorism in Chile.

The Dirty War in Argentina, 1976–1983

As noted earlier, Juan Perón's populist presidency (1946–1955) left a legacy of an irreconcilably divided country that was virtually ungovernable. The anti-Peronists, anchored in the armed forces and the elites, sought to marginalize Perón's powerful bloc of supporters, while the Peronists demanded that their leader be allowed to return from his forced exile in Spain and run again for the presidency. Short-lived military and civilian governments succeeded one another after 1955, until by 1973 the radicalized Peronist labor movement and youth organizations backed by the urban guerrillas had become powerful enough to convince the military that only Perón's return could restore stability.

Tacitly acknowledging the failure of the military's strategy of marginalizing the Peronists, General Alejandro Lanusse called elections in which Perón's party, but not the aging icon himself, could participate. After Perón stand-in Héctor Cámpora was elected, he resigned, and Perón then was elected president in September 1973 with 62 percent of the vote. The former president's return to power, however, did little to quell the guerrilla violence and general turmoil. His death less than a year later left his widow and vice president, Isabel Perón, in nominal charge. The next two years witnessed a sharp increase in guerrilla actions and right-wing armed response led by the Argentine Anticommunist Alliance (Alianza Anticomunista Argentina, AAA), resulting in an alarming rise in the death toll on both sides, as well as among Uruguayan and Chilean leftists who had fled their countries after the 1973 coups. As violence escalated and the government's power deteriorated, Argentina appeared to be disintegrating.

The military overthrew the tottering government of Isabel Perón on March 24, 1976. Army commander General Jorge Rafael Videla and navy commander Admiral Emilio Massera, leaders of the governing junta, initially appeared to be moderates who had acted selflessly to save the *patria* from the guerrilla violence and disorder that characterized Isabel Perón's inept presidency. Accustomed to frequent coups and military governments, many Argentines welcomed the military coup as a reprieve. According to the *Buenos Aires Herald*, "The entire nation responded with relief. . . . This was not just another coup, but a rescue operation."[10] But in explaining The Process of National Reorganization (El Proceso de Reorganización Nacional), as the commanders named their regime, Videla said ominously that the coup signified "the final closing of a historical cycle and the opening of a new one."[11] Even as they introduced *El Proceso* to their countrymen, the commanders unleashed a lethal assault on civil society.

As in the other new-style military regimes, state terrorism in Argentina was not only a response to the threat of revolution, but also the instrument for imposing a final solution to the problem of Marxism and subversion. From the pinnacle of their power in 1973, the urban guerrillas had been weakened by police and military crackdowns and the work of the AAA, and by the time of the military takeover their ranks had thinned substantially. Reflecting this reality, two months prior to the coup General Videla had written that the guerrillas were "absolutely impotent," had "little fighting capability," were unable to "reach a military level," and remained capable of only isolated attacks on the authorities.[12] At no time after the coup were the guerrillas a threat to hold territory or overthrow the government, and their power continued to decline until the People's Revolutionary Army (ERP) ordered its surviving cadres to abandon Argentina in 1977, and the Montoneros followed suit two years later. Yet the Dirty War went on, as the military used an increasingly fictitious struggle against the guerrillas as cover for its project of permanently ending the threat of revolution by physically eliminating Marxists and "subversives," their supporters, and anyone who might fall under their influence, through state terrorism.

The Argentine military commanders had decided prior to their coup to install state terrorism to eradicate the left. Like their counterparts in Brazil, Uruguay, and Chile, they closed Congress; appointed military governors; imposed censorship; and purged unions, universities, and other potential sources of opposition. But they had learned from the nearly universal denunciation of the Chilean coup and the violence that accompanied it that open, uncontrolled state terrorism carried a price in the form of international condemnation and sanctions. Thus, the Argentine military's primary method for eliminating the revolutionary threat was the disappearance.

The regime jailed, tortured, exiled, and murdered individuals whose bodies were recovered, but the Dirty War became synonymous with disappearances; the term "disappear" became a sinister transitive verb. By disappearing their victims, the military left neither arrest records nor corpses and thus enjoyed plausible deniability. Disappearance also served to intensify and prolong the general state of terror and discourage opposition to the regime; for as long as one's family member was missing rather than certified as dead, the family was neutralized, fearful that making waves would cause their loved one's death. In Chile, the brunt of state terrorism

ARGENTINA

Salta•

San Miguel
de Tucuman
•

Formosa•

Resistencia
•

•Posadas

Pacific
Ocean

Catamarca•

La Ribja•

Santo Tome•

Cordoba• Santa Fe•

Rio
Parana

San Juan•

•Parana

Mendoza•

•Resario

Mercedes•

Venado•
Tuerto

Buenos Aires
★

San Rafael•

Realico•

La Plata•

Rio de la Plata

Santa Rosa•

Bahia
•Blanca

•Mar del Plata

Zapala• •Neuquen

Viedma
•

•San Carlos de Bariloche

Rawson•

Atlantic
Ocean

•Comodoro Rivadavia

Las Heras

•Puerto Deseado

•Puerto Santa Cruz

•Rio Gallegos

Falkland
Islands

N

•Ushuaia

Tierra del
Fuego

was directed at leaders and militants of the Communist and Socialist parties and the MIR, and most nonaffiliated people were not targeted for heinous human rights violations. In Argentina, broad segments of the population were subject to torture, murder, and disappearance as the military's definitions of "subversives" and "enemies of the state" were quite elastic. For Videla, subversives were those who embraced "ideas contrary to our western, Christian civilization," and General Reynaldo Bignone considered them both "anti-fatherland" and agents of the "anti-Christ."[13] Having thus dehumanized its victims, the dictatorship recognized no legal or moral constraints on its power in its war against subversion. According to Lieutenant Colonel Hugo Pascarelli, "The fight in which we are engaged does not recognize moral limits; it is conducted beyond good or evil."[14]

General Ibérico Saint Jean, military governor of Buenos Aires Province, articulated his understanding of the Dirty War in the following terms: "First we will kill all the subversives, then we will kill their collaborators, then . . . their sympathizers, then . . . those who remain indifferent; and, finally, we will kill the timid."[15] General Luciano Menéndez phrased his approach to ending subversion in quantitative terms: "We are going to have to kill 50,000 people: 25,000 subversives, 20,000 sympathizers, and we will make 5,000 mistakes."[16] These leaders' ambitions and plans may have overstated the reach of state terrorism in Argentina, but they offer chilling insights into the thinking that underpinned the Dirty War.

The junta divided the country into large "zones," smaller "subzones," and even smaller "areas" and placed them under military or police command. Under general orders from the top, zone, subzone, and area commanders established task groups of between half a dozen and a dozen police and military personnel that operated semi-autonomously to terrorize the populace. Disappearances began with abductions at the victim's home or workplace, or even on the street. Abducted persons were not taken to police stations, where their detention would become a matter of public record, but to one of over 400 secret detention centers established around the country, whose existence could be and was consistently denied. Upon arrival at a facility, prisoners were assigned numbers and taken to the torture chamber, where they faced up to a week or more of intense physical and psychological torture. Then they were normally taken to a holding area where, typically, they were handcuffed and shackled in spaces so tiny they were called "*tubos*," or tubes, and subjected to ongoing physical and psychological abuse and degradation. The Naval Mechanics' School (Escuela de Mecánica de la Armada, ESMA) in Buenos Aires, known as the Argentine Auschwitz, was one of the largest and the most notorious of the secret detention centers; over 5,000 abducted persons were detained there, and few survived.

Two categories of captured individuals suffered particularly savage treatment. Pregnant women were removed from the *tubos* as their delivery time approached. After giving birth, they were separated from their babies and either killed outright or held for later disposal. The infants, along with false documentation, were given to military families and others favored by the regime. Jews suffered disproportionately because of their overrepresentation in some of the occupations and professions that the military considered hotbeds of subversion and because of virulent anti-Semitism in the military and the right in general. As a result, though constituting less than 2 percent of the Argentine population, Jews comprised approximately 10 percent of the disappeared. According to surviving witnesses, they suffered even greater dehumanization and humiliation than gentiles.

Prisoners in the secret detention centers were ranked on their perceived degree of dangerousness: potentially dangerous, dangerous, and extremely dangerous. Some of the "potentially dangerous" were sent to public prisons or freed, but almost all the others faced death. The most common means of execution were gunfire and throwing live, drugged prisoners into the ocean from aircraft; great pains were taken to prevent the bodies from being discovered. After some bodies washed up on the Uruguayan shore of the Río de la Plata, death flights simply went further out over the Atlantic Ocean to drop their victims.

At the time of the coup that established the dictatorship, Argentines had no defense against the reign of terror unleashed upon them. In marked contrast to Chile, the Catholic Church hierarchy failed to intervene in favor of victims; in fact, many of the bishops and archbishops supported the Dirty War, whereas numerous priests worked at their peril to aid victims and their families. The best-known Argentine human rights organization was the Mothers of the Plaza de Mayo (Madres de Plaza de Mayo), a group of women who first met making their dreary rounds of police stations, military bases, and morgues in search of their disappeared children. After failing in an attempt to petition junta leader Videla for information about their children, they settled into a routine of marching in the Plaza de Mayo in front of the presidential palace on Thursday afternoons, bearing placards with their children's photographs and the phrase "*¿donde están?*" (where are they?). These brave women were vilified and beaten, and some of them were murdered, but they persisted and became the face of resistance to state terrorism. Another human rights organization, the Center for Legal and Social Studies (Centro de Estudios Legales y Sociales, CELS) tried legal approaches to protect individuals. Like the Chilean Vicaría, CELS filed thousands of writs of habeas corpus that were rejected but which eventually became critical evidence in the later trials of hundreds of practitioners of state terrorism.

The Argentine military expected to hold power indefinitely, until its mission was completed, and thus made no provision for an eventual return to civilian government, but the regime began to unravel after four years. Largely through the efforts of President Jimmy Carter, the Inter-American Commission on Human Rights conducted an on-site investigation of disappearances in 1980. Its damning report, banned in Argentina but circulated clandestinely, demonstrated conclusively that the missing people were indeed victims of a government conspiracy—not "terrorists" killed in confrontations with police or who had fled the country, as the military consistently claimed. A severe economic contraction in 1981 sparked the beginnings of overt opposition. To rally public support for its faltering government, in 1982 the military invaded the Malvinas/Falkland Islands, claimed by Argentina but long occupied by Britain. The brief war was a disaster for Argentina and quickly eroded any lingering support for the dictatorship. Having proved inept at governing, managing the economy, and fighting a war, the military beat a hasty retreat to the barracks. After granting itself amnesty and publishing a final document justifying its actions as patriotic service that saved the country from Marxists and subversives, the military surrendered power to civilians. After nearly eight years of state terrorism, President Raúl Alfonsín of the moderate Unión Cívica Radical Party and a new Congress took office on December 10, 1983.

The new government established a truth commission, the National Commission on the Disappearance of Persons (Comisión Nacional Sobre la Desaparición de Personas, CONADEP), that became a model for truth commissions around the world. In its chilling report, *Nunca más* (Never Again), the commission made an unmistakable reference to the Holocaust: "Many of the episodes described here will be difficult to believe. That is because the men and women of our country have only known such horrors through chronicles from other latitudes." It also quoted President Alfonsín: "Thousands of persons were illegally deprived of their liberty, tortured and killed as a result of the application of the totalitarian Doctrine of National Security."[17] CONADEP documented 8,960 disappearances, but acknowledged that its count was far from complete due to time constraints and military obfuscation. Human rights organizations put the number of disappeared at 30,000.

Notes

1. Frederick H. Gareau, *State Terrorism and the United States: From Counterinsurgency War to the War on Terrorism* (London: Zed Books, 2004), 14.

2. Archdiocese of São Paulo, *Torture in Brazil: A Report by the Archdiocese of São Paulo*, trans. Jaime Wright (New York: Vintage Books, 1986), x.

3. Alain Rouquié, *The Military and the State in Latin America*, trans. Paul Sigmund (Berkeley: University of California Press, 1987), 252.

4. Rouquié, *The Military*, 256.

5. Servicio Paz y Justicia, Uruguay, *Uruguay nunca más: Human Rights Violations, 1972–1985*, trans. Elizabeth Hampsten (Philadelphia: Temple University Press, 1992), 79.

6. Thomas C. Wright, *State Terrorism in Latin America: Chile, Argentina, and International Human Rights* (Lanham, MD: Rowman & Littlefield, 2007), 52, 53.

7. Thomas G. Sanders, "Military Government in Chile," in *The Politics of Antipolitics: The Military in Latin America*, ed. Brian Loveman and Thomas M. Davies. (Lincoln: University of Nebraska Press, 1978), 274.

8. Thomas C. Wright and Rody Oñate, *Flight from Chile: Voices of Exile* (Albuquerque: University of New Mexico Press, 1998), 82.

9. *Chile. Report of the National Commission on Truth and Reconciliation*, trans. Phillip E. Berryman (Notre Dame, IN: University of Notre Dame Press, 1993), 7.

10. *Buenos Aires Herald*, March 25, 1976.

11. Brian Loveman and Thomas M. Davies, Jr., *The Politics of Antipolitics: The Military in Latin America*, revised and updated ed. (Wilmington, DE: Scholarly Resources, 1997), 160.

12. *Clarín* (Buenos Aires), January 31, 1976.

13. Marguerite Feitlowitz, *A Lexicon of Terror: Argentina and the Legacies of Torture*, revised and updated ed. (New York: Oxford University Press, 2011), 27.

14. Eduardo Luis Duhalde, *El estado terrorista argentino* (Barcelona: Editorial Argos Vergara, 1983), 79 (author's translation).

15. Feitlowitz, *Lexicon*, 32.

16. Paul Lewis, *Guerrillas and Generals: The "Dirty War" in Argentina* (Westport, CT: Praeger, 2002), 147.

17. CONADEP, *Nunca más: Informe de la Comisión Nacional sobre la Desaparición de Personas*, 15, 473 (author's translation).

CHAPTER ELEVEN

State Terrorism in Central America

Although sharing essential traits with state terrorism in the Southern Cone, the Central American phenomenon unfolded in a different context and assumed different characteristics. Guatemala and El Salvador were far less developed economically than Argentina, Uruguay, Chile, and Brazil. The colonial legacy of a rigid social hierarchy, while somewhat modified over the years, held firm: Both countries were still dominated by the traditional coffee oligarchies in alliance with the armed forces. Both had small middle classes and large, predominantly rural lower classes—mostly Maya Indian in Guatemala and primarily mestizo in El Salvador. The impact of the Cuban Revolution was relatively weak in Central America, but it did create demands for change that gave rise to guerrilla action in Guatemala and, initially, calls for economic and social reform through the electoral process in El Salvador. Rather than concede even limited change, the oligarchy—military alliance in Guatemala relied on state terrorism to preserve its monopoly of power and economic dominance. Some of the Salvadoran elites flirted with cosmetic reforms, but they also relied on their military allies to utilize state terrorism in defense of their interests.

A few points of comparison illuminate the similarities and distinctions among the state terrorist regimes in Central and South America. Far more people were murdered or disappeared in Guatemala and El Salvador than in Argentina or Chile, and the state killed or disappeared still fewer in Brazil and Uruguay. The terrorist governments of Argentina and El Salvador faced insurrections, more serious in El Salvador than in Argentina; the

Guatemalan government confronted a long-running but relatively weak armed opposition; and the Brazilian, Uruguayan, and Chilean terrorist governments faced no immediate threat of successful insurrection when they took power. Military dictatorships conducted the repression in South America, whereas in Guatemala and El Salvador it was primarily elected governments, often headed by military men, that directed, sanctioned, or acquiesced in terrorism by the armed forces and death squads. The South American terrorist regimes ended under mostly internal pressures, while their Central American counterparts ended through UN-brokered peace processes.

Another difference between state terrorism in Central and South America largely accounts for the huge numbers of mortal victims in Guatemala and El Salvador. In the four South American countries, victims were largely defined by their politics: guerrillas, Marxists, "subversives," and their sympathizers were the repressors' primary targets. These individuals were predominantly urban, and they came from social groups ranging from working class to elite who had embraced leftist politics, described in Chile as "people who had always managed things, whose names were on street signs and wine bottles."[1] In Central America, race and class were key determinants of targeting. The elites and their military allies in Guatemala and El Salvador believed, or purported to believe, that the Indian and mestizo lower classes would naturally sympathize with or ally themselves with the guerrillas who promised to liberate them from their upper-class oppressors.

Moreover, many of these predominantly rural folk lived in or near zones of guerrilla activity. Rather than try to discriminate between peasants who supported the guerrillas and those who did not, the militaries and death squads adopted the easier solution of wiping out all those suspected of sympathizing or collaborating with the enemy, thereby depriving the guerrillas of their presumed support. A Guatemalan presidential spokesman explained to a U.S. journalist the rationale for killing Indians; the explanation fits in El Salvador also, with *"campesino"* replacing "Indian": "The guerrillas won over many Indian collaborators . . . Therefore, the Indians were subversives, right? And how do you fight subversion? Clearly, you had to kill Indians because they were collaborating with subversion . . ."[2]

Underlying this approach was the mentality of many of the elites, shared by much of the militaries' upper echelons: the lives of Indians and poor mestizos did not matter, even those of women, children, and infants. According to an authority on genocide, in Guatemala "the ideology of racism . . . played a profound role in establishing the preconditions for the genocide and in facilitating its perpetration."[3] This deeply ingrained racism was responsible for the savagery meted out to the thousands of noncombatants subjected to the most horrible tortures and agonizing deaths.

Guatemala: Repression and Genocide

State terrorism in Guatemala arose in the context of a guerrilla war that lasted from 1962 to 1996. The guerrilla movement in Guatemala, as elsewhere in Latin America, was heavily influenced by the Cuban Revolution and Che Guevara's advocacy of the rural guerrilla method. But recent Guatemalan history added impetus to the inspiration coming from Cuba and set the country apart from its Central American neighbors.

Following the lengthy dictatorship of General Jorge Ubico (1931–1944), Guatemala experienced a breach in the traditional elite–military governing alliance. Ubico's elected successor, Juan José Arévalo (1945–1951), aligned himself with moderates and leftists to enact reform measures favoring labor and the urban poor. Although unsettling to the right-wing forces, Arévalo's reforms were less threatening to vested interests than those of his successor, Jacobo Árbenz (1951–1954). While furthering urban-focused reforms, Árbenz simultaneously set out to change backward and impoverished rural Guatemala, where the country's exploited and oppressed Maya Indians constituted a majority of the population.

Unfortunately for this ambitious reform agenda, the Árbenz administration became embroiled in international politics. By 1950 the United States was fully engaged in the Cold War with the Soviet Union, and Guatemala became the first test of U.S. resolve to keep Communist influence out of Latin America. Árbenz committed two violations of U.S.-sanctioned conduct. First, he appeared to be, in the lexicon of the McCarthy era, "soft on Communism." Árbenz was on good terms with Guatemala's small Communist Party and appointed a few of its members and allies to posts in his administration. Moreover, blocked by the United States from acquiring weaponry in Western Europe, he turned to Communist Czechoslovakia for arms. Second, Árbenz's 1952 agrarian reform law authorized expropriation of unused agricultural property, of which the United Fruit Company (UFCO), an extremely powerful entity throughout Central America, owned thousands of acres. Following implementation of the law, the Guatemalan government offered compensation in bonds based on value reported on the tax rolls, while UFCO, backed by the U.S. State Department, demanded payment in cash based on its estimate of the land's market value: $620,000 versus $15.9 million. The combination of alleged Communist sympathies and expropriation of U.S.-owned property without adequate compensation—reminiscent of the situation in Cuba a few years later—created a drumbeat in the United States for action against Árbenz. In the dramatic words of a prominent magazine, "The battle of the Western Hemisphere has begun."[4]

After pressuring the OAS to adopt the 1954 Declaration of Caracas, which named Communism the hemispheric enemy, the Eisenhower administration orchestrated the overthrow of the Guatemalan government. Following an intense CIA-conducted propaganda and psychological campaign, a small CIA-trained and -equipped armed group crossed into Guatemala from Honduras and El Salvador. The Guatemalan military, which could easily have crushed the invaders, refused to engage them; President Árbenz was forced to flee; and Guatemala fell back into the traditional pattern of repressive dictatorship. But having experienced the tantalizing taste of reform, some Guatemalans proved receptive to a renewed reform message in the early 1960s.

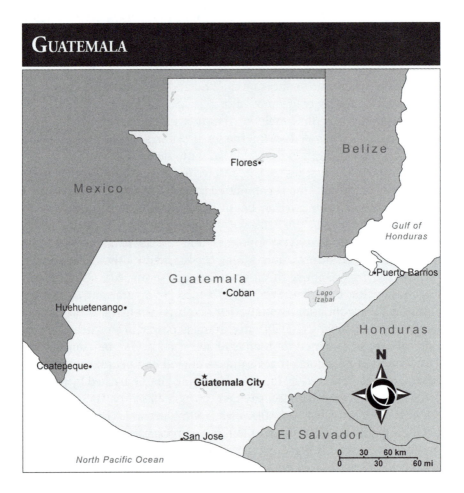

The first Guatemalan guerrilla movement grew out of a failed November 1960 coup by young nationalist army officers who, in addition to their commitment to reform, opposed the government's permitting the CIA to train the Bay of Pigs invasion force in Guatemala. After fleeing into exile, Marco Antonio Yon Sosa and Luis Turcios Lima returned in 1962 to establish the Rebel Armed Forces (Fuerzas Armadas Rebeldes, FAR), composed of a mix of reformers, Communists, peasants, and officers. Other guerrilla groups followed, but all faced the challenges of U.S.-trained counterinsurgency troops, Green Berets on the battlefields, and disunity within their ranks. Guerrilla activity varied in intensity over the following years but never reached the level of threatening to overthrow the government.

Despite the guerrillas' limited success, the military regimes of the 1960s inaugurated the response followed by Guatemalan governments over the next three decades: severe repression against all potential guerrilla sympathizers or collaborators, including peasants, left and moderate political parties, intellectuals, students, teachers, and union leaders. Governments used not only army troops, including U.S.-trained Ranger units, but also death squads, themselves composed largely of army and police personnel. The most notorious of these was the Organized National Anti- Communist Movement (Movimiento Anticomunista Nacional Organizado, MANO), referred to as the Mano Blanca (White Hand). Together, the repressive forces carried out assassinations and kidnappings in the urban areas and large-scale massacres of the predominantly Mayan peasantry in the countryside. Additional death squads formed in the 1970s and 1980s.

Colonel Carlos Arana Osorio, elected president in 1970, promised to eliminate the guerrillas even "if it was necessary to turn the country into a cemetery."[5] He was successful in killing the surviving leader of the FAR, Yon Sosa, the same year, leading to the group's dissolution; but by that time, the deadly cycle of guerrilla activity and state terrorism was entrenched. During the ensuing 16 years, with military men in the presidency, there was no realistic possibility of a resumption of the reforms begun under Árbenz. Whenever new guerrilla outbreaks occurred, the U.S.-trained and -supplied army and the death squads swung into action intimidating, assassinating, and massacring in the name of anti-Communism.

A 1978 massacre of Maya Indians in the town of Panzós, Alta Verapaz Department, marked a turning point in the conflict. Some 700 Indians converged on Panzós on May 29 to petition for their historic rights to lands that had recently been illegally appropriated by military and political elites. Soldiers fired on the crowd, killing some 150 and wounding around 300. Others drowned trying to escape across a river or were hunted down after fleeing the town. The bodies were buried in a mass grave. The army claimed that the Indians had attacked the soldiers, the president blamed Fidel Castro, and the defense minister accused local priests and nuns of inciting the peasants to violence. Although the scope of the Panzós massacre became the norm in coming years, this event, unlike those that preceded it, spurred protests that reached the capital. After sporadic demonstrations the week following the massacre, some 80,000 people from left parties, labor unions, and student organizations marched in Guatemala City on June 8 demanding accountability for the slaughter.

In January 1980, a group of Maya peasants marched to the capital to protest the murders and disappearances in the Quiché area. Denied a congressional hearing, and in the company of urban leftist groups, the protesters occupied the Spanish embassy in an effort to publicize their cause. They presented a letter to the ambassador and announced a press conference for noon. Rebuffing the ambassador's plea for negotiations, the authorities stormed in and set fire to the building, killing over 30 people including embassy officials, the protesters, and Guatemalan officials visiting the site. Spain broke diplomatic relations in response, but the repression continued unabated.

In fact, the protests and increased guerrilla activity led to heightened state terrorism. General Fernando Romeo Lucas García, president from June 1978 to June 1982, escalated the war against leftists, trade unionists, and peasants. In 1980, 27 leaders of the national labor confederation were kidnapped and never seen again. In 1981 Lucas García launched a scorched earth campaign designed to "drain the sea to kill the fish", or to isolate the guerrillas from the population and thus from their presumed base of support.[6] In pursuing this policy, military intelligence evaluated Maya villages and towns based on the degree of their suspected support of the guerrillas. Communities deemed free of subversives escaped the worst repression; those considered to be infiltrated but not fully supportive of the guerrillas received selective repression such as kidnappings or assassinations; and villages where support for guerrillas was strong were slated for destruction, meaning mass killings and physical eradication of villages by burning.

General Lucas García's repressive measures paled in comparison with the state terrorism unleashed by his successor. General Efraín Ríos Montt, an evangelical Protestant, overthrew Lucas García in March 1982, served as president for 17 bloody months, and faced a renewed guerrilla effort led by the Guatemalan National Revolutionary Union (Unidad Revolucionario Nacional de Guatemala, URNG), an amalgamation of four guerrilla groups that coalesced in January 1982. Ríos Montt accepted no limits to the slaughter of Maya Indians and leftists. He launched a scorched earth policy against the peasantry that virtually annihilated some smaller subgroups of Maya. The two general/presidents' actions accounted for the great majority of over 600 villages completely destroyed, 1 million internally displaced (of a total population of 8 million), 200,000 refugees driven across the border to Mexico where they were often attacked by Guatemalan forces, and 200,000 civilians killed or disappeared. In the genocide of villagers, troops and death squads raped women, then killed them along with men and boys, and bayoneted babies or smashed them against rocks. They also tore fetuses from the wombs of pregnant women.

Ríos Montt set up "civilian self-defense patrols," which forcibly enrolled over 700,000 men and boys in lightly armed squads under military control, allegedly to defend their villages against the guerrillas. The patrols' other purpose was to report suspected subversive activity in order to dissuade villagers from collaborating with the guerrillas. If accused of failing in their duties, patrol members faced severe reprisals. Ríos Montt also established "model villages" based loosely on the "strategic hamlet" program that the United States instituted during the Vietnam War. Peasants were moved from active guerrilla areas and resettled in new or renovated villages under the complete control of the army. Their villages of origin were razed, crops uprooted, and animals slaughtered so that the displaced persons would have nothing to return to. In the model villages, military men monitored residents' movements and prevented them from leaving without special permission from the local commanding officer. A scholar described the model villages as "forced resettlement camps in which every aspect of people's lives was subject to direct military control . . ."[7]

U.S. military aid to Guatemala had been suspended during the administration of President Jimmy Carter (1977–1981), who made respect for human rights a centerpiece of his foreign policy and a condition for offering military aid. With the accession of Ronald Reagan in January 1981, full U.S. financial, logistical, and moral support for state terrorism resumed and the genocide escalated. Reagan visited the country in December 1982 in an effort to offset negative U.S. reactions to his support of Ríos Montt. He declared that the Guatemalan government had been getting a "bum rap" on human rights and that Ríos Montt was "totally dedicated to democracy in Guatemala."[8] In a separate conversation, Ríos Montt took a different view of human rights: he reportedly said, "The subject of human rights is an international topic which they use to annoy a government which is against Communism."[9] Ríos Montt was eventually tried and convicted of genocide and crimes against humanity in 2013, but Guatemala's highest court overturned the verdict.

The strongest voice of Indian protest was that of Rigoberta Menchú, a Quiché Mayan born to a poor peasant family and an activist for Indian and women's rights from an early age. After her parents and brother were murdered by government forces, she became prominent in the opposition until forced to flee to Mexico for her safety. She received the Nobel Peace Prize in 1992 and has continued her work for Indian rights and reconciliation not only in Guatemala but throughout Latin America. She told her story, including the torture and murder of her brother, in a book.

> My name is Rigoberta Menchú. I am 23 years old. This is my testimony . . . It's not only my life, it's also the testimony of my people . . . My story is the story of all poor Guatemalans. My personal experience is the reality of a whole people. They took my brother away, bleeding from different places. When they'd done with him, he didn't look like a person any more. His whole face was disfigured . . . He couldn't see any more; they'd even forced stones into his eyes. My brother was tortured more than sixteen days. They cut off his fingernails, they cut off his fingers, they cut off his skin, they burned parts of his skin . . . They cut the skin off his head and pulled it down on either side and cut off the fleshy part of his face. They lined up the tortured and poured petrol on them; and then the soldiers set fire to each one of them.[10]

The story of Rigoberta Menchú's brother is the story of the genocide of Maya Indians, and it is repeated ad nauseam in testimonies recorded by individuals and human rights organizations. Two additional testimonies confirm that Rigoberta Menchú's story was the rule, not the exception:

> Government soldiers arrived in his village. The same soldiers had been there on two previous occasions to organize a civil patrol, an organization whose sole purpose, he says, is to keep watch on the town. The first time, in early July [1982], they said all the villagers were now soldiers . . . The second time, on July 20, they called everyone in the village enemies of the government. They drove off the cattle, killed many peasants, and burned the village. Those who had joined the civil patrol participated in the killing, then were themselves killed by the soldiers . . . He and other residents fled as their village burned . . .[11]

> In late 1982 Guatemalan army soldiers entered their village and began shooting men, women, children and livestock. Soldiers murdered children by cleaving their heads with machetes, strangling them with rope, and throwing them in the air and then impaling them on bayonets. Women who did not escape were raped. Those who survived fled to the hills and tried to live off the crops and food supplies the army had not destroyed. In January and February 1983, the army again returned to the village and burned crops that the survivors had recently cultivated in nearby *parcelas* [fields].

No longer able to subsist in the mountains, 221 survivors from Kaibil Balam fled to Mexico. They were pursued by army patrols and 14 of them, including women and children, were killed by those patrols.[12]

Violence declined under civilian governments beginning in 1986 but continued until UN-brokered talks between the government and the URNG led to a peace accord in 1996. As part of a preliminary agreement a truth commission, the Commission for Historical Clarification (Comisión para el Esclarecimiento Histórico, CEH), was formed in 1994. Among the Commission's findings: "agents of the Guatemalan State committed acts of genocide against the Maya people . . ."[13] The total number of people killed was over 200,000, 83 percent of them Maya; state forces and "related paramilitary groups" (death squads) committed 93 percent and the insurgents 3 percent of the human rights violations. State terrorism in Guatemala, then, was responsible for over half of the total slaughter carried out by Latin American governments in their war on the left.

El Salvador: State Terrorism and Civil War

In El Salvador, military officers served as presidents from 1931 until 1979, with one brief interlude. The first of these was General Maximiliano Hernández Martínez, who ordered troops to fire on striking coffee workers in 1932, killing between 10,000 and 30,000 in an event known simply as "*La Matanza*" (the massacre). These military presidents formed a close alliance with the coffee oligarchy, governing under a façade of democracy by holding regular elections from which the majority was excluded, until developments of the 1960s began to challenge that arrangement.

Although El Salvador possessed several distinct official military and police forces, including the army and the National Guard, right-wing elements reinforced the state's powers of repression by establishing the first of several death squads in the early 1960s. The Democratic Nationalist Organization (Organización Democrática Nacionalista, ORDEN), whose acronym means "order," was closely linked to the military's security agency, which had been created in close cooperation with U.S. agents. ORDEN was staffed by military and police personnel as well as right-wing civilians. A second death squad emerged from ORDEN later in the 1960s, and several more appeared in the 1970s and 1980s.

The death squads gathered intelligence and acted with complete impunity, intimidating the population and liquidating persons suspected of being leftist or even of having independent political opinions. Poor peasants were favorite targets, but the death squads also monitored and frequently

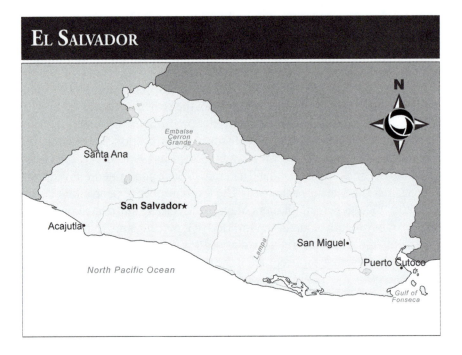

murdered members of groups they considered subversive: labor unions, left political parties, the press, and human rights organizations, as well as teachers, students, and peasant organizers. According to the international human rights organization Amnesty International, in El Salvador, "[t]he use of the 'death squad' strategy—murder through domestic covert action—serves as a short-term solution to both peaceful dissidence and armed opposition, while allowing governments to avoid accountability for criminal acts."[14]

As elsewhere in Latin America, both the Cuban Revolution and the Alliance for Progress gave rise to hopes for change in El Salvador. Governments of the mid-to-late 1960s adopted a more liberal tone and invested Alliance for Progress money in schools, food subsidies, and other social programs. Although the short-lived Central American Common Market, founded in 1960, brought economic growth, two developments increased landlessness among the country's majority rural population and accelerated the formation of urban slums. First, a boom in demand for cotton and sugar, both requiring large properties for efficient production, drove smallholders off their land. Second, as a consequence of the so-called Soccer War with Honduras in 1969, thousands of Salvadorans who had left their overpopulated country to farm vacant land across the border were forced to return.

Despite conservatives' opposition, President General Fidel Sánchez Hernández convened a National Agrarian Reform Congress in 1970 to address the issue. The congress called for expropriation of large estates and recognition of rural worker unions. Although right-wing parties swept legislative elections shortly after the congress and ended open discussion of agrarian reform for several years, the congress planted seeds of hope that persisted.

Guerrilla groups began to appear in El Salvador early in the 1970s. The first was the Popular Forces of Liberation (Fuerzas Populares de Liberación), formed in 1970 by a faction of the Salvadoran Communist Party and supported by left-wing university students. Next came the People's Revolutionary Army (Ejército Popular Revolucionario) the following year and the Armed Forces of National Resistance (Fuerzas Armadas de Resistencia Nacional) in 1975. Two others appeared later in the decade: the Armed Forces of Liberation (Fuerzas Armadas de Liberación) and the Revolutionary Party of Central American Workers (Partido Revolucinario de Trabajdores de Centro América). The proliferation of guerrilla groups reflected the fragmentation of the Salvadoran left; lacking cooperation and coordination, the small guerrilla bands made little headway against the government's repressive power.

Christian Democrat José Napoleón Duarte, former mayor of San Salvador and a political moderate, challenged the military–oligarchy alliance by running for president in 1972; despite Duarte's victory at the polls, the conservative candidate was declared the winner as the result of blatant fraud. Repression mounted, including a massacre of university students in which some 37 were killed and dozens were disappeared. The military–oligarchy alliance retained power in the 1977 election through even more blatant fraud: ballot boxes were openly stuffed for the government's candidate, opposition poll watchers were driven off or arrested, and the National Guard attacked and killed protesters. The fraudulent 1972 and 1977 elections demonstrated conclusively that change could not be achieved in El Salvador through peaceful means. Unrest mounted and, as in Guatemala, the army, National Guard, and death squads responded with heightened repression.

The years 1979 through 1981 were the most bloody of the Salvadoran conflict. They were also turning points. The July 1979 Sandinista victory in Nicaragua resonated strongly in El Salvador. Fearful that the Sandinistas' feat might stimulate a surge of domestic guerrilla activity, elements of the military overthrew the government in October 1979 and installed a mixed military–civilian junta that proposed reforms and promised to rein in human rights abuses. Frustrated by their inability to overcome the hard-liners' resistance to reform and to easing the repression, civilians abandoned the junta, and a series of unstable military-dominated regimes held power until 1982, when conservative, military-aligned civilian Álvaro Magaña was elected president. The 1979 rupture of the traditional military–elite governance thus failed to bring about meaningful change.

In October 1980, the five guerrilla groups that had formed in the 1970s combined into the Farabundo Martí National Liberation Front (Frente Farabundo Martí de Liberación Nacional, FMLN), named for the Communist leader of the rural workers' strike that led to *La Matanza* in 1932. From its beginning with a few hundred fighters, the FMLN grew to between 9,000 and 12,000 by 1984. With this rebel army in the field, El Salvador throughout the 1980s was wracked not only by state terrorism but also by civil war.

High on the list of the right-wing organizations' targets was the Catholic Church. Systematic repression of the Church distinguished state terrorism in El Salvador from that in other Latin American countries. Although more Church personnel were killed by state repressors in Argentina, the Argentine Church hierarchy supported the Dirty War. Those killed were dissidents, many of them "Third World priests" who worked with the poor and opposed the Dirty War, and thus were readily identified as "subversives." In El Salvador, the hierarchy as well as parish priests, nuns, lay workers, and members of the religious orders became victims of state or state-allied forces primarily because they embraced liberation theology and stood with the country's poor majority against injustice and exploitation.

Liberation theology was a movement within the Catholic Church based on doctrines that emerged from the Second Vatican Council (Vatican II) of 1962–1965 and the Conference of Latin American Bishops held at Medellín, Colombia, in 1968. Vatican II called for a realignment of the church from its traditional alliance with the elites to solidarity with the poor in seeking a more just world. The Latin American bishops fleshed out this principle, arguing that the church should embrace a "preferential option for the poor." They called for the formation of "Christian base communities" headed by priests and committed laypersons where the poor would be taught literacy by reading the Bible and organized to seek improved material conditions.

Conservatives inside and outside of the church considered liberation theology and its practitioners subversive. They viewed writings by leading liberation theologian Gustavo Gutiérrez denouncing "private ownership of the means of production" as synonymous with Marxism. The Vatican's Congregation for the Doctrine of the Faith, under the direction of future Pope Benedict XVI, denounced liberation theology for using "concepts uncritically borrowed from Marxist ideology."[15] But liberation theology's real threat to the status quo was not words; it was the focus of its practitioners on the millions of marginalized persons inhabiting the teeming slums that had proliferated in Latin America's cities and the impoverished rural landless and smallholders. Although nonviolent, liberation theology appeared as dangerous to the status quo as some of the armed revolutionary movements.

The Catholic Church in El Salvador became a target of repression because, in embracing the reformist currents within the church, it was the most prestigious national institution to challenge the status quo. Leftist parties, labor unions, human rights organizations, and others also called for reform, but none spoke with the authority of the Catholic Church. Archbishop Oscar Romero explained the animus of the Salvadoran establishment toward the church: "The persecution comes about because of the Church's defense of the poor, for assuming the destiny of the poor."[16] From the other side of the political divide, Major Roberto Molina confirmed the archbishop's understanding of the conflict: "the progressive clerics bear a great responsibility for what has happened to this country. They have launched the class struggle . . ."[17]

Archbishop Romero, known as "the voice of the voiceless," was an outspoken critic of the repression carried out by the military and the death squads. He was shot to death while saying Mass in a hospital on March 24, 1980. Roberto d'Aubisson, a military officer and fervent anti-leftist crusader, was suspected of orchestrating the murder but was not prosecuted. The previous day, Romero had said in a sermon: "In the name of God, in the name of this suffering people whose cries rise up more and more loudly to heaven, I ask you, I beg you, I order you in God's name: Stop the repression."[18] Death squads opened fire on the multitude attending Romero's funeral on March 30, killing approximately 40 mourners. Romero was succeeded in the church's highest office in El Salvador by Arturo Rivera Damas, another prelate committed to solidarity with the poor and to brokering peace, but who kept a lower profile than Romero and survived.

Another high-profile murder of church personnel occurred eight months after Romero's assassination. On December 2, 1980, three nuns and a layperson from the United States were abducted, raped, and murdered by members of the National Guard after arriving at San Salvador's international airport. They were traveling on the main highway linking the airport to the capital when abducted. Their bodies were discovered the following day. In response, President Jimmy Carter cut U.S. aid to El Salvador.

The year 1980 also marked an intensification of the government's repression of the peasantry. The sporadic but deadly war on the rural poor, carried out for years by government forces and death squads, gave way to systematic, large-scale massacres. In a military sweep of a suspected guerrilla stronghold near the Sumpul River on May 14, 1980, several thousand panicked peasants fled their homes before the advancing troops and sought to cross the river to safety in Honduras. Honduran soldiers drove many back across the river, where soldiers and death squads, backed by helicopters, slaughtered at least 600 men, women, and children. The Reverend Earl Gallagher, a Capuchin priest working in the area, went to the river the following day and observed: "There were so many vultures picking at the bodies in the water that it looked like a black carpet."[19] A Honduran fisherman reportedly found the bodies of five children in his fish trap. Both the Salvadoran and Honduran governments denied reports of the massacre. Two similar but smaller massacres occurred along the Lempa River in March and October 1981.

Ronald Reagan succeeded Jimmy Carter as U.S. president in January 1981. Reagan pursued dual strategies to defeat the insurgency. On one hand, he pushed for a moderate government and even advocated agrarian reform to quell peasant support of the insurgency; thus, he supported Christian Democrat Duarte's successful second bid for the presidency in 1984. Duarte initiated agrarian and other reforms and sought unsuccessfully to broker peace with the FMLN. While Duarte's election raised hopes for improvement in human rights, the powerful security forces rejected presidential control and continued to obstruct reform, using their military and death squads at will against civilians as well as insurgents.

The other face of U.S. policy was a military solution. Shortly after its inauguration, the Reagan administration issued a "white paper" which ignored the indigenous roots of the rebellion and the government's glaring use of terrorism against the populace. It declared the Salvadoran conflict, in Cold War terms, a case of Communist subversion directed by Moscow and channeled through Havana and Managua. Thus justifying intervention, the United States vastly increased the aid that had sustained the military effort for several years. Military support rose from $6 million in 1980 (President Jimmy Carter's last year) to $82 million in 1982 and $197 million in 1984. In authorizing that aid, Congress required the administration to certify every six months that the Salvadoran government was making progress on improving human rights and controlling the military. Certification was routinely issued every six months until Reagan killed the requirement in 1983. Reagan also dispatched contingents of military advisors, who virtually took charge of counterinsurgency operations from the Salvadoran military. U.S.-trained counterinsurgency units, including the notorious Atlacatl Batallion, routinely massacred and uprooted villagers in attempts to pacify the countryside. U.S. aid underwrote the quadrupling of the Salvadoran government's security forces between 1981 and 1989 to 56,000 personnel. Meanwhile, Cuba supplied aid to the FMLN through Nicaragua in amounts that paled in comparison with U.S. support of the government.

The most publicized of the many massacres occurred in and around the village of El Mozote in Morazán province in December 1981. It was carried out by the Atlacatl Battalion, which was conducting a sweep of guerrillas in the area. El Mozote's population had swelled with people from neighboring hamlets, who came seeking safety in the mistaken belief that the village would provide a safe haven during the military operation. According to eyewitnesses, the soldiers first attacked and beat the men, decapitated many, then shot the remainder. Next, they raped and killed young women and girls, then shot older women. Finally, children met their fate by bayonet, strangulation, and hanging from trees. When a soldier balked at the prospect of killing children, his captain allegedly told him: "If we don't kill them now . . . they'll just grow up to be guerrillas. We have to take care of the job now."[20] From El Mozote the soldiers fanned out to some 10 nearby hamlets, repeating the massacre. Following the killings, soldiers burned El Mozote and the other locales to the ground. The death toll was between 800 and 1,000 noncombatants of both sexes and all ages.

The U.S. press began reporting on El Mozote and the other massacres in early 1982. Salvadoran authorities denied the events, and the U.S. embassy cast doubt on the reports. Ambassador Deane Hinton cabled six months after El Mozote that "[t]he January 1982 embassy investigation concluded that civilians who were either willing or unwilling guerrilla collaborators did die in and around El Mozote, but not as a result of systematic massacre, and not in the numbers widely reported in the international press. Leftist propaganda to the effect is almost certainly exaggerated."[21] Assistant Secretary of State Thomas Enders assured two congressional committees that "there is no evidence to confirm that government forces systematically massacred civilians in the operations zone, or that the number of civilians even remotely approached the 733 or 936 cited in the press."[22] Yet in view of the adverse publicity, the U.S. government called for improving the human rights situation. As a result, the Salvadoran army cut back the scale of its operations involving civilian casualties. The El Mozote massacre, which took the highest toll in civilian deaths of any of the massacres, was the last of that scope, but hundreds of peasants were killed in smaller actions.

For the next couple of years, air strikes, allegedly against FMLN positions, took the greatest toll in civilian casualties. In testimony before the U.S. Congress, an eyewitness to the air war stated in March 1983 that for the past nine months he could not "remember a day that a village has not been bombed by A-37 jets, strafed by Huey helicopters, or rocketed by Cessna spotter planes . . ."[23] As a result of the ground and air assaults on civilians, 450,000 persons, or one-tenth of the Salvadoran population, were internally displaced by May 1984, according to the Red Cross.

There is little evidence that the army's fighting capabilities increased as a result of the massive injection of aid under Reagan. Indeed, by the mid-1980s, the civil war had reached the point where the government held the main cities and kept the major highways open by day, and the FMLN held large swaths of territory and operated freely by night, disrupting transportation and sabotaging utilities and military installations. While the U.S.-financed and -trained counterinsurgency battalions and death squads continued to terrorize and kill civilians, both rural and urban, the FMLN focused on preparing for a final battle for the capital, San Salvador.

On the evening of November 11, 1989, rebels entered San Salvador, descending from the nearby hills that the FMLN had held for several years. The rebels occupied the poor neighborhoods that ringed the capital and also took the fight into several elite districts, targeting the homes of prominent government officials and capturing and briefly holding the Sheraton Hotel, where several U.S. Green Berets and OAS Secretary-General João Berna Soares were lodged. The FMLN hoped to provoke a popular uprising with its offensive, but rather than fight, many residents of the poor neighborhoods fled. The offensive inflicted major casualties on both sides as well as on noncombatants. After three weeks, the FMLN withdrew. Defeated in its immediate objective, the FMLN nonetheless showed unexpected strength and demonstrated that the war had reached a stalemate with neither side capable of victory.

In the midst of the FMLN offensive, government forces carried out their most brazen attack on the Catholic Church since the murder of Archbishop Romero. On November 16, uniformed soldiers of the Atlacatl Battalion entered the Jesuit-run Central American University in San Salvador where, directed by a high-ranking official, they killed six Jesuits, including the rector, vice-rector, and head of the Human Rights Institute along with their housekeeper and her daughter. The Central American University was the country's leading institution of higher learning. The Jesuits had been under threat for several years, due to their sympathy with liberation theology and advocacy of peace negotiations. They had been warned to abandon the country or be killed, and the university had been bombed over a dozen times.

This high-profile operation in the capital could not be swept under the rug, and it swayed U.S. public opinion, the U.S. Congress, and President George H. W. Bush to discontinue support of the government. Meanwhile, the Sandinistas' electoral defeat in 1990, combined with the end of the Soviet subsidy to Cuba and the resulting economic crisis on the island, undercut outside support for the FMLN. Brokered by the United Nations, a January 1992 peace accord ended the armed conflict. The comprehensive agreement called for reduction and restructuring of the security forces, reform of the justice system, and the long-debated agrarian reform. Transformed into a political party, the FMLN won the presidency in 2009 and 2014.

State terrorism and civil war in El Salvador took at least 75,000 lives, mostly civilian; created hundreds of thousands of refugees; and launched the migration stream that made Salvadorans the fastest-growing Latino group in the United States in the late 20th century. The truth commission established by the peace accord determined that state agents, including death squads, were responsible for 85 percent of the human rights violations and the FMLN 5 percent. Both the military and the government rejected the report's findings, and five days after the report's release the national legislature enacted a general amnesty. As a result, very few prosecutions have occurred in El Salvador.

Notes

1. Pamela Constable and Arturo Valenzuela, *A Nation of Enemies: Chile under Pinochet* (New York: W. W. Norton, 1991), 143.

2. Americas Watch, "Human Rights in Guatemala: No Neutrals Allowed" (New York: Americas Watch, 1982), 17.

3. Roderick Leslie Brett, *Origins and Dynamics of Genocide: Political Violence in Guatemala* (London: Palgrave Macmillan, 2016), 63.

4. Peter H. Smith, *Talons of the Eagle: Latin America, the United States, and the World*, 4th ed. (New York: Oxford University Press, 2013), 152.

5. Jim Handy, *Gift of the Devil: A History of Guatemala* (Boston: South End Press, 1984), 167.

6. Brett, *Origins*, 34.

7. Susanne Jonas, *Battle for Guatemala: Rebels, Death Squads, and U.S. Power* (Boulder, CO: Westview Press, 1991).

8. Thomas Carothers, *In the Name of Democracy: U.S. Policy toward Latin America in the Reagan Years* (Berkeley: University of California Press, 1991), 62.

9. Americas Watch, "Human Rights," 8.

10. Rigoberta Menchú, *I, Rigoberta Menchú: An Indian Woman in Guatemala*, ed. Elisabeth Burgos-Debray, trans. Ann Wright, 2nd ed. (London: Verso, 2009), 1, 203, 204, 209.

11. Americas Watch, "Human Rights," 19–20.

12. Americas Watch, "Creating a Desolation and Calling It Peace: May 1983 Supplement to the Report of Human Rights in Guatemala" (New York: Americas Watch, 1983), 16–17.

13. Daniel Rothenberg, ed., *Memory of Silence: The Guatemalan Truth Commission Report* (New York: Palgrave Macmillan, 2012), 77.

14. Americas Watch, *El Salvador's Decade of Terror: Human Rights since the Assassination of Archbishop Romero* (New Haven, CT: Yale University Press, 1991), 22.

15. Paul E. Sigmund, "The Development of Liberation Theology: Continuity or Change?", in Richard L. Rubenstein and John K. Roth (eds.), *The Politics of Latin American Liberation Theology: The Challenge to U.S. Public Policy* (Washington, D.C.: The Washington Institute Press, 1988), 21, 22.

16. Americas Watch, *El Salvador's Decade*, 33.

17. Americas Watch, *El Salvador's Decade*, 33.

18. Jeffrey Davis, *Justice Across Borders: The Struggle for Human Rights in U.S. Courts* (New York: Cambridge University Press, 2008), 44.

19. *New York Times*, June 8, 1991.

20. Mark Danner, *The Massacre at El Mozote: A Parable of the Cold War* (New York: Vintage Books, 1994), 75.

21. Leigh Binford, *The El Mozote Massacre: Human Rights and Global Implications* (Tucson: University of Arizona Press, 2016), 74.

22. Russell Crandall, *The Salvador Option: The United States in El Salvador, 1977–1992* (New York: Cambridge University Press, 2016), 227.

23. Tommie Sue Montgomery, *Revolution in El Salvador: From Civil Strife to Civil Peace* (Boulder, CO: Westview Press, 1995), 173.

PART 6

The Continuing Impact of the Cuban Revolution

CHAPTER TWELVE

Major Political Trends Since 1990

On the 30th anniversary of his death, Che Guevara was resurrected. His body was "discovered" buried under a runway at the air field at Vallegrande, Bolivia, where he had been killed on October 9, 1967, following his capture by Bolivian rangers. Bolivian authorities delivered the body to Cuban officials, who transported it to Havana, where it was received in a massive ceremony before its burial in Santa Clara, the city whose liberation by Che's column had put Batista to flight and Castro into power.

Elsewhere in Latin America, ceremonies and memorials were staged in honor of the apostle of revolution. Thousands made the pilgrimage to the site of Che's *foco* and death, overwhelming the meager capacity of Vallegrande. In Santiago, Chile, the scene was poignant with memories. The three Cuban survivors of Che's *foco* had escaped into Chile, where then-Senator Salvador Allende welcomed them. On October 9, 1997, a warm spring evening, some 50,000 people gathered to hear revolutionary music and speeches extolling Che in the National Stadium, where thousands of Allende supporters had been detained and many tortured and murdered in the wake of the coup that overthrew Allende 24 years earlier.

The crowd was diverse: old leftists, disaffected youth, contingents of the Communist Party of Chile marching in formation, curiosity seekers. The figure of Che, emblazoned on a huge banner and reproduced on thousands of handheld flags, meant something different to each of these groups, indeed probably to every individual in attendance. But whether paying their respects to Che and his legend in Havana, Vallegrande, or Santiago, people were drawn by a common sentiment: nostalgia. Nostalgia for a time when utopia had seemed within reach. Nostalgia for the era of the Cuban Revolution.

The End of an Era

A series of developments in the early 1990s signaled the end of the era of the Cuban Revolution. Between 1989 and 1991 the fall of the Communist regimes in Eastern Europe and the collapse of the Soviet Union deprived Cuba of its primary allies and crucial economic support. Two hemispheric events of 1990 were milestones of different sorts: the Sandinistas' electoral defeat ended the only revolutionary government to seize power through insurrection since Cuba's, and the end of the Pinochet dictatorship in Chile closed out the long phase of the South American state terrorist regimes established to combat Cuban-style revolution. That "something new, exciting, dangerous, and infectious" that Herbert Matthews had detected at the beginning of the 1960s was gone.[1] The situation was exactly the opposite of that 30 years earlier: having placed the United States and the Latin American elites on the defensive in the early years of his revolution, Castro was on the defensive in the 1990s. The issue now was the very survival of his revolution.

While the collapse of the Soviet Union was the final blow to Cuba's three decades as the driving force in Latin American politics, the eclipse of the Cuban Revolution's outsized influence was a long and gradual process resulting from the dialectic of revolution and reaction within the Western Hemisphere. A primary factor in the decline of Cuban influence was the secular tarnishing of the revolution's luster. Fidel's revolution had its broadest appeal in its first three or four years, when the great accomplishments were made and savored: the seizure of power, portrayed as the work of heroic guerrillas; the social revolution carried out with lightning speed; and the successful break with the United States. Later, it proved impossible to match those spectacular successes or to sustain the dizzying pace of the early years. After 1961 there were no more electrifying developments of the magnitude of the guerrillas' entry into Havana, the first agrarian reform, the literacy campaign, or the Bay of Pigs defense. Inevitably, as consolidation replaced innovation, routine settled in. As the 1960s became the 1970s and 1980s, Fidel's speeches were still riveting but redundant; volunteer labor in the cane fields seemed less joyous and spontaneous; the Soviet presence became more visible; and Cuban soldiers returned home from Africa in body bags. The postponement of political democracy and individual liberties became permanent. The virtues of egalitarianism were overshadowed by the drabness of a society without consumer goods. In sum, the revolution's great accomplishments had been institutionalized early on, while its shortcomings became more evident as the years passed.

Also central to the waning of Cuban influence was the failure of revolution in Latin America. From his first moment in power, Castro had publicly staked his prestige on the exportation of the Cuban model of revolution. But his calls to arms, his threat to turn the Andes into another Sierra Maestra, his and Che's advocacy of two, three, many Vietnams rang hollow after a while, validating the skeptics' thesis that the Cuban Revolution was an exception, an aberration that could not be replicated. Although revolutions began in Peru, Chile, and Nicaragua, all ended prematurely. The results of three decades of attempted revolution were grim. A generation of revolutionaries and hundreds of thousands of sympathizers, innocent victims, government troops, and police were killed, jailed, tortured, and exiled. The popular classes of Latin America paid the price of unprecedented political repression and socially retrograde economic policies that exacerbated their poverty and shattered their illusions of betterment.

The apparent ease of Castro's victory in Cuba undoubtedly led to a serious underestimation of the resilience of Latin America's elites and of the United States' resolve to prevent other revolutions. Fidel and Che themselves bore major responsibility for this fatal misperception by fostering the idea that others could repeat the Cuban experience with reasonable certainty by establishing *focos* and following Che's guidelines. Despite the launching of scores of guerrilla *focos* based on the embellished Cuban model, the "heroic guerrilla" formula for insurrection yielded no victories. Nicaragua's Sandinistas, the one successful rural guerrilla group, initially embraced *foquismo* but only achieved victory following a protracted campaign and the assiduous cultivation of mass support. One is led to wonder whether an accurate recounting of the Cuban insurrection might have inspired some successes during the height of the revolutionary impulse of the 1960s, whereas promoting the official version as a model led to failure.

Despite the political effervescence and the unprecedented pan–Latin American mobilization ignited by the Cuban Revolution, the habits and the mechanisms of domination that underpinned Latin America's established societies did not suddenly crumble. Although some peasants shook off their traditional lethargy and joined the ranks of the mobilized, it was quite another thing to join a guerrilla band or even to offer aid to city-bred guerrillas operating in their areas. Shantytown dwellers might join the clamor for material improvements, but few could set aside their transplanted rural attitudes and values to join revolutionary movements.

Reinforcing these obstacles to revolution was the determination of Latin America's elites and much of its middle classes to fight to preserve their way of life. The widespread recourse to military solutions, including in several cases the institutionalization of state terrorism when political systems collapsed in the face of revolutionary threats, reflected this resolve. The willingness of the elites, most notably in Chile and Nicaragua, to stay and fight the revolutionaries rather than, as in Cuba, to abandon the battlefield to the class enemy further illustrated the deeply rooted resistance to change. The heroic guerrilla model, as broadcast from Cuba, simply did not take into account the inherent conservatism of the Latin American lower classes and the resolve and superior resources of the establishment.

Revolution also ran squarely into the historic, unswerving resistance of the United States to radical change in the hemisphere. From its first challenge, the Mexican Revolution of 1910, the United States consistently opposed revolution and was normally hostile even to reform. During the era of the Cuban Revolution, U.S. governments repeatedly demonstrated their willingness to use all the power necessary to thwart revolution and preserve U.S. hegemony and economic interests, casting aside all but the pretenses of principled behavior and adherence to international law. U.S. training and arming of the Latin American militaries and police for counterinsurgency and the numerous instances of overt and covert U.S. military and CIA intervention generally proved effective in keeping revolutionaries and suspect reformers from power. U.S. support of the state terrorist regimes was an effective means of dampening the momentum of revolution not only in the countries where they were established but throughout the hemisphere. And things were not easier for the few progressives who, despite the odds, attained power: whereas Peru's Velasco, being head of a military government, was harder to handle, U.S. treatment of Allende's Chile and Sandinista Nicaragua demonstrated an iron will to use war, subversion, and economic strangulation to bring down those offending governments.

Concomitant to the defeat of the revolutionaries and the aging of his own revolution, Castro saw his influence in Latin America decline over the years. It was a slow and uneven process—one that eludes the neat periodization that historians seek—but a decade-by-decade overview reveals the gradual eclipse of the era of the Cuban Revolution.

The decade of the 1960s was clearly the crest of the revolutionary wave. The Cuban model was broadly appealing throughout Latin America, revolutionary forces were active virtually everywhere, and the United States and Latin American elites reacted defensively. The death of Che Guevara in 1967 dampened the revolutionary momentum, but within a short time urban guerrilla warfare began to yield promising results, while the Peruvian military created hope for revolution from above. The rise of the urban guerrillas and the Peruvian experiment in the late 1960s marked a maturing of the revolutionary trend in Latin America. Inspired by the Cuban Revolution, both represented important innovations that went beyond the sterile "heroic guerrilla" model and broadened the currents of change.

The 1970s brought mixed signals about the continuing influence of the Cuban Revolution. On one hand, several moderate to conservative governments normalized relations with Cuba during the decade, and the OAS in 1975 lifted its economic and diplomatic sanctions against Cuba, demonstrating confidence that the danger of revolution had passed. Few important insurrectionary movements took the field during the 1970s, yet the decade began and ended with major victories for the forces of revolution. Allende's election in September 1970 and the Sandinista victory in July 1979 bracketed the decade, and the Velasco regime in Peru became increasingly radical until its removal in 1975.

Most revealing of the continuing influence of the Cuban Revolution was the establishment of the state terrorist regimes in the 1970s or, in the case of the Brazilian government, its evolution into a more repressive state after 1968. These regimes were clearly responses to threats of revolution, and their ambitious goals and extreme methods were testimony to the profound effects of the revolutionary current still flowing strong in Latin America. On balance, despite some signs of relaxation of tensions, the Cuban Revolution continued as a major influence in Latin American politics during the decade of the 1970s.

During the 1980s there was unmistakable evidence of the waning of the era of the Cuban Revolution, the most convincing indication being the return to civilian rule throughout most of Latin America. From a low point in the late 1970s, civilian governments had returned through the 1980s until only Cuba, Haiti, and Chile ended the decade under governments that had not been elected in a minimally competitive process. The phasing out of the South American state terrorist regimes was the most revealing confirmation of the passing of threats of revolution. The 1980s also brought a marked decline of ideological politics. Saddled with massive foreign debts and reeling from a decade of severe recession, Latin America turned from redistributive issues to the pragmatic matter of inducing economic growth. With the left tamed by repression and the right tainted by the dictatorships' human rights records, the appeal of both extremes declined and the political spectrum contracted toward the center, giving rise to a new politics of pragmatism.

Yet these trends of the 1980s did not close out the era of the Cuban Revolution in all of Latin America. In Peru, the Sendero Luminoso insurrection gained strength throughout the decade. The destabilization of Central America in the 1980s resulted to a large extent from the Sandinista victory in Nicaragua, which had grown from seeds planted in the heady early days of the Cuban Revolution. The extremism of the U.S. reaction to the FSLN government and the massive military aid to El Salvador and Guatemala underscored Washington's preoccupation with Nicaragua and Cuba. The revolutionary impulse unleashed by Fidel's revolution reached its high point in Central America only in the 1980s, even while South America showed signs of returning to a calmer and more orderly political life after long years of revolutionary effervescence and antirevolutionary violence. It was not until the early 1990s that the flame of revolution was finally reduced to smoldering embers and the fury of reaction spent, but as the following years would show, the impact of the Cuban Revolution lingered.

An Unprecedented Time of Democracy

The period since 1990 has been unique in Latin America's political history. With the exceptions of Cuba and Haiti, elected civilian governments have held sway throughout the region. By 2000 all these governments had passed the most basic test of democracy: they took power through elections that, despite blemishes in some cases, were essentially free, fair, and open. Latin America's transition to democracy took place in the face of serious obstacles. One of these was the lack of democratic culture in many countries. Uruguay, Chile, and Costa Rica were the main exceptions, and the first two experienced the eclipse, but not the extinction, of their democratic cultures and values under state terrorism. Some countries had almost no experience with democracy, having been under military or oligarchic rule during much or most of their independent histories. The first democratic president following the end of Argentina's Dirty War, Raúl Alfonsín, explained the problem facing his country, which had had more experience with democracy than many: "It was not a matter of reconstructing a system that was functioning well until it was interrupted by authoritarianism, but of establishing new foundations for an authentic democratic system."[2]

That challenge was more acute in countries such as Guatemala, El Salvador, Paraguay, or Mexico, where a second fundamental test of democracy had rarely or never been met: the peaceful transfer of power to the opposition following an election. Another challenge in several countries was the legacy of state terrorism. The civilian governments that succeeded highly repressive regimes faced profoundly divided societies. On one side were the armed forces and the civilians who had supported their policy of exterminating the left; on the other were victims of repression and the human rights movements formed during the dictatorships. The main issue dividing these societies was impunity versus justice. Would the amnesty decrees left in place by exiting military regimes protect former repressors from prosecution? Would victims, their families, and the human rights movements be satisfied with the reports of truth commissions, or would they demand trials? Would the militaries submit to prosecution after, from their perspective, heroically saving their countries from Marxism and subversion? These were some of the dilemmas facing the new civilian governments intent on shoring up their fragile democracies. Two countries have had considerable success in meeting this challenge: hundreds of former repressors have been tried and convicted since 2000 in Argentina and Chile, while the poisonous legacy of state terrorism is largely unresolved elsewhere.

Latin America's trend toward democratic governance was part of a global wave of democratization, as identified by political scientist Samuel P. Huntington.[3] The wave began with the fall of dictatorships in Portugal and Greece in 1974 and Spain the following year. It accelerated in the 1990s with the end of the Eastern European Communist regimes and the disintegration of the Soviet Union and Yugoslavia. The spread of democracy was, in large measure, a reaction against authoritarianism. In Latin America, where only Mexico, Costa Rica, Venezuela, and Colombia remained free of military domination between the 1960s and 1990s, the reaction was particularly potent, manifested both in support for democracy and for the human rights so severely abused in many countries.

Since the Paraguayan armed forces ended the 35-year dictatorship of Alfredo Stroessner in 1989, Latin America has been virtually free of military coups. The military regimes established in response to the threat of Cuban-style revolution gave way to civilian governments, mostly in the 1980s and 1990s. In South America, the Argentine state terrorist dictatorship ended in 1983, followed by the Uruguayan and Brazilian in 1985 and the Chilean in 1990. State terrorism in El Salvador and Guatemalan ended in 1992 and 1996, respectively. Since that time, democratic governance has prevailed, and military influence in politics has diminished. The recent period compares favorably with the previous high tide of democracy in the 1950s, which ended under the destabilizing impact of the Cuban Revolution.

The OAS has promoted democracy in recent years. Article 21 of the 2001 Inter-American Democratic Charter calls for suspending a member state, by a two-thirds vote, in the case of an "unconstitutional interruption of the democratic order."[4] That rule was tested in 2009 when the Honduran armed forces arrested and exiled President José Manuel Zelaya. However, this was not a standard or clear-cut military coup, as the Honduran Supreme Court had ordered Zelaya's arrest for defying its orders and, the day after the military acted, Congress voted overwhelmingly to remove Zelaya from office and install his constitutionally designated successor as president. Nonetheless, demonstrating that the Democratic Charter was more than rhetoric, the OAS suspended Honduras, an action it had not taken since suspending Cuba in 1962. The issue was resolved, and Honduras's membership was restored in 2011.

There have been other tests of Latin America's commitment to democratic governance. In earlier periods, political instability frequently triggered military coups designed to restore order or, in the era of the Cuban Revolution, to cleanse countries of Marxism and "subversion." However, the military generally has refrained from staging coups when irregular situations, such as interruptions of presidential terms, have occurred. In Bolivia, Paraguay, Peru, Argentina, and Brazil, all historically susceptible to military coups, these interrupted presidencies were resolved by constitutional rules of succession. In Ecuador, five presidencies ended prematurely between 1997 and 2005, but only one provoked military intervention. Military officers removed the president in 2000, but rather than retaining power themselves, restored constitutional government after only 18 hours by turning over power to the elected vice-president. In Venezuela a 1992 coup failed and a 2002 coup succeeded temporarily but ultimately collapsed.

Mexico is a special case of democratization. While avoiding military rule and extreme repression during the 1970s and 1980s, and despite holding regular elections, Mexico before the 21st century was not a functioning democracy. Since 1929 it had been under the complete control of the PRI, which used all means to maintain its monopoly of power in a system that Peruvian Nobel Laureate novelist Mario Vargas Llosa labeled "the perfect dictatorship."[5] During its early decades in power, the PRI had carried out revolutionary change and engineered strong economic growth, but by the 1980s recurring economic problems, heightened and blatant corruption, and electoral fraud had eroded its support. Developments in the 1990s further weakened the PRI's hold on power until, finally, internal pressures and the region-wide wave of democratization forced a reform of the corrupt electoral system that led to the party's loss of its congressional majority in 1997 and the presidency in 2000. By that time a competitive three-party system had emerged and Mexico joined the burgeoning ranks of Latin America's democracies.

Proclamations about democracy and human rights have not been empty words: numerous countries enacted laws or amended constitutions to translate the rhetoric of democracy and human rights into reality. Human rights have been strengthened by legislation and by ratifying international human rights treaties. Argentina has gone the furthest in guaranteeing human rights: in 1994, it incorporated the nine international human rights treaties that the country had ratified directly into its constitution and declared them superior to domestic law. Human rights are more respected than ever across Latin America, and both governmental agencies and private organizations constantly monitor compliance; but one need only read Human Rights Watch's *Annual Report* to be reminded that the human rights situation still needs improvement.

Countries have fortified democracy by making elections more transparent and politics more inclusive. They have expanded participation by lowering the voting age, making the vote obligatory, and mandating quotas for women candidates for office. In 1991 Argentina became the world's first country to legislate a requirement that a fixed percentage of all political parties' candidates for the national Congress be women. In succeeding years, the Argentine innovation has spread, making Latin America the world's region with the greatest concentration of gender quota laws. As of 2016, seven countries had raised the quota to 50 percent, and only five countries had not enacted quotas. The result has been a spectacular growth of female representation: from less than 1 percent of national legislative seats in 1979, by 2016 women held 27 percent (the corresponding figure for the United States was 19 percent), and some countries had extended quotas to local and regional elections. Reflecting heightened women's political activism, Nicaragua, Costa Rica, Panama, Chile, Argentina, and Brazil have elected women presidents since 1990.

Public opinion surveys find broad support for democracy in Latin America. Since its founding in 1995, the respected polling firm Latinbarómetro has asked about attitudes toward governance. At 10-year intervals, respondents across the region agreed that democracy is better than any other form of government, by 58.3 percent in 1995, 52.7 percent in 2005, and 57.0 percent in 2015. The firm also asked whether an autocratic government could be preferable to a democratic one in some circumstances, to which respondents answered affirmatively by 16.9 percent in 1995, 14.8 percent in 2005, and 15.6 percent in 2015. The consistency of these responses over time suggests that the current ascendancy of democracy rests on firm foundations.

Despite notable advances, consolidation of democracy in Latin America is still a work in progress. Voter apathy and distrust of election results are problems in some countries. Nor has authoritarianism been vanquished: Peru's elected President Alberto Fujimori (1990–2000) in 1992 shut down Congress, suspended the constitution, and assumed dictatorial powers; Argentina's President Carlos Menem (1989–1999) packed the Supreme Court with unqualified cronies in order to push his agenda; Venezuela's Hugo Chávez (1999–2013) created a cult of personality that underpinned his great personal power, and his successor, Nicolás Maduro, established a virtual dictatorship as Venezuela descended into crisis. Large-scale corruption tarnished several Latin American governments, most notably Brazil. Although far from perfect, democracy has become the new normal in Latin America.

The Pink Tide

One of the salient political developments of the early 21st century has been the emergence of a number of leftist governments collectively known as the "Pink Tide." Underlying this leftward shift in the political landscape is the Washington Consensus, known in Latin America as neoliberalism. The roots of neoliberalism lie in the 1970s and 1980s. Crude oil prices quadrupled in 1973–1974 when the Organization of Petroleum Exporting Countries (OPEC) embargoed shipments to the United States and cut production. While damaging to the economies of oil-importing countries, OPEC's action created a bonanza for petroleum exporters and flooded the world's banks with cash. International banks, in turn, promoted massive loans, which Latin American countries readily accepted, pushing the region's external debt from around 30 billion dollars in 1970 to some 230 billion in 1980. Then came the worldwide recession of the 1980s, which depressed the prices of Latin American exports and stopped the region's economic growth, creating a crisis of debt repayment. To prevent potential defaults, international lenders led by the IMF and the World Bank offered to renegotiate the loans to reduce interest rates and payments. They also offered new bridge loans, further expanding Latin America's external debt.

As the condition for refinancing billions of dollars of debt and offering emergency loans, the international lenders demanded radical policy changes. These neoliberal policies involved fiscal austerity to balance national budgets, opening closed or protected markets to foreign investment, and privatization of state-owned assets. In almost every country, government services and subsidies to the poor were slashed, protective tariffs fell, and transnational corporations and national conglomerates bought up the public sector at bargain prices.

Combined with Latin America's economic contraction in the "lost decade" of the 1980s, the implementation of neoliberal policies had severe human consequences. Many jobs were lost due to the reduction in government employment, privatization of government enterprises, and the new competition of imported consumer goods that reduced employment in the manufacturing sectors. Already weakened by the dictatorships of the 1970s and 1980s, labor unions' bargaining power was further eroded by the contraction of manufacturing and public-sector employment, leaving workers vulnerable to cuts in wages and benefits. Many who lost their jobs or suffered wage cuts joined the masses living in burgeoning slums and surviving in the informal economy, guarding parked cars, selling pencils on buses, or performing tricks for motorists stopped at traffic signals. In this period of heightened need, the mandated reductions in government spending on health care, education, and subsidies for transportation and food, such as the tortilla subsidy in Mexico, were particularly onerous, as illustrated by sporadic but often violent protests against austerity measures and price increases. As poverty rates increased dramatically, income and wealth inequality grew apace.

The precarious situation of Latin America's workers, peasants, and marginalized slum dwellers did not go unnoticed. A number of voices, including those of populist politicians, Fidel Castro, and even conservative Pope John Paul II, arose in the 1990s to denounce neoliberalism. The Latin American Council of Bishops condemned "economism," or "the absolutizing of market forces and the power of money, forgetting that the economy is to be at the service of the people and not the other way around."[6] Having discovered the extent of poverty in the developing world, including Latin America, the World Bank by the turn of the century began recommending strong measures to reverse the damage done by the very neoliberal policies of which it had been a primary architect.

The new leftist governments constituting the Pink Tide came to power largely through their opposition to neoliberalism. Elected president of Venezuela in 1998, Hugo Chávez pioneered the Pink Tide. He was followed by Brazil's Luiz Inácio Lula da Silva (known simply as Lula) and Argentina's Néstor Kirchner in 2003, by Uruguay's Tabaré Vásquez in 2005, Bolivia's Evo Morales in 2006, Ecuador's Rafael Correa and Nicaragua's Daniel Ortega in 2007, and El Salvador's Mauricio Funes in 2009.

These governments were more moderate than the revolutionary regimes that took power during the era of the Cuban Revolution. Although they were often described or self-identified as "socialist" or proponents of "21st-century socialism," most did not nationalize the basic components of their countries' economies as occurred in Cuba and, to a lesser extent, in

Peru, Chile, and Nicaragua. Rather, most of the new left leaders attempted to humanize neoliberalism, rather than vanquish it altogether, by initiating antipoverty, nutrition, education, housing, and other programs to establish a social safety net for as many of their citizens as possible. Despite these differences, there is a direct connection between the era of the Cuban Revolution and the revival of the left. Four sitting presidents in 2015 were former guerrilla fighters: El Salvador's Salvador Sánchez Cerén, a commander in the FMLN; Uruguay's José Mujica, a Tupamaro; Nicaragua's Daniel Ortega, a Sandinista guerrilla and president during the Sandinista revolution; and Brazil's Dilma Rousseff, a guerrilla fighter during the Brazilian military dictatorship.

A colonel in the Venezuelan army, Hugo Chávez achieved prominence as leader of a failed 1992 coup. Following a long history of dictatorship, Venezuela's promising experiment in democracy, begun in 1959, had spiraled into a corrupt, elitist regime that had squandered much of the country's oil income and adopted the neoliberal formula in the late 1980s. Chávez's attempted coup aimed to replace that discredited regime with new principles vaguely called "Bolivarian," after the great liberator of South America and founder of Venezuela, Simón Bolívar. Despite its failure, the military uprising made Chávez popular among the country's poor majority and positioned him for a future in electoral politics following his 1994 release from prison.

That future arrived in 1998, when Chávez was elected president with 56 percent of the vote on a promise to clean house and write a new constitution. The following year, he got his new constitution, which named the country the "Bolivarian Republic of Venezuela" and called for broad popular participation in governance. In 2000 he was elected to a six-year term under the terms of the new constitution and began a sustained attack on Venezuela's widespread poverty by enlisting the army to build housing, clinics, schools, and subsidized markets in the slums and in rural areas.

Four years later, Chávez formed the Bolivarian Alliance for the Peoples of Our America (Alianza Bolivariana para los Pueblos de Nuestra América, ALBA), a trade and solidarity agreement initially with Cuba that later spread to other left-governed countries, including Bolivia, Ecuador, Nicaragua, and several Caribbean islands. ALBA allowed Chávez to intensify his social "missions," as he named them, by trading oil for Cuban human capital—some 20,000 medical personnel and teachers who were deployed to Venezuela's poorest areas. He also raised government oil royalties and invested heavily in health, education, nutrition, and literacy programs while agrarian reform benefited some 180,000 families, around half of the rural population. By some estimates, these programs reduced poverty up to 50 percent.

Chávez's authoritarian style was controversial, particularly to the business and conservative political groups that opposed his agenda and to the U.S. government. With its Bolivarian majority, the Congress in 2001 granted Chávez decree powers, which he used extensively. As opposition to his programs and powers grew and the privately owned media openly called for his ouster, a military coup briefly overthrew him in April 2002, but loyal army units and massive protests by his supporters turned the tide, and he was back in office 48 hours later. Washington denied involvement in the coup. The opposition then turned to the new constitution's referendum provision to force a recall election, but the president prevailed with 59 percent of the vote.

Chávez continued to build his personal power, winning reelection in 2006 with 63 percent of the vote, forming his United Socialist Party of

Venezuela (Partido Socialista Unido de Venezuela, PSUV) the following year, and in 2009 winning a referendum to allow unlimited presidential reelections. The opposition and U.S. media began labeling Chávez a dictator, despite international observers' validation of all the elections and referenda. The U.S. government was spending some 40 million dollars annually to shore up the opposition to a regime it considered increasingly hostile, even dangerous, to U.S. interests. Chávez responded by assailing "American imperialism" and calling U.S. President George W. Bush "the devil."

Diagnosed with cancer in 2011, Chávez went to Cuba several times for treatment and died in March 2013 after winning another presidential term in 2012. His preserved body reposes in an impressive mausoleum with an eternal flame and a military guard. His vice president, Nicolás Maduro, succeeded him and won a six-year term in a narrow victory over opposition leader Henrique Capriles a month after Chávez's death. The outlook for Maduro was not rosy. While Chávez was enormously popular with his base of poor Venezuelans, he had governed as a charismatic leader who developed a cult of personality and established relationships with his followers through his social programs and his Sunday television and radio show, *"Aló Presidente"* (Hello President). Thus he had not needed to build institutions to translate his vision of participatory democracy and 21st-century socialism into concrete forms. Nor could he transfer his charismatic leadership to the new president, although Maduro constantly invoked Chávez's name and legacy. With falling oil prices beginning in 2014 and resulting shortages of consumer goods and increased unrest eroding his popularity, Maduro turned to heightened repression of the opposition. That opposition won two-thirds control of Congress in December 2015 and set about trying to terminate Maduro's presidency. By 2017 the future of Chávez's Bolivarian dream hung in the balance.

Along with Rafael Correa of Ecuador and Evo Morales of Bolivia, Chávez represented the more radical, populist version of the Pink Tide. Brazil's Lula followed a less flamboyant, more moderate approach to humanizing neoliberalism. As the long Brazilian military dictatorship (1964–1985) prepared to return governance to civilians and began to allow political activity, one of those taking advantage of the opening was Lula, who formed an independent labor union and, in 1980 the Workers' Party (Partido dos Trabalhadores, PT). Lula ran for president in 1990 and lost. The victor, Fernando Collor de Mello, followed the Latin American trend by introducing neoliberal policies of austerity, lowered tariffs, and privatization of government-owned enterprises. The persistent Lula lost in the two subsequent elections before prevailing on his fourth try in 2002.

During his two presidential terms, Lula focused on dual goals: gaining Brazil an international status commensurate with the world's eighth-largest economy and alleviating the country's endemic, widespread poverty. Internationally, he promoted Brazil's traditional exports as well as its new products such as ethanol and airplanes. He advocated unsuccessfully for a permanent seat on the UN Security Council, but gave Brazil a prominent role in the new Group of Twenty (G-20), an international forum for major economies. Taking advantage of enhanced export earnings, he paid off Brazil's foreign debt in 2006. Finally, Lula lured the world's greatest sporting events to Brazil: the World Cup soccer tournament in 2014 and, for only the second time in Latin America, the Olympic Games in 2016.

Lula's war on poverty was a multipronged endeavor that included raising the minimum wage and expanding social security, but the centerpiece and most widely recognized element was the policy of making cash payments to families living below the poverty line. He launched the Zero Hunger (*Fome Zero*) program to combat the malnutrition that accompanied poverty. Then he combined that program with one started by his predecessor, Fernando Henrique Cardoso, that paid cash to families for keeping their children in school and getting them vaccinated. The hybrid Family Stipend (*Bolsa Familia*) eventually reached nearly a quarter of Brazil's population. These combined approaches reduced poverty dramatically; government figures indicate that "extreme poverty" fell from 9 percent to 4 percent by 2012. Graduation rates increased significantly, due to the powerful financial incentive for parents to school their children. Critics of the cash subsidy approach claimed that it created attitudes of dependency and pointed out the potentially dangerous consequences of the program ending and returning millions to poverty. Nonetheless, variants of the *Familia Bolsa* program were introduced in other Latin American countries.

Lula's former chief of staff, Dilma Rousseff, the daughter of Bulgarian immigrants, succeeded him as president in 2010 and continued most of his international and domestic initiatives. She faced major popular protests in 2013 that were initially aimed at price increases for public transportation but escalated into a mobilization against poor public education and health services, corruption, and what many saw as excessive spending on new facilities for the World Cup and Olympic Games. Against this background, Rousseff barely won reelection in 2014 and continued to face the challenge of a faltering economy, growing corruption scandals, low approval ratings, and growing popular opposition. She was impeached on charges unrelated to corruption, removed from office by Congress in 2016, and replaced by a conservative acting president. This development, along with the victory of conservative Mauricio Macri in Argentina's 2016 presidential election and the daunting challenges facing Venezuela's Maduro, suggested that by the mid-2010s, after nearly two decades, the Pink Tide was becoming an ebb tide.

Indigenous Activism

Among the notable political developments since 1990 are heightened political awareness and activism among Latin America's native peoples. The genocide of Guatemala's Maya peasantry under state terrorism raised consciousness of the plight of indigenous groups, and the 1992 quincentennial of Columbus's voyage of "discovery" catalyzed Indians to protest the legacies of European imperialism and their continued marginalization under republican governments. After decades of frustration with their degraded condition, Maya Indians in the southern Mexican state of Chiapas organized as the Zapatista National Liberation Army (Ejército Zapatista de Liberación Nacional, EZLN) and rose in rebellion on January 1, 1994. Not coincidentally, that was the day that the North American Free Trade Agreement (NAFTA), which links Mexico with Canada and the United States in a free trade zone, took effect, threatening to further impoverish the Maya farmers facing competition from more efficient northern agricultural producers. Led by a non-Indian, Subcomandante Marcos, the rebels captured San Cristóbal de las Casas, the state capital, skirmished briefly with government forces, then settled into a protracted war that relied more on Web sites than bullets.

The EZLN's program soon expanded from economic grievances to include broad claims of rights and identity for all of Mexico's indigenous groups, approximately 10 percent of the country's population. Rejecting the historic approach that promoted assimilation of native peoples, the EZLN demanded autonomy and self-determination along with land rights for Indians. The 1996 San Andrés Accords negotiated with government representatives incorporated the Zapatistas' key demands: "A judicial framework that establishes a new relationship between indigenous peoples and the State, based on their right to self determination and the judicial, political, social, economic and cultural rights that obtain from it."[7] However, President Ernesto Zedillo failed to submit the accords to Congress for ratification, and the conflict in Chiapas simmered well into the 21st century.

The rise of native consciousness and militancy led to a different outcome in Bolivia, Latin America's only majority-Indian country. In 2005

Bolivians elected Evo Morales, an Aymara Indian, as president. Morales had been leader of the coca growers' organizations that strongly opposed U.S. efforts to suppress cultivation of the coca leaf that yields cocaine but is also a traditional Andean product with important cultural significance. He was inaugurated twice: in the traditional ceremony in La Paz and an indigenous ritual at a native religious site. One of the more militant Pink Tide leaders, Morales took office determined to institutionalize and protect Bolivia's native heritage. While nationalizing important sectors of the economy and restarting the agrarian reform that had originated in Bolivia's 1952 revolution, he also pushed for a new constitution. Enacted in 2009, the new document created the "Plurinational State of Bolivia." It defines indigenous peoples as "every human collective that shares a cultural identity, language, historic tradition, institutions, territory and world view, whose existence predates the *Spanish colonial invasion*" [italics added].[8] Among recognized indigenous rights are self-determination, collective ownership of land (the *ayllu*), cultural identity, religious beliefs, and practices and customs. The constitution also allowed for presidential reelection, and Morales was easily reelected in 2009 and 2014, although a 2016 referendum on allowing another reelection narrowly failed.

The End of Latin America's Longest Insurgency

Several rural guerrilla movements appeared in the 1960s in Colombia, the largest and most durable of which were the National Liberation Army (Ejército de Liberación Nacional, ELN) and the Revolutionary Armed Forces of Colombia (Fuerzas Armadas Revolucionarias de Colombia, FARC), both established in 1964 by Communist factions. Over time, FARC became the larger and more effective fighting force. By the late 1990s its army comprised some 17,000 fighters who held substantial amounts of territory as a liberated zone while operating in other rural areas as well as in cities. To finance its operations, the FARC engaged in two lucrative pursuits: taxing coca farmers and cocaine traffickers, and kidnapping for ransom. These revenue sources gave the FARC a solid financial foundation with which to recruit soldiers and acquire materiel.

The FARC's situation began to deteriorate early in the new century under dual pressures. Plan Colombia, a U.S.-funded multibillion-dollar program initiated in 2000, provided financial aid and intelligence, a fleet of helicopters, and U.S. advisors to the Colombian government. Officially labeled an antidrug campaign, Plan Colombia also targeted the guerrillas. Álvaro Uribe, elected president in 2002, turned up the heat on FARC using expanded landowner-run paramilitary forces to supplement the national armed forces. Under this multipronged assault, FARC ranks thinned, falling to an estimated 7,000 fighters by 2013.

Uribe's successor, Juan Manuel Santos, offered to renew peace negotiations in 2010. Government and FARC representatives met in Havana for five years, finally striking a deal in August 2016 that called for hostilities to end and the FARC to become a political party with a small number of guaranteed seats in Congress. FARC fighters would be subjected to a regimen of restorative justice in which full confessions of minor crimes would result in absolution, whereas perpetrators of more serious crimes would face penalties short of prison time. The agreement also called for a program of agrarian reform—long a goal of the Colombian left. An October referendum narrowly rejected the deal for being too lenient on the FARC, according to observers. Undaunted, the FARC and Santos resumed negotiations. With the support of his party's congressional majority, Santos succeeded in resurrecting the rejected agreement with minor changes and getting it approved without a referendum. President Santos and the FARC commander known as Temochenko signed the agreement ending the protracted conflict on November 24, 2016. For his efforts, Santos received the Nobel Peace Prize.

Although its long struggle for a Marxist state failed, the FARC vowed to pursue the same goal in the political arena as a political party. The FARC's transformation left only the much-weakened ELN in the field. Peace negotiations underway in 2017 between the government and the ELN appeared promising. Should they succeed, Latin America's longest insurgency—one launched in the heyday of the Cuban Revolution—would end.

Cuba in Transition

The collapse of Communism in Europe, the elimination of the Soviet subsidy, and the end of the Soviet bloc's trading system, COMECON, plunged Castro's regime into profound crisis. Still heavily reliant on sugar exports, which beginning in the early 1990s had to compete in the world market without subsidies, the Cuban economy contracted by a third between 1989 and 1993. Castro responded to this severe blow to an already austere economy by proclaiming a "special period in peacetime" and invoking the familiar calls to sacrifice for the revolution. Reflecting on the crisis several years later, he remarked: "When the Soviet Union and the Socialist camp disappeared, no one would have wagered one cent on the survival of the Cuban Revolution."[9]

Castro also instituted economic reforms, including modest openings for private small businesses and legalization of the use of dollars. Bypassed earlier by the spectacular development of Caribbean tourism, Cuba opened up in the 1990s to controlled foreign investment in beach resorts: from 2,000 hotel rooms and 3 airlines serving the island in 1989, Cuba boasted 30,000 rooms and 47 airlines a decade later—and the expansion has continued, fueled by tourists from Europe and Canada. Remittances from family members in the United States and medical tourism brought in additional hard currency.

The West's victory in the Cold War pressured Castro to conform to Western norms of democracy and human rights. Yet Castro successfully met the challenge of establishing international legitimacy for his increasingly anachronistic regime in the post-Soviet world. By the end of the 1990s, almost all Latin American countries had reestablished diplomatic and trade relations with the island. Rather than calling for the overthrow of their governments, Castro now hobnobbed with presidents and prime ministers at international conferences. Three popes visited the island between 1998 and 2015. Beginning in the early 1990s, the UN annually condemned the United States for continuing its long-running trade embargo. But while relations with the rest of the world normalized, the chill between Havana and Washington deepened. The 1992 Cuban Democracy Act and the 1996 Helms–Burton Act sought to stem the influx of Western capital that had begun to undermine U.S. sanctions. These laws also codified the embargo, heretofore based on presidential discretion, as law and prohibited lifting it until a democratic, post-Castro government was in place.

In declining health, Castro surprised the world in 2008 by stepping down from the presidency at age 81. He was succeeded by his younger brother Raúl Castro, a veteran of the Sierra Maestra guerrilla campaign and Castro's second in command over the decades. More pragmatic than Fidel, Raúl began instituting a series of market-oriented reforms designed to improve living standards and stanch the flow of thousands of Cubans who abandoned the island in search of better lives abroad. In order to create a mixed state–private economy, the government announced its intention to reduce government employment, which still amounted to nearly 100 percent of Cubans, by 20 percent. As areas for legal private business expanded, Cubans opened thousands of small shops, restaurants, and services, including renting rooms to tourists in private homes. A new real estate market allowed individuals to buy and sell houses and apartments. And important infrastructural improvements were undertaken in partnership with foreign capital, including a deepwater port at Mariel. Personal freedoms are still restricted, but Cubans with the means to do so can now travel abroad without seeking permission, and numerous Cuban baseball players have joined the U.S. major leagues.

Salvation through economic innovation has carried a high and growing price. The basic tenet of the revolution, egalitarianism, has given way to a glaring division in Cuban society between those with access to dollars or euros, and thus to consumer goods, and those without who still depend on low-paying state jobs and the ration card. Medical doctors and university professors turn to driving taxis and serving food in order to enter the hard-currency economy. Although most Cubans appear to support the recent changes, there is a deep-seated fear that exiles may return some day and, supported by capitalist law, reclaim their properties and businesses and reestablish the old order.

Under Presidents Raúl Castro and Barack Obama, relations have recently thawed in ways that were unthinkable just a few years earlier. Following 18 months of talks brokered by Pope Francis, in December 2014, the presidents announced the resumption of full diplomatic ties severed in 1961. Despite objections from Republicans in the U.S. Congress, Obama and Castro reopened the shuttered embassies in July 2015. During a state visit to the island in March 2016, President Obama stated: "I have come here to bury the last remnant of the Cold War in the Americas."[10] Following the easing of restrictions on U.S. tourism, commercial flights linking the two countries resumed in August 2016.

According to opinion surveys, this rapprochement is strongly supported by Cubans and by the U.S. public, including many Cuban Americans, whose U.S.-born younger generations seem to embrace good relations with the island over the adamant anti-Castro position of their elders. It was also well received throughout Latin America. The next step in normalizing relations—lifting the embargo—faced the prospect of opposition in the U.S. Congress, which, thanks to the two laws of the 1990s, must approve the measure if the current Cuban political system remains in place, as Raúl has emphatically vowed that it will even after his announced 2018 retirement.

The icon of the Cuban Revolution and hero of the Latin American left, Fidel Castro, died on November 25, 2016, at the age of 90. Thus ended the life and career of a man from a small island nation who became a giant on the world stage. His revolution brought hope for a better life to millions of Latin Americans, but when the wave of revolution that it launched became too threatening to vested interests in Latin America and the United States, hope turned to despair under the crushing repression of state terrorism. Even after the era of the Cuban Revolution had passed, Castro continued to influence Latin American politics in a variety of ways. Now in his grave, Fidel Castro continues to be either worshipped or vilified, but not ignored.

Notes

1. Herbert Matthews, *The Cuban Story* (New York: George Braziller, 1961), 185.

2. Rebecca Bill Chávez, *The Rule of Law in Nascent Democracies: Judicial Politics in Argentina* (Stanford, CA: Stanford University Press, 2004), 29.

3. Samuel P. Huntington, *The Third Wave: Democratization in the Late Twentieth Century* (Norman: University of Oklahoma Press, 1991).

4. www.oas.org/charter/docs/resolution1_en_p4.htm.

5. Jonathan Schlefer, *Palace Politics: How the Ruling Party Brought Crisis to Mexico* (Austin: University of Texas Press, 2008), 1.

6. Thomas W. Walker, *Nicaragua without Illusions: Regime Transition and Structural Adjustment in the 1990s* (Wilmington, DE: Scholarly Resources, 1997), 300.

7. See flag.blackened.net/revolt/mexico/ezln/san_andres.html.

8. Article 30 of the 2009 Bolivian constitution: https://www.constituteproject .org/constitution/Bolivia_2009.pdf.

9. Fidel Castro and Ignacio Ramonet, *Fidel Castro: My Life, a Spoken Autobiography*, trans. Andrew Hurley (New York: Scribner, 2008), 365.

10. *New York Times*, March 22, 2016.

Suggested Further Reading

These suggestions for further reading are limited to books in English.

Chapter 1

Aguilar, Luis E. *Cuba 1933—Prologue to Revolution*. Ithaca, NY: Cornell University Press, 1972.

Ameringer, Charles D. *The Cuban Democratic Experience: The Auténtico Years, 1944–1952*. Gainesville: University of Florida Press, 2000.

Argote-Freyre, Frank. *Fulgencio Batista*. New Brunswick, NJ: Rutgers University Press, 2006.

Benjamin, Jules R. *The United States and Cuba: Hegemony and Dependent Development, 1880–1934*. Pittsburgh: University of Pittsburgh Press, 1977.

Bonachea, Rolando, and Marta San Martín. *The Cuban Insurrection, 1952–1958*. New Brunswick, NJ: Transaction Books, 1974.

Castro, Fidel. *History Will Absolve Me*. Translator not indicated. Havana: Editorial de Ciencias Sociales, 1975.

Castro, Fidel. *Revolutionary Struggle, 1947–1958*. Ed. Rolando Bonachea and Nelson P. Valdés. Cambridge, MA: MIT Press, 1972.

Castro, Fidel and Ignacio Ramonet. *Fidel Castro: My Life, a Spoken Autobiography*. Trans. Andrew Hurley. New York: Scribner, 2008.

Chase, Michelle. *Revolution within the Revolution: Women and Gender Politics in Cuba, 1952–1962*. Chapel Hill: University of North Carolina Press, 2015.

Dosal, Paul J. *Comandante Che: Guerrilla Soldier, Commander, and Strategist, 1956–1967*. State Park: Pennsylvania State University Press, 2003.

Franqui, Carlos. *Diary of the Cuban Revolution*. Trans. Georgette Felix et al. New York: Viking, 1980.

González, Edward. *Cuba under Castro: The Limits of Charisma*. Boston: Houghton Mifflin, 1974.

Guevara, Ernesto (Che). *Reminiscences of the Cuban Revolutionary War*. Trans. Victoria Ortiz. New York: Grove Press, 1968.

Hart, Armando. *Aldabonazo: Inside the Cuban Revolutionary Underground: A Participant's Account.* Ed. Mary-Alice Waters. New York: Pathfinder Press, 2004.

Marel García-Pérez, Gladys. *Insurrection and Revolution: Armed Struggle in Cuba, 1952–1959.* Trans. Juan Ortega. Boulder, CO: Lynne Rienner, 1998.

Matthews, Herbert L. *The Cuban Story.* New York: George Braziller, 1961.

Palmer, Steven Paul, José Antonio Arenas Piqueras, and Amparo Sánchez Cobos, eds. *State of Ambiguity: Civic Life and Culture in Cuba's First Republic.* Durham, NC: Duke University Press, 2014.

Pérez, Louis A., Jr. *Cuba: Between Reform and Revolution.* 5th ed. New York: Oxford University Press, 2014.

Pérez, Louis A. *Cuba under the Platt Amendment, 1902–1934.* Pittsburgh: University of Pittsburgh Press, 1986.

Pérez, Louis A. *Intervention, Revolution, and Politics in Cuba, 1913–1921.* Pittsburgh: University of Pittsburgh Press, 1978.

Suchlicki, Jaime. *Cuba from Columbus to Castro and Beyond.* 5th ed. Washington, DC: Brassey's, 2002.

Suchlicki, Jaime. *University Students and Revolution in Cuba, 1920–1968.* Coral Gables, FL: University of Miami Press, 1969.

Sweig, Julia E. *Inside the Cuban Revolution: Fidel Castro and the Urban Underground.* Cambridge, MA: Harvard University Press, 2002.

Szulc, Tad. *Fidel: A Critical Portrait.* New York: William Morrow, 1986.

Chapter 2

Balfour, Sebastian. *Castro.* 3rd ed. Harlow, UK: Pearson Longman, 2009.

Bernardo, Robert M. *The Theory of Moral Incentives in Cuba.* Tuscaloosa: University of Alabama Press, 1971.

Blasier, Cole, and Carmelo Mesa-Lago, eds. *Cuba in the World.* Pittsburgh: University of Pittsburgh Press, 1979.

Blight, James G. and Peter Kornbluh, eds. *Politics of Illusion: The Bay of Pigs Invasion Reexamined.* Boulder, CO: Lynne Rienner, 1998.

Brundenius, Claes. *Revolutionary Cuba: The Challenge of Economic Growth with Equity.* Boulder, CO: Westview Press, 1984.

Bunck, Julie Marie. *Fidel Castro and the Quest for a Revolutionary Culture in Cuba.* University Park: Pennsylvania State University Press, 1994.

Carbonell, Nestor T. *And the Russians Stayed: The Sovietization of Cuba: A Personal Portrait.* New York: Morrow, 1989.

Castro, Fidel. *The First and Second Declarations of Havana: Manifestos of Revolutionary Struggle in the Americas Adopted by the Cuban People.* 3rd ed. Ed. Mary-Alice Waters. New York: Pathfinder Press, 2007.

Chomsky, Aviva. *A History of the Cuban Revolution.* 2nd ed. Hoboken, NJ: John Wiley and Sons, 2015.

Domínguez, Jorge I. *Cuba: Order and Revolution*. Cambridge, MA: Harvard University Press, 1978.

Domínguez, Jorge I. *To Make a World Safe for Revolution: Cuba's Foreign Policy*. Cambridge, MA: Harvard University Press, 1989.

Duncan, W. Raymond. *The Soviet Union and Cuba: Interests and Influence*. New York: Praeger, 1985.

Fagen, Richard R. *The Transformation of Political Culture in Cuba*. Stanford, CA: Stanford University Press, 1969.

Farber, Samuel. *The Origins of the Cuban Revolution Reconsidered*. Chapel Hill: University of North Carolina Press, 2006.

Franqui, Carlos. *Family Portrait with Fidel: A Memoir*. Trans. Alfred MacAdam. New York: Random House, 1984.

Geyer, Georgie Anne. *Guerrilla Prince: The Untold Story of Fidel Castro*. 3rd ed. Kansas City, MO: Andrews McMeel, 2001.

Horowitz, Irving Louis, and Jaime Suchlicki, eds. *Cuban Communism, 1959–1995*. 11th ed. New Brunswick, NJ: Transaction Publishers, 2003.

Kenner, Martin, and James Petras, eds. *Fidel Castro Speaks*. New York: Grove Press, 1969.

Kornbluh, Peter, ed. *The Bay of Pigs Declassified: The Secret CIA Report on the Invasion of Cuba*. New York: New Press, 1998.

LeoGrande, William M. *Cuba's Policy in Africa, 1959–1980*. Berkeley: University of California, Institute of International Studies, 1980.

Leonard, Thomas M. *Castro and the Cuban Revolution*. Westport, CT: Greenwood Press, 1999.

Leonard, Thomas M. *Fidel Castro: A Biography*. Westport, CT: Greenwood Press, 2004.

Lockwood, Lee. *Castro's Cuba, Cuba's Fidel*. 2nd ed. Boulder, CO: Westview Press, 1990.

Munton, Don, and David A. Welch. *The Cuban Missile Crisis: A Concise History*. New York: Oxford University Press, 2012.

Paterson, Thomas G. *Contesting Castro: The United States and the Triumph of the Cuban Revolution*. New York: Oxford University Press, 1994.

Pérez-Stable, Marifeli. *The Cuban Revolution: Origins, Course, and Legacy*. 3rd ed. New York: Oxford University Press, 2011.

Rabkin, Rhoda P. *Cuban Politics: The Revolutionary Experiment*. New York: Praeger, 1991.

Schoultz, Lars. *That Infernal Little Cuban Republic: The United States and the Cuban Revolution*. Chapel Hill: University of North Carolina Press, 2009.

Stern, Sheldon M. *The Cuban Missile Crisis in American Memory: Myth versus Reality*. Stanford, CA: Stanford University Press, 2012.

Thomas, Hugh. *Cuba, or, the Pursuit of Freedom*. 2nd ed. New York: Da Capo Press, 1998.

Yafee, Helen. *Che Guevara: The Economics of Revolution*. London: Palgrave Macmillan, 2009.

Chapter 3

Aguilar, Luis E. *Marxism in Latin America*. New York: Alfred A. Knopf, 1968.

Alexander, Robert J. *Agrarian Reform in Latin America*. New York: Macmillan, 1974.

Blanco, Hugo. *Land or Death: The Peasant Struggle in Peru*. New York: Pathfinder Press, 1972.

Brands, Hal. *Latin America's Cold War*. Cambridge, MA: Harvard University Press, 2010.

Brown, Jonathan C. *Cuba's Revolutionary World*. Cambridge, MA: Harvard University Press, 2017.

Castro, Daniel, ed. *Revolution and Revolutionaries: Guerrilla Movements in Latin America*. Wilmington, DE: SR Books, 1999.

Dorner, Peter. *Latin American Land Reforms in Theory and Practice: A Retrospective Analysis*. Madison: University of Wisconsin Press, 1992.

Feder, Ernest. *The Rape of the Peasantry: Latin America's Landholding System*. Garden City, NY: Doubleday, 1971.

Frank, Andre Gunder. *Latin America: Underdevelopment or Revolution*. New York: Monthly Review Press, 1969.

Garrard-Burnett, Virginia, Mark Atwood Lawrence, and Julio E. Moreno, eds. *Beyond the Eagle's Shadow: New Histories of Latin America's Cold War*. Albuquerque: University of New Mexico Press, 2013.

Goldenberg, Boris. *The Cuban Revolution and Latin America*. New York: Praeger, 1966.

Hodges, Donald C. *The Latin American Revolution: Politics and Strategy from Apro-Marxism to Guevarism*. New York: William Morrow, 1974.

Horowitz, Irving Louis, Josué de Castro, and John Gerassi, eds. *Latin American Radicalism*. New York: Vintage Books, 1969.

Jackson, Bruce D. *Castro, the Kremlin, and Communism in Latin America*. Baltimore: Johns Hopkins University Press, 1969.

Johnson, Ollie A. *Brazilian Party Politics and the Coup of 1964*. Gainesville: University Press of Florida, 2001.

Landsberger, Henry A., ed. *Latin American Peasant Movements*. Ithaca, NY: Cornell University Press, 1969.

Levinson, Jerome, and Juan de Onís. *The Alliance That Lost Its Way*. Chicago: Quadrangle Books, 1970.

Mercier Vega, Luis. *Roads to Power in Latin America*. Trans. Robert Rowland. New York: Praeger, 1969.

Parker, Phyllis R. *Brazil and the Quiet Intervention, 1964*. Austin: University of Texas Press, 1979.

Petras, James F., and Robert LaPorte, Jr. *Cultivating Revolution: The United States and Agrarian Reform in Latin America*. New York: Random House, 1971.

Petras, James F., Robert LaPorte, Jr., and Maurice Zeitlin, eds. *Latin America: Reform or Revolution?* New York: Fawcett, 1968.

Ratliff, William E. *Castroism and Communism in Latin America, 1959–1976: The Varieties of Marxist-Leninist Experience.* Washington, D.C.: American Enterprise Institute for Public Policy Research, 1976.

Skidmore, Thomas E. *Politics in Brazil, 1930–1964: An Experiment in Democracy.* Updated ed. New York: Oxford University Press, 2007.

Stavenhagen, Rodolfo, ed. *Agrarian Problems and Peasant Movements in Latin America.* Garden City, NY: Doubleday, 1970.

Thiesenhusen, William C. *Broken Promises: Agrarian Reform and the Latin American Campesino.* Boulder, CO: Westview Press, 1995.

Thiesenhusen, William C. *Searching for Agrarian Reform in Latin America.* Boston: Unwin Hyman, 1989.

Véliz, Claudio, ed. *The Politics of Conformity in Latin America.* London: Oxford University Press, 1967.

Wickhan-Crowley, Patrick J. *Revolution in Latin America: A Comparative Study of Insurgents and Regimes since 1956.* Princeton, NJ: Princeton University Press, 1992.

Chapter 4

Alexander, Robert J. *Rómulo Betancourt and the Transformation of Venezuela.* New Brunswick, NJ: Transaction Books, 1982.

Ayers, Bradley E. *The War That Never Was: An Insider's Account of CIA Covert Operations Against Cuba.* Indianapolis: Bobbs-Merrill, 1976.

Ball, M. Margaret. *The OAS in Transition.* Durham, NC: Duke University Press, 1969.

Barber, Willard F., and C. Neale Ronning. *Internal Security and Military Power: Counterinsurgency and Civic Action in Latin America.* Columbus: Ohio State University Press, 1966.

Blasier, Cole. *The Hovering Giant: U.S. Responses to Revolutionary Change in Latin America, 1910–1985.* Rev. ed. Pittsburgh: University of Pittsburgh Press, 1985.

Blight, James A. and Peter Kornbluh. *Politics of Illusion: The Bay of Pigs Invasion Reexamined.* Boulder, CO: Lynne Rienner, 1998.

Child, John. *Unequal Alliance: The Inter-American Military System, 1938–1978.* Boulder, CO: Westview Press, 1980.

Immerman, Richard H. *The CIA in Guatemala: The Foreign Policy of Intervention.* Austin: University of Texas Press, 1982.

Jones, Howard. *Bay of Pigs.* New York: Oxford University Press, 2008.

Klare, Michael T., and Cynthia Arnson. *Supplying Repression: U.S. Support for Authoritarian Regimes Abroad.* Washington, D.C.: Institute for Policy Studies, 1981.

Latham, Michael E. *Modernization as Ideology: American Social Science and "Nation Building" in the Kennedy Era.* Chapel Hill: University of North Carolina Press, 2000.

Levinson, Jerome, and Juan de Onís. *The Alliance That Lost Its Way.* Chicago: Quadrangle Books, 1970.

Lowenthal, Abraham F. *The Dominican Intervention.* Reprint. Baltimore: Johns Hopkins University Press, 1995.

Martz, John D., ed. *United States Policy in Latin America: A Quarter Century of Crisis and Challenge, 1961–1986.* Lincoln: University of Nebraska Press, 1988.

Martz, John D., and Lars Schoultz, eds. *Latin America, the United States, and the Inter-American System.* Boulder, CO: Westview Press, 1980.

Morley, Morris T. *Imperial State and Revolution: The United States and Cuba, 1952–1986.* Cambridge: Cambridge University Press, 1987.

Parkinson, F. *Latin America, the Cold War, and the World Powers, 1945–1973.* Beverly Hills, CA: Sage Publications, 1974.

Rabe, Stephen G. *The Killing Zone: The United States Wages Cole War in Latin America.* New York: Oxford University Press, 2011.

Rabe, Stephen G. *The Most Dangerous Area in the World: John F. Kennedy Confronts Communist Revolution in Latin America.* Chapel Hill: University of North Carolina Press, 1999.

Rodriguez, Felix I., and John Weisman. *Shadow Warrior.* New York: Simon and Schuster, 1989.

Scheman, Ronald L., ed. *The Alliance for Progress: A Retrospective.* New York: Praeger, 1988.

Schlesinger, Arthur M., Jr. *A Thousand Days.* Boston: Houghton Mifflin, 1966.

Schlesinger, Stephen, and Stephen Kinzer. *Bitter Fruit: The Untold Story of the American Coup in Guatemala.* Garden City, NY: Doubleday & Co., 1982.

Schoultz, Lars. *Human Rights and United States Policy toward Latin America.* Princeton, NJ: Princeton University Press, 1981.

Smith, Peter H. *Talons of the Eagle: Latin America, the United States, and the World.* 4th ed. New York: Oxford University Press, 2013.

Taffet, Jeffrey F. *Foreign Aid as Foreign Policy: The Alliance for Progress in Latin America.* New York: Routledge, 2007.

Welch, Richard E., Jr. *Response to Revolution: The United States and the Cuban Revolution, 1959–1961.* Chapel Hill: University of North Carolina Press, 1985.

Williams, Mark Eric. *Understanding U.S.-Latin American Relations: Theory and History.* New York: Routledge, 2012.

Chapter 5

Alexander, Robert J. *The Bolivian National Revolution.* New Brunswick, NJ: Rutgers University Press, 1958.

Anderson, Jon Lee. *Che Guevara: A Revolutionary Life.* 2nd ed. New York: Grove Press, 2010.

Béjar, Héctor. *Peru 1965: Notes on a Guerrilla Experience.* Trans. William Rose. New York: Monthly Review Press, 1970.

Blackburn, Robin, ed. *Strategy for Revolution: Essays on Latin America by Régis Deb-ray.* New York: Monthly Review Press, 1970.

Bonachea, Rolando, and Nelson P. Valdés. *Che: Selected Works of Ernesto Guevara.* Cambridge, MA: MIT Press, 1969.

Braun, Herbert. *Our Guerrillas, Our Sidewalks: A Journey into the Violence of Colom-bia.* 2nd ed. Lanham, MD: Rowman & Littlefield, 2003.

Bravo, Douglas. *Douglas Bravo Speaks: Interview with Venezuelan Leader.* New York: Merit, 1970.

Brittain, James J. Revolutionary *Social Change in Colombia: The Origins and Direc-tion of the FARC-EP.* London: Pluto Press, 2010.

Bustos, Ciro. *Che Wants to See You: The Untold Story of Che in Bolivia.* Trans. Ann Wright. London: Verso, 2013.

Castañeda, Jorge G. *Compañero: The Life and Death of Che Guevara.* Trans. Marina Castañeda. New York: Knopf, 1997.

Debray, Régis. *Che's Guerrilla War.* Trans. Rosemary Sheed. Harmondsworth, UK: Penguin Books, 1975.

Debray, Régis. *Revolution in the Revolution? Armed Struggle and Political Struggle in Latin America.* Trans. Bobbye Ortiz. New York: Grove Press, 1967.

Gadea, Hilda. *Ernesto: A Memoir of Che Guevara.* Garden City, NY: Doubleday, 1972.

Gerassi, John, ed. *Revolutionary Priest: The Complete Writings and Messages of Camilo Torres.* New York: Random House, 1972.

Gerassi, John, ed. *Venceremos! The Speeches and Writings of Che Guevara.* New York: Macmillan, 1968.

González, Luis J., and Gustavo A. Sánchez Salazar. *The Great Rebel: Che Guevara in Bolivia.* Trans. Helen R. Lane. New York: Grove Press, 1969.

Gorriti Ellenbogen, Gustavo. *The Shining Path: A History of the Millenarian War in Peru.* Trans. Robin Kirk. Chapel Hill: University of North Carolina Press, 1999.

Gott, Richard. *Guerrilla Movements in Latin America.* Garden City, NY: Anchor Books, 1972.

Guevara, Che. *Guerrilla Warfare.* 3rd ed. Revised and updated introduction and case studies by Brian Loveman and Thomas M. Davies, Jr. Wilmington, DE: Scholarly Resources, 1997.

Harris, Richard L. *Death of a Revolutionary: Che Guevara's Last Mission.* Revised and Updated edition. New York: W. W. Norton, 2007.

Hodges, Donald C., ed. *The Legacy of Che Guevara: A Documentary Study.* London: Thomas and Hudson, 1977.

James, Daniel. *Che Guevara: A Biography.* New York: Stein and Day, 1969.

James, Daniel, ed. *The Complete Bolivian Diaries of Che Guevara and Other Captured Documents.* 1st Cooper Square ed. New York: Cooper Square Press, 2000.

Leech, Garry. *The FARC: the Longest Insurgency.* London: Zed Books, 2011.

Llorente, Renzo. *The Political Theory of Che Guevara.* Lanham, MD: Rowman & Littlefield, 2017.

Malloy, James M. *Bolivia: The Uncompleted Revolution*. Pittsburgh: University of Pittsburgh Press, 1970.

McClintock, Cynthia. *Revolutionary Movements in Latin America: El Salvador's FMLN and Peru's Shining Path*. Washington, D.C.: United States Institute of Peace Press, 1998.

Palmer, David Scott, ed. *The Shining Path of Peru*. New York: St. Martin's Press, 1992.

Stern, Steve J., ed. *Shining and Other Paths: War and Society in Peru, 1980–1995*. Durham, NC: Duke University Press, 1998.

Chapter 6

Brum, Pablo. *The Robin Hood Guerrillas: The Epic Journey of Uruguay's Tupamaros*. No place of publication: CreateSpace Independent Publishing Platform, 2014.

Churchill, Lindsey Blake. *Becoming the Tupamaros: Solidarity and Transnational Revolutionaries in Uruguay and the United States*. Nashville: Vanderbilt University Press, 2014.

Generals and Tupamaros: The Struggle for Power in Uruguay, 1969–1973. London: Latin American Review of Books, Ltd., 1974.

Gilio, María Esther. *The Tupamaro Guerrillas*. Trans. Anne Edmondson. New York: Ballantine Books, 1973.

Gillespie, Richard. *Soldiers of Perón: Argentina's Montoneros*. New York: Oxford University Press, 1983.

Gregory, Stephen. *José 'Pepe' Mujica: Warrior, Philosopher, President*. Brighton, UK: Sussex Academic Press, 2016.

Halperin, Ernst. *Terrorism in Latin America*. Vol. 4 of *The Washington Papers*. Beverly Hills, CA: Sage Publications, 1976.

Hodges, Donald C. *Argentina, 1943–1987: The National Revolution and Resistance*. Rev. ed. Albuquerque: University of New Mexico Press, 1988.

Hodges, Donald C., ed. and trans. *Philosophy of the Urban Guerrilla: The Revolutionary Writings of Abraham Guillén*. New York: William Morrow, 1973.

Jackson, Sir Geoffrey. *Surviving the Long Night: An Autobiographical Account of a Political Kidnapping*. New York: Vanguard, 1974.

Kohl, James, and John Litt, eds. *Urban Guerrilla Warfare in Latin America*. Cambridge, MA: MIT Press, 1974.

Labrousse, Alain. *The Tupamaros: Urban Guerrillas in Uruguay*. Trans. Dinah Livingstone. Harmondsworth, UK: Penguin, 1973.

Lewis, Paul H. *Guerrillas and Generals: The Dirty War in Argentina*. Westport, CT: Praeger, 2002.

Marighela, Carlos. *For the Liberation of Brazil*. Trans. John Butt and Rosemary Sheed. Harmondsworth, UK: Penguin Books, 1971.

Marighela, Carlos. *The Terrorist Classic: Manual of the Urban Guerrilla*. Trans. Gene Hanrahan. Chapel Hill, NC: Documentary Publications, 1985.

Markarian, Vania. *Uruguay, 1968: Student Activism from Global Counterculture to Molotov Cocktails*. Trans. Laura Pérez Carrara. Oakland: University of California Press, 2017.

Moreira Alves, Marcio. *A Grain of Mustard Seed: The Awakening of the Brazilian Revolution*. Garden City, NY: Doubleday, 1973.

Moss, Robert. *Urban Guerrillas in Latin America*. London: Institute for the Study of Conflict, 1970.

Moyano, María José. *Argentina's Lost Patrol: Armed Struggle, 1969–1979*. New Haven, CT: Yale University Press, 1995.

Núñez, Carlos. *The Tupamaros: Urban Guerrillas of Uruguay*. New York: Times Change Press, 1970.

Porzecanski, Arturo C. *Uruguay's Tupamaros: The Urban Guerrillas*. New York: Praeger, 1973.

Quartim, João. *Dictatorship and Armed Struggle in Brazil*. Trans. David Fernbach. London: New Left Books, 1971.

Ronfledt, David F. *The Mitrione Kidnapping in Uruguay*. Santa Monica, CA: Rand Corporation, 1987.

Weinstein, Martin. *Uruguay: The Politics of Failure*. Westport, CT: Greenwood Press, 1975.

Wilson, Major Carlos. *The Tupamaros: The Unmentionables*. Boston: Branden Publishers, 1974.

Chapter 7

Aguirre, Carlos and Paulo Drinot, eds. *The Peculiar Revolution: Rethinking the Peruvian Experiment under Military Rule*. Austin: University of Texas Press, 2017.

Alberts, Tom. *Agrarian Reform and Rural Poverty: A Case Study of Peru*. Boulder, CO: Westview Press, 1983.

Alexander, Robert J., ed. *Aprismo: The Ideas and Doctrines of Victor Raúl Haya de la Torre*. Kent, OH: Kent State University Press, 1973.

Becker, David G. *The New Bourgeoisie and the Limits of Dependency: Mining, Class, and Power in "Revolutionary" Peru*. Princeton, NJ: Princeton University Press, 1983.

Booth, David, and Bernardo Sorj, eds. *Military Reformism and Social Classes: The Peruvian Experience, 1968–1980*. New York: St. Martin's Press, 1983.

Chaplin, David, ed. *Peruvian Nationalism: A Corporatist Revolution*. New Brunswick, NJ: Transaction Books, 1976.

Chavarría, Jesús. *José Carlos Mariátegui and the Rise of Modern Peru, 1890–1930*. Albuquerque: University of New Mexico Press, 1979.

Cleaves, Peter S., and Martin J. Scurrah. *Agriculture, Bureaucracy, and Military Government in Peru*. Ithaca, NY: Cornell University Press, 1980.

Goodsell, Charles T. *American Corporations and Peruvian Politics*. Cambridge, MA: Harvard University Press, 1974.

Gorman, Stephen M. *Post-Revolutionary Peru: The Politics of Transformation*. Boulder, CO: Westview Press, 1982.

Kantor, Harry. *The Ideology and Politics of the Peruvian Aprista Movement*. New York: Octagon Books, 1966.

Kruijt, Dirk. *Revolution by Decree: Peru, 1968–1975*. Amsterdam: Thela Publishers, 1994.

Lowenthal, Abraham F., ed. *The Peruvian Experiment: Continuity and Change under Military Rule*. Princeton, NJ: Princeton University Press, 1975.

Mariátegui, José Carlos. *Seven Interpretive Essays on Peruvian Reality*. Trans. Marjory Urquidi. Austin: University of Texas Press, 1971.

Mayer, Enrique. *Ugly Stories of the Peruvian Agrarian Reform*. Durham, NC: Duke University Press, 2009.

McClintock, Cynthia. *Peasant Cooperatives and Political Change in Peru*. Princeton, NJ: Princeton University Press, 1982.

McClintock, Cynthia, and Abraham F. Lowenthal, eds. *The Peruvian Experiment Reconsidered*. Princeton, NJ: Princeton University Press, 1983.

Middlebrook, Kevin J., and David Scott Palmer. *The Military and Political Development: Lessons from Peru*. Beverly Hills, CA: Sage Publications, 1975.

North, Liisa, and Tanya Korovkin. *The Peruvian Revolution and the Officers in Power, 1967–1976*. Montreal: McGill University Centre for Developing-Area Studies, 1981.

Palmer, David Scott, ed. *Peru: The Authoritarian Tradition*. New York: Praeger, 1980.

Philip, George D. E. *The Rise and Fall of the Peruvian Military Radicals, 1968–1976*. London: The Athlone Press, 1978.

Saba, Raúl. *Political Development and Democracy in Peru: Continuity and Change in Crisis*. Boulder, CO: Westview Press, 1987.

Stein, Steve. *Populism in Peru: The Emergence of the Masses and the Politics of Social Control*. Madison: University of Wisconsin Press, 1980.

Stepan, Alfred. *The State and Society: Peru in Comparative Perspective*. Princeton, NJ: Princeton University Press, 1978.

Stephens, Evelyne Huber. *The Politics of Workers' Participation: The Peruvian Approach in Comparative Perspective*. New York: Academic Press, 1980.

Vanden, Harry E. *National Marxism in Latin America: José Carlos Mariátegui's Thought and Politics*. Boulder, CO: Lynne Rienner, 1986.

Wils, Frits. *Industrialization, Industrialists, and the Nation-State in Peru: A Comparative/Sociological Analysis*. Berkeley: University of California, Institute of International Studies, 1979.

Chapter 8

Alexander, Robert J. *The Tragedy of Chile*. Westport, CT: Greenwood Press, 1978.

Allende, Salvador. *Chile's Road to Socialism*. Ed. Joan E. Garcés, trans. J. Darling. Harmondsworth, UK: Penguin Books, 1973.

Bitar, Sergio. *Chile: Experiment in Democracy*. Trans. Sam Sherman. Philadelphia: Institute for the Study of Human Issues, 1986.

Castro, Fidel. *Fidel Castro on Chile*. New York: Pathfinder Press, 1982.

Davis, Nathaniel. *The Last Two Years of Salvador Allende*. Ithaca, NY: Cornell University Press, 1985.

Debray, Régis. *The Chilean Revolution: Conversations with Allende*. New York: Pantheon, 1971.

de Vylder, Stefan. *Allende's Chile: The Political Economy of the Rise and Fall of the Unidad Popular*. Cambridge: Cambridge University Press, 1976.

Faúndez, Julio. *Marxism and Democracy in Chile: From 1932 to the Fall of Allende*. New Haven, CT: Yale University Press, 1988.

Figueroa Clark, Víctor. *Salvador Allende: Revolutionary Democrat*. London: Pluto Press, 2013.

Fleet, Michael. *The Rise and Fall of Chilean Christian Democracy*. Princeton, NJ: Princeton University Press, 1985.

Gil, Federico, Ricardo Lagos, and Henry A. Landsberger, eds. *Chile at the Turning Point: Lessons of the Socialist Years, 1970–1973*. Trans. John S. Gitlitz. Philadelphia: Institute for the Study of Human Issues, 1979.

Gustafson, Kristian. *Hostile Intent: U.S. Covert Operations in Chile, 1964–1974*. Washington, D.C.: Potomac Books, 2007.

Harmer, Tanya. *Allende's Chile and the Inter-American Cold War*. Chapel Hill: University of North Carolina Press, 2011.

Haslam, Jonathan. *The Nixon Administration and the Death of Allende's Chile: A Case of Assisted Suicide*. London: Verso, 2005.

Hite, Catherine. *When the Romance Ended: Leaders of the Chilean Left, 1968–1998*. New York: Columbia University Press, 2000.

Kaufman, Edy. *Crisis in Allende's Chile: New Perspectives*. New York: Praeger, 1988.

Loveman, Brian. *Struggle in the Countryside: Politics and Rural Labor in Chile, 1919–1973*. Bloomington: Indiana University Press, 1976.

Morris, David J. *We Must Make Haste—Slowly: The Process of Revolution in Chile*. New York: Vintage Books, 1973.

O'Brien, Philip, ed. *Allende's Chile*. New York: Praeger, 1976.

Petras, James F., and Morris H. Morley. *The United States and Chile: Imperialism and the Overthrow of the Allende Government*. New York: Monthly Review Press, 1975.

Pollack, Benny. *Revolutionary Social Democracy: The Chilean Socialist Policy*. New York: St. Martin's Press, 1986.

Roxborough, Ian, Philip O'Brien, and Jackie Roddick. *Chile: The State and Revolution*. New York: Holmes and Meier, 1977.

Sigmund, Paul E. *The Overthrow of Allende and the Politics of Chile, 1964–1976*. Pittsburgh: University of Pittsburgh Press, 1977.

Stallings, Barbara. *Class Conflict and Economic Development in Chile, 1958–1973*. Stanford, CA: Stanford University Press, 1978.

Valenzuela, Arturo. *The Breakdown of Democratic Regimes: Chile*. Baltimore: Johns Hopkins University Press, 1978.

Valenzuela, Arturo, and J. Samuel Valenzuela, eds. *Chile: Politics and Society*. New Brunswick, NJ: Transaction Books, 1976.

Winn, Peter. *Weavers of Revolution: The Yarur Workers and Chile's Road to Social-ism.* New York: Oxford University Press, 1986.

Wolpin, Miles D. *Cuban Foreign Policy and Chilean Politics.* Lexington, MA: D. C. Heath & Co., 1972.

Chapter 9

Arnove, Robert F. *Education and Revolution in Nicaragua.* New York: Praeger, 1986.

Black, George. *Triumph of the People: The Sandinista Revolution in Nicaragua.* London: Zed Books, 1981.

Booth, John A. *The End and the Beginning: The Nicaraguan Revolution.* 2nd ed. Boulder, CO: Westview Press, 1985.

Burns, E. Bradford. *At War in Nicaragua: The Reagan Doctrine and the Politics of Nostalgia.* New York: Harper and Row, 1987.

Cabezas, Omar. *Fire from the Mountain: The Making of a Sandinista.* Trans. Kathleen Weaver. New York: Crown, 1985.

Colbourn, Forrest. *Post-Revolutionary Nicaragua: State, Class, and the Dilemmas of Agrarian Policy.* Berkeley: University of California Press, 1986.

Cruz, Arturo J. *Memoirs of a Counterrevolutionary.* New York: Doubleday, 1989.

Everingham, Mark. *Revolution and the Multiclass Coalition in Nicaragua.* Pittsburgh: University of Pittsburgh Press, 1996.

Gilbert, Dennis. *Sandinistas: The Party and the Revolution.* New York: Basil Blackwell, 1988.

Harris, Richard L., and Carlos M. Vilas, eds. *Nicaragua: A Revolution under Siege.* London: Zed Books, 1985.

Hodges, Donald C. *Intellectual Foundations of the Nicaraguan Revolution.* Austin: University of Texas Press, 1986.

Kinzer, Stephen. *Blood of Brothers: Life and War in Nicaragua.* 1st David Rockefeller Center for Latin American Studies ed. Cambridge, MA: David Rockefeller Center for Latin American Studies, Harvard University, 2007.

Kombluh, Peter. *Nicaragua, the Price of Intervention: Reagan's Wars against the Sandinistas.* Washington, D.C.: Institute for Policy Studies, 1987.

Millett, Richard. *Guardians of the Dynasty: A History of the U.S.-Created Guardia Nacional de Nicaragua and the Somoza Family.* Maryknoll, NY: Orbis Books, 1977.

Morley, Morris H. *Washington, Somoza, and the Sandinistas: State and Regime in U.S. Policy toward Nicaragua, 1969–1981.* Cambridge: Cambridge University Press, 1994.

Nolan, David. *FSLN, the Ideology of the Sandinistas and the Nicaraguan Revolution.* Miami: Institute of Latin American Studies, University of Miami, 1984.

O'Shaughnessy, Laura Nozzi, and Luis H. Serra. *The Church and Revolution in Nicaragua.* Athens: Ohio University, Center for International Studies, Latin American Studies Program, 1986.

Pastor, Robert A. *Condemned to Repetition: The United States and Nicaragua.* Princeton, NJ: Princeton University Press, 1987.

Ramírez, Sergio. *Adiós Muchachos: A Memoir of the Sandinista Revolution.* Trans. Stacey Alba D. Skar. Durham, NC: Duke University Press, 2012.

Robinson, William I. *David and Goliath: The U.S. War against Nicaragua.* New York: Monthly Review Press, 1987.

Rosset, Peter, and John Vandermeer, eds. *Nicaragua: Unfinished Revolution. The New Nicaragua Reader.* New York: Grove Press, 1986.

Ruchwarger, Gary. *People in Power: Forging a Grassroots Democracy in Nicaragua.* South Hadley, MA: Bergin and Garvey, 1987.

Spalding, Rose J., ed. *The Political Economy of Revolutionary Nicaragua.* Winchester, MA: Allen and Unwin, 1987.

Vilas, Carlos. *State, Class, and Ethnicity in Nicaragua: Capitalist Modernization and Revolutionary Change on the Atlantic Coast.* Trans. Susan Norwood. Boulder, CO: Lynne Rienner, 1989.

Walker, Thomas W., ed. *Nicaragua: The First Five Years.* New York: Praeger, 1985.

Walker, Thomas W., ed. *Reagan versus the Sandinistas: The Undeclared War on Nicaragua.* Boulder, CO: Westview Press, 1987.

Walker, Thomas W. *Revolution and Counterrevolution in Nicaragua, 1979–1990.* Boulder, CO: Westview Press, 1991.

Chapter 10

Andersen, Martin Edwin. *Dossier Secreto: Argentina's Desaparecidos and the Myth of the "Dirty War."* Boulder, CO: Westview Press, 1993.

Angell, Alan, and Benny Pollack, eds. *The Legacy of Dictatorship: Political, Economic, and Social Change in Pinochet's Chile.* Liverpool, UK: Institute of Latin American Studies, University of Liverpool, 1993.

Archdiocese of São Paulo. *Torture in Brazil: A Shocking Report on the Pervasive Use of Torture by Brazilian Military Governments, 1964–1985.* Trans. Jaime Wright. Austin: Institute of Latin American Studies, University of Texas Press, 1985.

Argentina. Comisión Nacional sobre la Desaparición de Personas. *Nunca más: The Report of the Argentine National Commission on the Disappeared.* 1st American edition. New York: Farrar, Straus, Giroux, 1986.

Arriagada, Genaro. *Pinochet: The Politics of Power.* Trans. Nancy Morris. Boston: Unwin Hyman, 1988.

Bacchus, Wilfred A. *Mission in Mufti: Brazil's Military Regimes, 1964–1985.* Westport, CT: Greenwood Press, 1990.

Bouvard, Marguerite Guzmán. *Revolutionizing Motherhood: The Mothers of the Plaza de Mayo.* Wilmington, DE: Scholarly Resources, 1994.

Chile. Comisión Nacional de Verdad y Reconciliación. *Report of the Chilean National Commission on Truth and Reconciliation.* Trans. Phillip E. Berryman. Notre Dame, IN: University of Notre Dame Press, 1993.

Constable, Pamela, and Arturo Valenzuela. *A Nation of Enemies: Chile under Pinochet*. New York: W. W. Norton, 1991.

Dinges, John. *Condor Years: How Pinochet and his Allies brought Terrorism to Three Continents*. New York: New Press, 2004.

Drake, Paul, and Iván Yaksic, eds., *The Struggle for Democracy in Chile, 1982–1990*. Rev. ed. Lincoln: University of Nebraska Press, 1995.

Esparza, Marcia, Henry R. Huttenbach, and Daniel Feierstein, eds. *State Violence and Genocide in Latin America: The Cold War Years*. London: Routledge, 2010.

Feitlowitz, Marguerite. *A Lexicon of Terror: Argentina and the Legacies of Torture*. Revised and updated ed. New York: Oxford University Press, 2011.

Finchelstein, Federico. *The Ideological Origins of the Dirty War: Fascism, Populism, and Dictatorship in Twentieth Century Argentina*. New York: Oxford University Press, 2014.

Gillespie, Charles Guy. *Negotiating Democracy: Politicians and Generals in Uruguay*. Cambridge: Cambridge University Press, 1991.

Guest, Iain. *Behind the Disappearances: Argentina's Dirty War against Human Rights and the United Nations*. Philadelphia: University of Pennsylvania Press, 1990.

Hodges, Donald C. *Argentina's "Dirty War": An Intellectual Biography*. Austin: University of Texas Press, 1991.

Kobut, David R. and Olga Vilella. *Historical Dictionary of the "Dirty Wars."* 2nd ed. Lanham, MD: Scarecrow Press, 2010.

Kornbluh, Peter. *The Pinochet File: A Declassified Dossier on Atrocity and Accountability*. New York: New Press, 2003.

Loveman, Brian, and Thomas M. Davies, Jr., eds. *The Politics of Antipolitics: The Military in Latin America*. Revised and updated ed. Wilmington, DE: Scholarly Resources, 1997.

McSherry, J. Patrice. *Predatory States: Operation Condor and Covert War in Latin America*. Lanham, MD: Rowman & Littlefield, 2005.

Morello, Gustavo, S. J. *The Catholic Church and Argentina's Dirty War*. New York: Oxford University Press, 2015.

Muñoz, Heraldo. *The Dictator's Shadow: Life under Augusto Pinochet*. New York: Basic Books, 2008.

Schneider, Nina. *Brazilian Propaganda: Legitimizing an Authoritarian Regime*. Gainesville: University Press of Florida, 2014.

Servicio Paz y Justicia, Uruguay. *Uruguay Nunca Más: Human Rights Violations, 1972–1985*. Trans. Elizabeth Hampsten. Philadelphia: Temple University Press, 1992.

Skidmore, Thomas E. *The Politics of Military Rule in Brazil, 1964–1985*. New York: Oxford University Press, 1988.

Sosnowski, Saúl, and Louise B. Popkin, eds. *Repression, Exile, and Democracy: Uruguayan Culture*. Trans. Louise B. Popkin. Durham, NC: Duke University Press, 1993.

Spooner, Mary Helen. *Soldiers in a Narrow Land: The Pinochet Regime in Chile.* Berkeley: University of California Press, 1994.

Taylor, Diana. *Disappearing Acts: Spectacles of Gender and Nationalism in Argentina's "Dirty War."* Durham, NC: Duke University Press, 1997.

Timerman, Jacobo. *Prisoner without a Name, Cell without a Number.* Trans. Tony Talbot. Madison: University of Wisconsin Press, 2002.

Valenzuela, J. Samuel, and Arturo Valenzuela, eds. *Military Rule in Chile: Dictatorship and Oppositions.* Baltimore: Johns Hopkins University Press, 1986.

Verbitsky, Horacio. *The Flight: Confessions of an Argentine Dirty Warrior.* Trans. Esther Allen. New York: New Press, 1996.

Weinstein, Martin. *Uruguay: Democracy at the Crossroads.* Boulder, CO: Westview Press, 1988.

Wright, Thomas C. *State Terrorism in Latin America: Chile, Argentina, and International Human Rights.* Lanham, MD: Rowman & Littlefield, 2007.

Wright, Thomas C. and Rody Oñate. *Flight from Chile: Voices of Exile.* Albuquerque: University of New Mexico Press, 1998.

Chapter 11

Americas Watch. *El Salvador's Decade of Terror: Human Rights since the Assassination of Archbishop Romero.* New Haven, CT: Yale University Press, 1991.

Archdiocese of Guatemala, Recovery of Historical Memory Project. *Guatemala Nunca Más: The Official Report of the Human Rights Office, Archdiocese of Guatemala.* Maryknoll, NY: Orbis Books, 1999.

Berryman, Phillip. *Liberation Theology: Essential Facts about the Revolutionary Movement in Latin America—and Beyond.* Philadelphia: Temple University Press, 1987.

Betancur, Belisario, Reinaldo Figueredo Planchart, and Thomas Buergenthal. *From Madness to Hope: The Twelve-Year War in El Salvador: Report of the Commission on the Truth for El Salvador.* New York: United Nations, 1993.

Binford, Leigh. *The El Mozote Massacre: Human Rights and Global Implications.* 2nd ed. Tucson: University of Arizona Press, 2016.

Brett, Roderick Leslie. *Origins and Dynamics of Genocide: Political Violence in Guatemala.* London: Palgrave Macmillan, 2016.

Brett, Roderick Leslie. *Social Movements, Indigenous Politics, and Democratization in Guatemala, 1985–1996.* Boston: Brill, 2008.

Carmack, Robert M., ed. *Harvest of Violence: The Maya Indians and the Guatemalan Crisis.* Norman: University of Oklahoma Press, 1988.

Carothers, Thomas. *In the Name of Democracy: U.S. Policy toward Latin America in the Reagan Years.* Berkeley: University of California Press, 1991.

Castellanos, Miguel. *The Comandante Speaks: Memoirs of an El Salvadoran Guerrilla Leader.* Ed. Courtney E. Prisk. Boulder, CO: Westview, 1991.

Crandall, Russell. *The Salvador Option: The United States in El Salvador, 1977–1992.* New York: Cambridge University Press, 2016.

Cruden, Alexander, ed. *Genocide and Persecution: El Salvador and Guatemala.* Detroit: Greenhaven Press, 2013.

Danner, Mark. *The Massacre at El Mozote: A Parable of the Cold War.* New York: Vintage Books. 1994.

Doggett, Martha. *Death Foretold: The Jesuit Murders in El Salvador.* Washington, D.C.: Georgetown University Press, 1993.

Eisenbrandt, Matt. *Assassination of a Saint: The Plot to Murder Óscar Romero and the Quest to Bring his Killers to Justice.* Oakland: University of California Press, 2017.

Fish, Joe, and Cristina Sganga. *El Salvador: Testament of Terror.* London: Zed, 1988.

Gleijeses, Piero. *Shattered Hopes: The Guatemalan Revolution and the United States.* Princeton, NJ: Princeton University Press, 1991.

Grandin, Greg. *The Last Colonial Massacre: Latin America in the Cold War.* Revised ed. Chicago: University of Chicago Press, 2011.

Higonnet, Etelle, ed. *Quiet Genocide: Guatemala 1981–1983.* New Brunswick. NJ: Transaction Publishers, 2009.

Jonas, Suzanne. *The Battle for Guatemala: Rebels, Death Squads, and U.S. Power.* Boulder, CO: Westview Press, 1991.

LaFeber, Walter. *Inevitable Revolutions: The United States in Central America.* 2nd ed. New York: W. W. Norton, 1993.

LeoGrande, William M. *Our Own Backyard: The United States in Central America, 1977–1992.* Chapel Hill: University of North Carolina Press, 1998.

McAllister, Carlota, and Diane M. Nelson, eds. *War by Other Means: Aftermath in Post-Genocide Guatemala.* Durham, NC: Duke University Press, 2013.

Menchú, Rigoberta. *I, Rigoberta Menchú: An Indian Woman in Guatemala.* Ed. Elisabeth Burgos-Debray, trans. Ann Wright. 2nd English ed. London: Verso, 2009.

Montgomery, Tommie Sue. *Revolution in El Salvador: From Civil Strife to Civil Peace.* 2nd ed. Boulder, CO: Westview Press, 1995.

Peterson, Anna L. *Martyrdom and the Politics of Religion: Progressive Catholicism in El Salvador's Civil War.* Albany, State University of New York Press, 1997.

Perera, Victor. *Unfinished Conquest: The Guatemalan Tragedy.* Berkeley: University of California Press, 1993.

Rothenberg, Daniel, ed. *Memory of Silence: The Guatemalan Truth Commission Report.* New York: Palgrave Macmillan, 2012.

Sanford, Victoria. *Buried Secrets: Truth and Human Rights in Guatemala.* New York: Palgrave Macmillan, 2003.

Schirmer, Jennifer G. *The Guatemalan Military Project: A Violence Called Democracy.* Philadelphia: University of Pennsylvania Press, 1998.

Stoll, David. *Between Two Armies: In the Ixil Towns of Guatemala.* New York: Columbia University Press, 1993.

Whitfield, Teresa. *Paying the Price: Ignacio Ellacuria and the Murdered Jesuits in El Salvador.* Philadelphia: Temple University Press, 1995.

Wilkinson, Daniel. *Silence on the Mountain: Stories of Terror, Betrayal, and Forgetting in Guatemala*. Durham, NC: Duke University Press, 2004.

Chapter 12

Arnson, Cynthia J., ed. *Comparative Peace Processes in Latin America*. Stanford, CA: Stanford University Press, 1999.

Arnson, Cynthia J. *In the Wake of War: Democratization and Internal Armed Conflict in Latin America*. Washington, D.C.: Woodrow Wilson Center Press, 2012.

Barahona de Brito, Alexandra. *Human Rights and Democratization in Latin America: Uruguay and Chile*. New York: Oxford University Press, 1997.

Berry, Albert, ed. *Poverty, Economic Reform, and Income Distribution in Latin America*. Boulder, CO: Lynne Rienner, 1998.

Brenner, Philip et al. *A Contemporary Cuba Reader: The Revolution under Raúl Castro*. 2nd ed. Lanham, MD: Rowman & Littlefield, 2015.

Brysk, Alison. *The Politics of Human Rights in Argentina: Protest, Change, and Democratization*. Stanford, CA: Stanford University Press, 1994.

Camp, Roderic Ai. *Politics in Mexico: The Democratic Consolidation*. 5th ed. New York: Oxford University Press, 2007.

Carroll, Rory, *Myth and Reality in Hugo Chávez's Venezuela*. New York: Penguin, 2013.

de Castro, Fabio, Kees Koonings, and Marianne Wiesebron, eds. *Brazil under the Workers' Party: Continuity and Change from Lula to Dilma*. Houndmills, UK: Palgrave Macmillan, 2014.

de la Torre, Carlos, and Cynthia J. Arnson, eds. *Latin American Populism in the Twenty-First Century*. Washington, D.C.: Woodrow Wilson Center Press, 2013.

Domínguez, Jorge I., and Michael Shifter, eds. *Constructing Democratic Governance in Latin America*. 4th ed. Baltimore: Johns Hopkins University Press, 2013.

Ellner, Steve, ed. *Latin America's Radical Left: Challenges and Complexities of Political Power in the Twenty-First Century*. Lanham, MD: Rowman & Littlefield, 2014.

Farthing, Linda C., and Benjamin H. Kohl. *Evo's Bolivia: Continuity and Change*. Austin: University of Texas Press.

Feinberg, Richard E. *Open for Business: Building Cuba's New Economy*. Washington, D.C.: Brookings Institution Press, 2016.

Goodale, Mark, and Nancy Postero. *Neoliberalism, Interrupted: Social Change and Contested Governance in Contemporary Latin America*. Stanford, CA: Stanford University Press, 2013.

Harten, Sven. *The Rise of Evo Morales and the MAS*. London: Zed Books, 2011.

Harvey, Neil. *The Chiapas Rebellion: The Struggle for Land and Democracy*. Durham, NC: Duke University Press, 1998.

Hershberg, Eric, and William M. LeoGrande, eds. *A New Chapter in US-Cuban Relations: Social, Political, and Economic Implications.* New York: Palgrave Macmillan, 2016.

Huntington, Samuel P. *The Third Wave: Democratization in the Late Twentieth Century.* Norman: University of Oklahoma Press, 1991.

Levistky, Steven, and Kenneth M. Roberts, eds. *The Resurgence of the Latin American Left.* Baltimore: Johns Hopkins University Press, 2011.

López-Segrera, Francisco. *The United States and Cuba: From Closest Enemies to Distant Friends.* Lanham, MD: Rowman & Littlefield, 2017.

McSherry, J. Patrice. *Incomplete Transition: Military Power and Democracy in Argentina.* New York: St. Martin's Press, 1997.

Mesa-Lago, Carmelo, and Jorge Pérez-López. *Cuba under Raúl Castro: Assessing the Reforms.* Boulder, CO: Lynne Rienner Publishers, 2013.

Piatti-Crocker, Adriana. *Diffusion of Gender Quotas in Latin America and Beyond: Advances and Setbacks in the last Two Decades.* New York: Peter Lang, 2011.

Postero, Nancy. *The Indigenous State: Race, Politics, and Performance in Plurinational Bolivia.* Oakland: University of California Press, 2017.

Prevost, Gary, Carlos Oliva Campos, and Harry E. Vanden, eds. *Social Movements and Leftist Governments in Latin America: Confrontation or Co-optation?* London: Zed Books, 2012.

Sieder, Rachel, ed. *Guatemala after the Peace Accords.* London: Institute of Latin American Studies, 1998.

Smilde, David, and Daniel C. Hellinger, eds. *Venezuela's Bolivarian Democracy: Participation, Politics, and Culture under Chávez.* Durham, NC: Duke University Press, 2011.

Smith, Peter H. *Democracy in Latin America: Political Change in Comparative Perspective.* 2nd ed. New York: Oxford University Press, 2012.

Solimano, Andrés. *Chile and the Neoliberal Trap: The Post-Pinochet Era.* New York: Cambridge University Press, 2012.

Vanden, Harry E., and Gary Prevost. *Politics of Latin America: The Power Game.* 5th ed. New York: Oxford University Press, 2014.

Walker, Thomas W., ed. *Nicaragua without Illusions: Regime Transition and Structural Adjustment in the 1990s.* Wilmington, DE: Scholarly Resources, 1997.

Walker, Thomas W., and Ariel C. Armony, eds. *Repression, Resistance, and Democratic Transition in Central America.* Wilmington, DE: Scholarly Resources, 2000.

Webber, Jeffery R., and Barry Carr, eds. *The New Latin American Left: Cracks in the Empire.* Lanham, MD: Rowman & Littlefield, 2013.

Wright, Thomas C. *Impunity, Human Rights, and Democracy: Chile and Argentina, 1990–2005.* Austin: University of Texas Press, 2014.

Index

About the Author

Thomas C. Wright is Distinguished Professor of History, Emeritus, at the University of Nevada, Las Vegas. He became interested in the impact of the Cuban Revolution on Latin America during his junior year at the University of San Marcos in Lima, where student politics and a national election focused his attention on the pervasive influence of *fidelismo* in the early 1960s. Wright's recent books include *State Terrorism in Latin America: Chile, Argentina, and International Human Rights* (2007); *Impunity, Human Rights, and Democracy: Chile and Argentina, 1990–2005* (2014); and *Latin America since Independence: Two Centuries of Continuity and Change* (2017).